**Advance praise for James**

"Have you ever thought, 'I wish I knew then what I know now?' Most people have. *Wealth Is a Choice* can give you 20 years of hindsight in just the few hours it takes to read this book."

–Ray Rowe, Attorney at Law

"James Studinger offers proactive and positive solutions to manage money that will help you make smart decisions."

–Greg Baker, President, The Baker Group

"Money is one of life's tools that comes without an instruction manual. Until now, that is. *Wealth Is a Choice* offers fantastic insight on how to build and maintain wealth in an easy-to-understand format. This book will redefine the way people understand and use money."

–Joseph Samples, Personal Financial Advisor

"It may seem strange to some that a book about creating personal wealth also talks about charitable giving. Studinger, however, demonstrates that giving can be deeply fulfilling while also advancing personal wealth goals. In this way, the author reminds us that true wealth also has a mission and higher purpose. *Wealth Is a Choice* is a remarkable book, both for the individual and society as a whole."

–Tim Smith, Development Director, VFW National Home for Children

"Studinger's integrity and style stem from his upbringing in the rural Upper Peninsula of Michigan. As an avid outdoorsman, he is keenly attuned to the physical world surrounding him. In *Wealth Is a Choice*, Studinger masterfully correlates logic from the natural world into actionable financial practices. Simply put, the financial environment, like nature itself, is governed by timeless universal truths, and understanding these truths puts readers on the path to financial freedom."

*–James T. Flynn, Flynn Benefits Group*

"Many financial books irresponsibly promise quick riches. Studinger's approach is smarter and more realistic. Building financial independence takes time and dedication. Studinger shows you how in *Wealth Is a Choice*."

*–Rod Charles, CFP, President, Financial Freedom Group*

"An intelligent yet simple read on the importance of taking control of your financial future."

*–Richard J. Keil, CPA, PFS, CFP®*

"Studinger set out to write a financial guide for his young sons. What he accomplished was far more significant. This book will redefine the way we understand money."

*–David Petoskey, RFC, Managing Principal, Wealth Management Services*

# Wealth *Is a* Choice

GREEN FROG BOOKS
www.greenfrogbooks.com

GREEN FROG BOOKS
www.greenfrogbooks.com

Published by Green Frog Books
www.greenfrogbooks.com

Copyright © 2008 by James P. Studinger

Copy editing by Dan Shenk
Layout by Norman T. Klebba
Cartoons by Dan Gibson
Cover design by George Foster
Photography by Brad Ziegler

All rights reserved. This book, or parts thereof, may not be reproduced in any form without written permission from the author or publisher. The scanning, uploading and distribution of this book via the Internet or via any other means without permission of the publisher is illegal and punishable by law. Please purchase only authorized electronic editions, and do not participate in or encourage electronic piracy of copyrighted materials. Your support of the author's rights is greatly appreciated.

Studinger, James P.
    Wealth Is a Choice / James P. Studinger.

ISBN 978-0-9800075-6-5

Printed in the United States of America

*For Eller and Owen*

*"Success and failure are not usually final destinations, just road markings along the way."*
—Patrick F. Irwin

## Contents

Acknowledgments .................................................................. 1
Disclosures ............................................................................ 5
Introduction ......................................................................... 11
PRINCIPLE 1: Know That Values Determine Decisions ......................... 25
PRINCIPLE 2: Pursue Visionary Goals ..................................... 41
PRINCIPLE 3: Take Ownership in Your Future: 'My Word Is Good' ....... 53
PRINCIPLE 4: Play Both Offense *and* Defense ......................... 69
PRINCIPLE 5: Buy Things That Go Up in Value ....................... 83
PRINCIPLE 6: Ask Yourself, 'Am I Spent?' ............................. 101
PRINCIPLE 7: Leverage Others' Expertise for Personal Gain ................ 115
PRINCIPLE 8: Choose Your Team Wisely ............................... 123
PRINCIPLE 9: Decide What Motivates You, Then Pursue It .................. 143
PRINCIPLE 10: Play the Game and Execute the Plan ............... 151
PRINCIPLE 11: Ask Three Telling Questions ........................... 163
PRINCIPLE 12: Don't Forget That Your Story's Ending Is Predictable .. 187
PRINCIPLE 13: Stay Financially Healthy ................................. 205
PRINCIPLE 14: Get Organized and Stay Organized ............... 221
PRINCIPLE 15: Put Your Money on a Mission ....................... 243
PRINCIPLE 16: Share the Wealth of Experiences ................... 253
PRINCIPLE 17: Always Remember the *Why* ......................... 263
Glossary .............................................................................. 267
Index .................................................................................. 291
About the Author .............................................................. 299

# ACKNOWLEDGMENTS

I'd like to give a big thank you to the many people who helped make this book a reality. For me, the writing and production of a book was an entirely new endeavor. This was another project in my life that if you asked me "Why did you go there?" the answer would be "Because I was naïve." Had I been better informed, I might not have even ventured into the wilderness of writing. I'm blessed, however, that I am surrounded by special people who provided encouragement and talent to help bring it all together.

To …

Kris Replogle, my wife and dear friend, not to mention business partner and mother extraordinaire, without whom I can't imagine where I'd be right now. We've taken a journey together, one that at times has been all-consuming. You have gracefully supported the late-night writing sessions, overcome new challenges, and even stayed with me while my mind was somewhere else, stuck on a paragraph that wasn't quite coming together. Much love and gratitude—more than I know how to express!

My boys, Eller and Owen, you have been my inspiration to finish this project. Living jumped to a whole new level since having you. I couldn't ask for a better family. You are my *why* in life.

All my associates at JPStudinger Group, present and past, whose efforts in the development and growth of our firm provided much of the work necessary to put the principles in this book into motion. For your attention to detail to all our clients, treating them with respect and always putting their needs first.

All of the countless clients and people who have, over the years, entrusted us to help guide them through the financial maze and get set on the path to financial independence. You grew with us over the years, from the development of a new firm identifying its culture, to what we are today. Your support, encouragement, and feedback are welcomed and much appreciated.

All those who read parts of the book during the early writing stages and provided me the peer review absolutely necessary to hone my writing skills and establish my style. Especially Susan Studinger, Marj Replogle, Nancy Archambeau, Tim Smith, Roger and Janet Pratt, Darrick Mitchell, Jonnie Sullivan, Steve Cosgrove, Amir Tamiz, Andrea Wolf, Harold and Nancy Brown, Wayne and Judy Lintz, Debbie Kalp, Melissa Jones, Melissa Allen, Dana Maschke and Janna Henderson. Without your honest opinions, the book would not be nearly what it has become.

All those inside the book industry who have helped untangle the mystery of what it takes to "birth" a book—from conception through all the stages up to production.

To …

Joyce Weiss and Greg Kowalski, a very big thank you for encouraging me to put the first words on paper. You helped me realize (or at least made me believe) that I was capable of actually doing this.

Dawn Josepheson, who first organized and edited my work, putting a whole mess of ideas and words into a substantive organized manuscript.

My brother Jakob Studinger, for your early illustrations that gave me the framework and helped create images from the text.

Pat Liebler, who continues to make me a better writer. You have a way with words, and your depth of insight is always spot-on.

My good friend Beth Wilkins, a tremendous thank you for the hours of work, the candid feedback, support and ideas. I'm not sure what I would have done without you.

Dan Poynter, for instantly answering my questions no matter where you were in the world and graciously opening your network of other professionals to me.

Steve Lemm, who demystified the printing business.

Brad Ziegler, for the wonderful pictures and life you helped bring to the back cover.

Dan Gibson, without humor we have nothing. Because of your cartoons, a great many more people will actually make it from cover to cover.

George Foster, seeing your cover design made it real.

Norm Klebba, thank you for your creative and tireless work on the interior design. You helped create something that we can all be proud of.

Dan Shenk, I cannot express enough how wonderful an editor, and person, you are. I'm very fortunate to have been put in touch with you and will forever value what you have done.

And finally to you, dear reader, thank you for picking up—and perhaps even embracing—this book. I hope it brings you as much help and enjoyment reading it as it has for me writing it.

Thank you all.

*James*

James

## Disclosures

This information included herein is for educational purposes only and not intended to solicit or sell any products or services. The information should not be applied or relied upon in any particular situation without the advice of your tax, legal and/or financial services professional. The views/concepts expressed may not be suitable for every situation. This material was created to provide accurate and reliable information on the subjects covered. It is not intended to provide specific legal, tax or other professional advice. The services of an appropriate professional should be sought regarding your individual situation.

Investments are not guaranteed and are subject to investment risk, including the possible loss of principal. The investment return and principal value of the security will fluctuate so that when redeemed, may be worth more or less than the original investment. Generally, the greater an investment's possible reward over time, the greater its level of price volatility or risk.

## ASSET-CATEGORY DEFINITIONS

### *Growth*

Growth-oriented stocks typically sell at relatively high valuations compared with other types of stocks. Historically, growth-oriented stocks have been more volatile than value-oriented stocks.

### *Mid-Sized-Company Stocks*

In exchange for higher growth potential, one's investment in stocks of small and mid-sized companies may entail greater price volatility and less liquidity than investing in stocks of larger companies.

### *Mid-Cap*

Securities of mid-sized companies may be more susceptible to price swings and are less liquid than investments in larger companies.

### *Real Estate*

REITs (real estate investment trusts) involve such risks as refinancing, economic impact on the industry, changes in property value, dependency on management skills and risks similar to small company investing.

### *Small Cap*

Small company stocks offer greater potential for growth, but there are additional market and business risks associated with them, such as low trading volumes, a greater degree of change in earnings and greater short-term volatility.

### *Internal Revenue Service Circular 230*

These materials are not intended to be used to avoid tax penalties and were prepared to support the matter addressed in this document. The taxpayer would do well to seek advice from an independent tax advisor.

Variable annuities are long-term insurance contracts designed for investing for retirement. They offer the opportunity to allocate premiums among fixed and variable investment options that have the potential to grow income tax-deferred, with an option to receive a stream of income at a later date.

Variable universal life insurance combines the protection and tax efficiencies of life insurance with the investment potential of a comprehensive selection of variable investment options. The insurance component provides the death-benefit coverage, and the variable component gives the flexibility to potentially increase the policy's cash value.

All withdrawals reduce the death benefit and may reduce the value of any optional benefits. Early withdrawals and other distributions of taxable amounts may be subject to ordinary income tax, a surrender charge and, if taken prior to age 59½, a 10% federal tax penalty may apply.

## INVESTING RISKS

### Credit Risk

The likelihood that a debtor will be unable to pay interest or principal payments as planned is typically referred to as default risk. Default risk for most debt securities is constantly monitored by several nationally recognized statistical rating agencies, such as Moody's Investors Services Inc. and Standard & Poor's Corporation. Even if the likelihood of default is remote, changes in the perception of an institution's financial health will affect the valuation of its debt securities. This extension of default risk is typically known as credit risk. Bonds rated BBB/Baa, although investment grade, may have speculative characteristics because their issuers are more vulnerable to financial setbacks and economic pressures than issuers with higher ratings.

### Current-Income Risk

A short-term interest rate target is set by the Federal Reserve Bank Open Market Committee. As the committee changes its target rate in response to the business cycle, rates in the Money Market Fund will change correspondingly. It is this mechanism of changing with the short-term interest rate that allows the fund to achieve the goal of maintaining principal value.

### Economic Risk

The prevailing economic environment is important to the health of all businesses. Some companies, however, are more sensitive to changes in the domestic or global economy than others. These types of companies are often referred to as cyclical businesses. Countries in which a large portion of businesses are in cyclical industries are thus economically sensitive and carry a higher amount of economic risk.

### *Growth-Stock Risk*

Because the prices of most growth stocks are based on future expectations, these stocks tend to be more sensitive than value stocks to bad economic news and negative earnings surprises. While the prices of any type of stock may rise and fall rapidly, growth stocks in particular may underperform during periods when the market favors value stocks. A fund's performance also may suffer if certain stocks don't perform as the fund's subadvisor expected. To the extent that a fund's subadvisor sells stocks before they reach their market peak, the fund may miss out on opportunities for higher performance.

### *Inflation Risk*

Inflation risk is the risk that the price of an asset, or the income generated by an asset, will not keep up with the cost of living. Almost all financial assets have some inflation risk.

### *Interest-Rate Risk*

Changing interest rates may adversely affect the value of an investment. An increase in interest rates typically causes the value of bonds and other fixed-income securities to fall. Because of this risk, a fund that invests in fixed-income securities is subject to risk even if all the fixed-income securities in that fund's portfolio are paid in full at maturity. Changes in interest rates will affect the value of longer-term fixed-income securities more than shorter-term securities.

### *Liquidity and Valuation Risk*

Securities that were liquid when purchased by a fund may become temporarily hard to value and difficult or impossible to sell, especially in declining markets. Many below-investment-grade securities are subject to legal or contractual restrictions that limit their resale to the general public at desired prices.

### *Management Risk*

Each fund is subject to management risk because it's an actively managed investment portfolio. Management risk is the chance that poor security selection will cause a fund to underperform other funds with similar objectives. The success of each fund's investment strategy depends significantly on the skill of the management company, and/or subadvisor to the funds, in assessing the potential of the securities in which the fund invests. The management company will apply its investment techniques and risk analyses in making investment decisions for each fund, but there can be no guarantee that these will produce the desired result.

## *Market Risk*

The market value of a fund's investments will fluctuate as the stock and bond markets fluctuate. Market risk may affect a single issuer, industry or sector of the economy. It also may affect the market as a whole.

## *Prepayment Risk*

Issuers may prepay fixed-rate bonds when interest rates fall, forcing a fund to reinvest in obligations with lower interest rates than the original bonds.

## *Price Risk*

As investors perceive and forecast good business prospects, they are willing to pay higher prices for securities. Higher prices therefore reflect higher expectations. If expectations aren't met, or if expectations are lowered, the prices of the securities will drop. This happens with individual securities or the financial markets overall. For stocks, price risk is often measured by comparing the price of any security or portfolio to the book value, earnings, or cash flow of the underlying company or companies. A higher ratio denotes higher expectations and higher risk that the expectations will not be sustained.

## *Real Estate-Industry Risk*

The stock prices of companies in the real estate industry are typically sensitive to changes in real estate values, property taxes, interest rates, cash flow of underlying real estate assets, occupancy rates, government regulations affecting zoning, land use and rents, as well as the management skill and creditworthiness of the issuer. Companies in the real estate industry also may be subject to liabilities under environmental hazardous-waste laws that could negatively affect their value.

### Restricted-Securities Risk

It may be difficult to find a buyer for restricted securities. In addition, the selling price for restricted securities may be less than originally anticipated because they may be sold only as privately negotiated transactions.

### Sector Risk

Companies that are in similar businesses may be similarly affected by particular economic or market events, which may, in certain circumstances, cause the value of securities of all companies in a particular sector of the market to decrease. Although a fund may not concentrate in any one industry, each fund may invest without limitation in any one sector. To the extent that a fund has substantial holdings within a particular sector, the risks associated with that sector increase.

### Tax-Management Risk

Risk management applies a variety of tax-management investment strategies designed to minimize taxable income and capital gains for shareholders. Notwithstanding the use of these strategies, the fund may have taxable income and may realize taxable capital gains. The ability of the fund to avoid realizing taxable gains may be affected by the timing of cash flows into and out of the fund, which are attributable to the payment of expenses and daily net sales and redemptions. In addition, investors purchasing shares when the fund has large accumulated capital gains could receive a significant part of the purchase price of their shares back as a taxable capital-gains distribution. Over time, securities with unrealized gains may comprise a substantial portion of the fund's assets.

### Volatility Risk

Volatility risk is the risk that performance will be affected by unanticipated events (e.g., significant earnings shortfalls or gains, war, or political events) that cause major price changes in individual securities or market sectors. Below-investment-grade securities are more susceptible to sudden and significant price movements because they're generally more sensitive to adverse developments.

# INTRODUCTION

I'm an avid outdoorsman and love to fish. There's a mystique about catching trout on a fly rod that has "hooked" anglers for centuries. Technologies with equipment change rapidly. Through it all, the basics of being able to catch big trout remain the same. A trout today looks, eats and swims the same way trout did 300 years ago. No amount of great equipment or technology will help you catch a trout if you don't understand the principles of trout. Experienced anglers can catch nearly as many fish on $50 worth of gear as they can on $2,000.

I feel the same way about money. It's easy to get caught up in the technical language and financial trends, even fads, of today. The basic principles of making money and building wealth, however, are the same ones that have been around for generations. I won't be giving you get-rich schemes. The truth is that very few get-rich schemes actually work. If money comes too fast, it all too often goes even faster. Why? Because the easy-come method doesn't generally include an understanding of what it takes to sustain wealth.

Here's my story. I grew up in the Upper Peninsula of Michigan in a small town. My dad was the breadwinner, while my mom took care of eight kids. I didn't have a clue how to make money and didn't give much thought to it. Living in a traditional small American town, I didn't see wealth around me, but I did daydream of what it would be like to have money. I envisioned a garage full of exotic luxury cars in a sprawling mansion with secret passageways. My real passion is the outdoors, so of course woods and my own private lake surrounded the house. Those were fun childhood dreams.

I worked all through high school, but I didn't save my money. I moved away from small-town living and went to college in Lower Michigan with $100 in my pocket. I worked all through college—many times 40 hours or more a week and frequently three jobs at a time. No matter how much I worked, though, I didn't accumulate a worthwhile balance in my bank account. It seemed just about everyone from downstate had more money than I did, and I wanted to do all the things they did. Credit cards made that possible—temporarily. Soon I found myself up to my neck in nasty debt, shifting money around to make the payments. My credit rating was taking a beating and, to make matters worse, I had my name on all the utilities at the college house. As it turned out, one of my roommates responsible for making utility payments wasn't paying the bill. He was using the money for "other" things. I know … Why would I have someone else be responsible to pay the bill if my name was on it? I realized this mistake after the damage had been done. It got so bad that summer it looked as if I might need to live in a public campground. Thankfully, I got a couple of breaks and was able to avoid that experience.

I concluded that there must be a better way to go about this. Nobody had taught me how to make ends meet—much less build wealth—and I was stuck in the rut of thinking that the whole point of income was simply to keep up with expenses. One day I saw an internship position posted at a financial services firm. That seemed like an obvious solution. I desperately needed to understand how money worked. What better opportunity than to learn from people in the consulting business. I took that job, and I did learn some things about money. I became quite passionate about the internship and eventually pursued it as a career. I soon was out of debt and began investing money. To be sure, it would take a number of years and many mistakes before I finally understood how money really worked.

Some of you may go through the same nasty financial cycles that I did before you realize that there's a better way. I hope you don't have to. While the experiences certainly are an important part of what has molded me into what I am today, we don't all need to undergo major financial hardship in order to succeed. In *Wealth Is a Choice* I share my own and others' experiences so that you can learn from our successes and, just as important, our failures. Most of the people profiled in this book are real and quite normal. Their names and some circumstances have been altered to protect their privacy; a few represent an amalgam of more than one person or couple. Some weren't very successful when we first met. As they focused on primary initiatives, however, they gained control—and their finances improved.

Consider the story of two couples, both of whom have similar resources, but they made very different decisions. Which situation most resembles yours today or the path you desire to be on?

Charles and Amy[1] worked for a company that didn't provide a pension. As such, they counted on no one else to fulfill their retirement. They erred on the side of being too frugal. After paying the bills, saving and buying the necessities, WAM (walking around money) seemed scarce. That was only in the beginning, though. When the commas started to show up in their balance sheet, saving money became fun.

By the time Charles and Amy reached middle age, the tables had definitely turned. Because they had money to invest, they were able to take advantage of great opportunities, while others only wished for them. They weren't investment gurus, and they made some mistakes, but years of systematic savings helped them accumulate a substantial nest egg.

Today they have no regrets. Now that they're retired, they reminisce about the old days as they watch the sun set over the mountains from the front porch of their lake-house retreat. Charles has developed a taste for wine and trout fishing, while Amy can tell you about the best chefs in town. The family pictures throughout their home tell an exciting story of happy times traveling around the world on family vacations. Charles and Amy lived their lives spending money on things that mattered, and they invested the rest. As a result, they are now wealthy and have the means to fulfill their fondest (and wildest) dreams.

They look back on life with a strong sense of accomplishment and satisfaction. Their decision to pursue wealth instead of bills has resulted in a very satisfying and well-rounded life for themselves and their family.

Ricky and Heather, on the other hand, have a very different story. Ricky worked at the same company as Charles and had a similar career path. Heather worked at another company that did in fact offer a pension.

---

[1] Not their real names. In this book when only first names are used it won't be their real names. If, however, both first and last names are used, the author has obtained permission from those persons for their names to appear in the book—or they are individuals in the public domain.

Heather and Ricky began their careers at the same time as Amy and Charles, yet they made very different decisions.

Ricky and Heather had neither the courage nor the foresight to save. They worked very hard and felt they deserved to play just as hard. Both Ricky and Heather actively fought for each promotion and knew their income would increase dramatically over the years. So they bought a large house soon after they were married, and they furnished every room as if it were from a showroom floor. They traveled, bought trendy clothes and wore expensive jewelry. They treated themselves for short-term accomplishments with large-ticket purchases, such as expensive cars and a couple of luxury cruises. They never took the time to calculate the thousands of dollars they would continue paying (through debt service and maintenance) beyond the initial excitement of their achievements.

Their children always expected to have the newest and nicest things. Ricky and Heather believed that once the children left home the financial drain would subside. They were wrong. Bad habits kept their children dependent on them far longer than they wished.

As time ticked by, rather than becoming more independent and carefree, Ricky and Heather became less so. When stark reality started to sink in about the future, they began to change their actions. They were tired of worrying about their job security and managing their debt load; they longed for a relaxed, stress-free environment. Ricky and Heather were done putting off learning about money—and finally decided to take ownership and build wealth.

So they learned what Charles and Amy had known for years: They took a step back in material things and a step forward in building wealth and independence. Now that they're a couple of years into their new way of life, they feel happier and more secure than they have in a long time. Additionally, because of their actions, their adult children are finally managing money and saving for their own future. Fortunately, it appears the children will take the more productive financial path of Charles and Amy.

Ricky and Heather don't have many regrets, and they treasure the good things in life, but if you ask them what they would have done differently, their answer would be *"Save sooner."* Because of the lessons they finally learned about the positive effects of money and how to build it, they can expect a comfortable retirement. Because they started late, however, retirement won't come as soon as it has for Charles and Amy. *Which scenario is more appealing to you?*

If you're like most people, the story of Charles and Amy is what you aspire to. Unfortunately for a great number of pre-retirees, the path of Ricky and Heather is what actually happens. Too many people, as they approach their retirement years, seem to think there will be a pot of gold at the end of their personal rainbow in the form of a massive payout—such as a large pension, inheritance, bonus, large commission check or stock options. So for most of the preceding decades they neglect the fundamental principles of wealth building that would have helped bring them security.

## WHAT THIS BOOK WILL SHOW YOU

Few people are used to having a lot of money. In fact, many still believe being a millionaire is "super rich," and they don't realize they actually may need to become millionaires sooner than expected. Those who make a good income often end up spending it on depreciating assets rather than discovering ways to grow it. Many individuals who don't make a great income believe there isn't enough left over to invest. Most people agree that having money is important, but they're still stuck in the age-old pattern of "income to goods" rather than "income to wealth."

This book will help show you how to build wealth by understanding the foundations. It will not give you specific investment strategies. Why? Because the foundations are solid and won't ever change, while strategies change virtually every year as tax laws, technology, new products and regulations constantly evolve. So by knowing the foundations—the 17 principles outlined in this book—you'll have the background and the back*bone* to capitalize on the appropriate strategies available in modern times. These principles will help you take ownership of your wealth-building process that, in turn, will help you develop strong financial strategies. You'll expand the tools necessary to help remove any present or future roadblocks that may keep you from accumulating the amount of money you really want to have.

## THE MONEY-SPENDING CYCLE

Throughout their lives, people generally go through varying stages of splurging and saving. While young and living with their parents, most individuals place very few boundaries on their money. They buy what they want, when they want it—and if they don't have enough money to get it, they simply ask Mom or Dad to buy it for them. Then while in college, money usually gets tighter as they balance a full-time course load and a part-time job. They struggle just to afford the rent, textbooks and some meager groceries. But with so many credit card companies building permanent booths in student lounges, today's college students are getting a premature introduction to bad debt.

Later, while single and on that first or second *real* job, the only thing that matters is today. Impressions count, and young people splurge on that name-brand suit, the trendy car and the top-dollar martinis. Retirement is *years* away, so why bother saving? Eventually, however (like Ricky and Heather), people realize they have to actively interact with their money and scale back, trade in the trendy car for a *responsible* one, and *start saving*.

If they've done things right as they near retirement, they now have a tidy sum—even wealth. Then comes the spending again with exotic trips, expensive toys and vacation property. Ideally, they don't go overboard, and the money will last through retirement, but sometimes it doesn't.

We all go through stages of our lives where money slips through the cracks (and our fingers) and other times when it accumulates nicely. I want you to experience and sustain great wealth accumulation by making better decisions more often and more consistently.

## SEVENTEEN WEALTH PRINCIPLES THIS BOOK WILL HELP YOU UNDERSTAND AND PUT INTO PRACTICE

### Principle 1: Know That Values Determine Decisions
While life has its share of uncertainties, the more secure you are in identifying actions truer to your goals, the more likely you'll reach them. In this opening principle (yes, I'm calling them principles instead of chapters) we'll discuss the importance of values as a key basis for making decisions.

### Principle 2: Pursue Visionary Goals
While you can't always predict what the future will hold, having an understanding of your personal needs and desires, building the framework for what that may look like, and identifying steps needed to get you there are key components toward having and accomplishing visionary goals. I'll explain how a swamp and a beaver helped me to realize this.

### Principle 3: Take Ownership in Your Future: 'My Word Is Good'
Most people today will retire on what they personally saved—not from a pension, Social Security, an inheritance, or lottery winnings. *You* are your greatest asset for building wealth. Believe in your ability to succeed.

### Principle 4: Play Both Offense *and* Defense
Earning lots of money is not as much of a factor in creating wealth as how you spend it. While financial offense (income) generally captures the greatest attention, focusing on financial defense (what you do with your income) will win the game. Without a strong defense, almost no amount of offense is enough.

### Principle 5: Buy Things That Go Up in Value
Do the rich really get richer and the poor get poorer? The answer, to a considerable degree, is in the habits of the rich, not because of their starting point. You don't need to *already* be rich in order to be wealthy. If

you engage in the habits of the poor, you will likely be poor—or become poor. You need to practice the habits of the wealthy in order to be rich and stay rich.

### Principle 6: Ask Yourself, 'Am I Spent?'
Are you in the ranks of the "not rich enough"? If so, you may need to take a step back from the lifestyle you're living and adopt the habits of the wealthy. Pursue real wealth rather than getting caught up in chasing the false appearance of wealth. Be careful that you aren't just borrowing a lifestyle that you'll never truly own.

### Principle 7: Leverage Others' Expertise for Personal Gain
Life is too complex to understand the maze on your own without a little direction. Money and the pursuit of wealth are no different. There's too much knowledge out there for you to ignore. But ignore it is exactly what you'll do if you attempt to get wealthy totally on your own. This book will show you how to learn from others' expertise and experiences.

### Principle 8: Choose Your Team Wisely
A wealth manager's role is to look out for your best interest, but that's in a perfect world. In the real world, every advisor enters the industry with a different set of motives. Learn how to evaluate and critique the advice of advisors.

### Principle 9: Decide What Motivates You, Then Pursue It
There are two main reasons people are motivated to take action—to avoid pain or to pursue pleasure. Pursuing pleasure often keeps you moving in the direction of your choice.

### Principle 10: Play the Game and Execute the Plan
While an idea may rev the heart, action moves it forward. Dreaming about the life you desire is important. The doers of this world, however, understand the difference between wishing and having.

### Principle 11: Ask Three Telling Questions
Evaluating the vast array of investment opportunities may seem too confusing a task to undertake. Rest assured, though, that there's an easier way to understand investments and determine which are appropriate for you. In this principle we'll discuss three key questions to ask before

investing—and how you can expand on them to become much more investment-savvy.

**PRINCIPLE 12: DON'T FORGET THAT YOUR STORY'S ENDING IS PREDICTABLE**
Do you identify what you're doing right and wrong by determining where your actions are taking you, based on those who have gone before? Fortunately, tens of millions of people have already retired to help show us the way. The decisions you make with money today will, in large measure, determine your financial future tomorrow.

**PRINCIPLE 13: STAY FINANCIALLY HEALTHY**
Measure and monitor your path to your desired end point, and you will likely succeed in reaching it. Dream up a goal, paying no attention to the means or conditions of accomplishing that goal, and it will likely become a vision of the past. You need to measure your effectiveness.

**PRINCIPLE 14: GET ORGANIZED AND STAY ORGANIZED**
Stay very organized with money, and you're likely one of those who have the most control over their money. Further, disorganized people are generally the ones struggling with wealth. This is not a coincidence. Learn how to make organization simple and effective for a positive outcome.

**PRINCIPLE 15: PUT YOUR MONEY ON A MISSION**
Save your money successfully, and you may amass more money than you'll actually use during your lifetime. Those with foresight may be able to significantly help themselves and others: those close to you, as well as charities.

**PRINCIPLE 16: SHARE THE WEALTH OF EXPERIENCES**
It would seem logical that each generation becomes more knowledgeable about money than the previous. Unfortunately, talking with others about money is generally taboo. This secrecy needs to change if we in the United States are to understand and advance in our efforts to become a nation of empowered and financially secure individuals, able to survive in a future with few pensions and little Social Security.

**PRINCIPLE 17: ALWAYS REMEMBER THE *WHY***
Your will must exceed the challenge at hand. Never forget your personal *why*, as it is the fuel of your will—and determines its strength. If you

forget *why* something is important, you lose the courage it takes to tackle the task.

## GAIN CONTROL

The main theme of each of these principles is to gain control over the financial factors that matter most. Each principle is necessary to round out the entire wealth-accumulation experience. Determine which of these principles you're already good at, as well as the ones you need help with. Then surround yourself with intelligent, wise people. Growing is a continuous process. Recognize and celebrate your strengths and convictions; don't dwell on what you don't do well. Spend your time using your unique abilities—and outsource the rest.

Learning about money and how to manage it can be dry for many people. New clients often have told me they were dreading our first meeting like they dread going to the dentist (no offense to dentists). But they soon realized that growing money is fun. I want you to have fun reading *Wealth Is a Choice,* so, along with my goal of writing engagingly, I've sprinkled some cartoons throughout the book to help lighten things up even more. Let's make this a positive experience!

## TODAY IS SOONER THAN TOMORROW

In writing this book I'm recognizing the sea change in U.S. society away from a pension mentality. What are the alternatives? An economic downward spiral for individuals *or* a society of individual wealth. Rather than fear this change, let's embrace it.

I believe that with individual wealth comes freedom. When people have enough money to support themselves and their families, they have more security, more options and the ability to make better decisions. I believe that this change, once realized, will prove to be most welcome for most Americans.

Not only are pensions becoming a thing of the past, it's no secret that there are problems with the U.S. Social Security system, as well as growing problems with healthcare. Both are destined to get worse before they get better as more and more Baby Boomers[2] reach retirement age. And it's no secret that these societal trends affect each and every one of us.

---
2  Generally considered to be those children born in the U.S. between 1947 and 1964.

I know that at one time people were taught to believe that they could work hard and somehow somebody, some company, some organization would make sure they would always have enough money. I know that most people don't believe this is true anymore. I also know that people struggle with knowing what to do about it. There's information overload. There's someone, it seems, on every block of every city in the United States ready to show you how to do it. Yet many people are still too scared of the responsibilities and unknowns of individual wealth to know exactly what to do or what advice to follow. We know that the game has changed, but many of us haven't yet taken action and committed to the new rules.

> *The angel and devil on the cover are taken from the memories of my childhood Saturday morning cartoons ... One tells you how much fun it is to be mischievous and irresponsible, whereas the other reminds you to have fun but stay true to your goals.*

I know what it's like to fear the unknown. For me, what makes a car run is a mystery. I fear the mechanic. I've had too many personal experiences when mechanics took advantage of my lack of knowledge. I know what it's like to be in a taxi in a strange city and believe the driver is taking me around the block a few too many times. We often fear what we don't fully understand. Sometimes we let that fear dictate our actions, while other times we're able to conquer our fear.

While it's abundantly clear that we as Americans need to become wealthier and much less dependent on social systems or pensions, it still seems as if *how* to attain that wealth is shrouded in mystery. It's no wonder many people don't yet have enough money invested for their future. How do you welcome change with conviction if you don't understand what it takes to win—to come out on top?

I wrote *Wealth Is a Choice* in order to share with you the "secrets" of what I believe it takes to win.

The extent of your success is driven by the quality of your decisions. The angel and devil on the cover are taken from the memories of my childhood Saturday morning cartoons. At an early age I was reminded through humor that quality decisions eventually beat those decisions that sometimes were more enticing or intriguing. The devil in one ear and the angel in the other: One tells you how much fun it is to be mischievous and irresponsible, whereas the other reminds you to have fun but stay true to your goals. We all need that reminder in life—the realization that, with each choice we make, there will be subsequent effects and consequences. With each quality choice, we invite bigger and better opportunities. With each negative choice, however, knowingly or unknowingly, an opportunity is lost.

My wife and I recently welcomed our second son into the world. It will be years before our boys are old enough to understand how money works. In the meantime, there will be blankets and toys, hockey and fishing, best friends and girlfriends. Even at this young age they learn there are choices in life. As a child, I could refuse to clean my room and be punished, or I could be productive with my time and get it done as quickly as possible. What I soon realized was that cleaning my room was inevitable. By refusing to promptly attend to my chores, I was merely postponing the inevitable and delaying the freedom I would have afterward.

I'll help my boys learn the positive effects of productive decisions and, in so doing, instill that "secret" of wealth accumulation that eludes too many people today. I'm going to share those same "secrets" with you—"secrets" I've learned during my career in wealth management. Most important is the understanding that becoming rich is not that difficult. Being a millionaire is within the mental and financial capacity of just about everyone. The principles of money are the same for everyone; the resources are equally available to almost all social and economic classes. Most of the wealthy people I know started out just as poor as everyone else.

As we prepare to move into the heart of the matter, I have two questions for reflection: Why do you work? And will you work forever?

People work hard to get ahead. Even so, it can feel like you're in the proverbial rat race with no finish line. If you work simply to pay your bills, then you'll probably be in that race for as long as you live. If, however, you work in order to advance your income by reinvesting your earnings, then you're embracing the transition—even transformation—to individual wealth. For many people, this change requires learning new behaviors, those of the wealthy. The learning curve requires effort and, unfortunately for too many people, the challenge ends there. You'll find that you can't be lazy and get rich at the same time. If you believe, as I do, that "your room must be cleaned," then the sooner you accept this fact the sooner you'll get ahead. You must take action and pursue opportunities. The good news is that you can attain wealth without turning into a business tycoon or analytical number cruncher. Indeed, some of my wealthiest clients have had modest careers.

In *Wealth Is a Choice* I go back to the basics and use logical, commonsense strategies that you can implement in your daily life. With each principle you gain more control of your money—and your outcomes—by removing the fear of the unknown. In today's environment, with smaller (or nonexistent) pensions and instability in the Social Security system, the average person has the ultimate motivator: He or she has no other option than to succeed!

I don't want you to ever look back on your life and say, "I should have gotten started sooner—and I wish I had made better decisions." *Today is sooner than tomorrow.* The principles in *Wealth Is a Choice* will show you the way. Now, together, let's embrace this change and take action to gain control for a successful future!

Ready? Let's get started!

Your financial freedom is just around the corner ...

## Principle 1

## Know That Values Determine Decisions

A wise friend of mine, John Dallas, once told me, "To be good at fishing for trout, you must understand the needs and life of a trout." I apply that same concept to wealth building when I say, "To live a fulfilled and financially secure life, you must understand the needs and meaning of your life."

What you believe about life (your values, philosophies, or religion) dictates virtually all your decisions on a conscious or subconscious level—even your monetary decisions. Remember, nothing good comes easy. To truly understand your beliefs requires self-discovery, which can be quite a challenge because your beliefs are a moving target. Nearly 2,500 years ago Socrates said, "Know thyself." It's still true today. The very fact that you are trying to discover your deepest values demonstrates that you are growing, evolving and changing. Therefore, once you believe that you have reached the *truth* of who you are and what you believe, your truth may have already changed. And that's good! It means you're alive and kickin'.

But before you throw in the towel, realize that it's the *pursuit* of knowledge that often leads to the greatest breakthroughs. At the core of the pursuit is the desire to understand your values. Why are values so important? Values crystallize your decision-making process. They help to give you a compass in an otherwise confusingly "gray" world. How intimately you understand your own sense of right and wrong will provide strength in decisions, most certainly monetary decisions. How often you act on your values identifies the strength of your potential outcomes.

## GET ANCHORED

The accuracy of a forward projected effort lies in a consistent foundation. In archery, we call this foundation your "anchor point."

If you've ever shot a bow, you know how difficult it can be to hit the broad side of a barn. I've shot a bow and arrow since age 10. Limestone cliffs surrounding my yard provided the neighborhood a 10-foot wall of protection from stray arrows. My target was usually a black quarter-sized marker dot in the middle of a paper plate. I attached the plate to a stack of three bales of hay and consistently hit the plate while practicing from 30 paces. But whenever I was under pressure when actually hunting, everything seemed off. I would raise my bow, find the notch in the corner of my mouth for proper placement, look at the deer and exhale. Then for some reason, I would adjust my position, missing the deer completely. This phenomenon has been called "buck fever," and, when the pressure is on, it can apply to many sports and pursuits in life.

For years this pattern baffled me. How could I be a consistent shot when I had no pressure, but when it mattered most, miss the target miserably? I found my answer years later one restless night at 2 o'clock in the morning.

I was in college living in a house with a large garage in the backyard. I had three bales of hay stacked against the outer garage wall. Late one night I went outside with three arrows, my bow and a paper plate. I drew a circle in the middle of the plate and pinned it to the bale of hay and stepped back 30 paces. The moonless night was dark and only a dim streetlight on the opposite corner provided slight illumination. I squinted to see the plate, but could barely see the circle in the middle. Nevertheless, I notched an arrow, drew and released a shot toward the center of the plate. I stared until my eyes watered searching for the arrow on the plate but couldn't see it. So I notched a second arrow, drew, shot at the plate and *spark!* Right in the center of the plate a spark flashed in the night and I could hear metal striking metal. Shocked that I might have hit my own arrow I notched a third arrow, drew and shot again. There was another spark and sound of metal striking metal. When I walked up to the target, I was amazed to see all three arrows, dead center in the plate, sharing a hole no larger than a dime! I had made three of my greatest shots in the worst shooting conditions ever.

**Archery anchor point**

In the morning light, I tried again. Not only did I miss the *center* of the plate, I didn't even hit the *plate*! I notched another arrow, drew the bowstring back and lined up my shot. My first alignment felt right, but it looked wrong, so I adjusted. I was sure the correction cost me an accurate shot, but I didn't trust myself to go with my instincts. Unlike shooting in the dark, now everything was visible. I could see the target and all the surrounding distractions. It gradually dawned on me, in the light of day: I now had *too much* information and didn't rely on my instincts as I had the night before.

That morning I discovered something that has helped me become a consistent bow marksman ... and has helped me in life, including investing. My inconsistent shooting was not because I was a poor shot. My problem was that I didn't know how good a shot I really was! While shooting at night, I had to rely on my anchor and instincts; I was able to focus on only what mattered, to sort the important from the unimportant. But during the daylight hours—with all the distractions, visual adjustments and distance checks—I doubted my original arrow placement and erroneously adjusted my shot.

What I had been lacking in my archery ability was confidence in my anchor—the key placement of my fingers consistently positioned the same way each time in the corner of my mouth and jaw. It's the starting point and basis for consistent and accurate shots. Without an anchor point, arrows fly everywhere. Likewise in life, we need an anchor point—a firm understanding and consistency in our values.

In *Wealth Is a Choice* I discuss the importance of establishing personal monetary values, which will become your anchor point while making financial decisions. You may like some of the financial values I list, values that have worked well for others; or you may establish financial values entirely on your own that best fit your situation. It's common for people to see the word *values* and associate it directly with a moral or ethical standard. That, however, isn't my intention as I use *values* to describe an anchor point. While some of your moral and ethical values may have a bearing on your money-related decisions, my use of *values* in this book is primarily to encourage you to establish a solid anchor point that helps you consistently make great decisions that are in line with your personal *financial* goals. That said, I do not believe in sacrificing personal ethics in order to make money.

> *In archery the arrow reaches the target almost instantaneously. So the feedback is immediate. With money, the results of decisions sometimes aren't known for years.*

## WHY VALUES MATTER

In their most basic function, our values help us make good decisions. Your values may not necessarily be consistent with everyone else's, but what matters is that you have a means of evaluating your decisions against a target or goal. The confidence that your anchor point (your values) will successfully guide you to the target (your goal) allows you to make decisions that some would perceive as extremely difficult. Conversely, if you subscribe mainly to values that someone else dictates for you—and you don't understand why you're following those values—then you truly don't have an anchor point, and your decisions will often appear inconsistent and lacking in empathy or depth. This is a common dilemma of political candidates who sometimes are so "scripted" that the essence of who they are is lost—until they throw away the script and assert their true identity.

When it comes to financial decisions, lacking a strong anchor point causes second-guessing. I have seen people fret even when they've made very good decisions. Without the proper anchor point, both good and bad decisions can cause people to stay up late, argue and stress about money. If you took the time to understand how your actions are attuned to your values and goals, you would be able to recognize the logic, then feel good about the decisions you've made. In archery the arrow reaches the target almost instantaneously. So the feedback is immediate. With money, the results of decisions sometimes aren't known for years. This is all the more reason why you need to be especially sound and solid in your anchors. If you make poor financial decisions, it might take you years to recover. In real life, there are only so many times people can miss their shots before they're out of arrows.

Much of the financial services industry is, truth be told, a sales industry. No matter how well you know people, if they are negotiating for your money there is a certain amount of sales involved. When someone is telling you a compelling investment story, having a firm understanding of your core values will help you determine whether this is the right investment for you. People who are confident in their values invest with conviction. They ask clarifying questions and don't give up until they understand the answer. Generally, after enough probing, you can better see the true colors of any message that might have ulterior motives behind it. Those with a strong foundation of values can weed through the stories they're told and discover the truth—or simply decide to invest where there's less smoke and fewer mirrors.

The more you understand your values, the more you may realize how they can differ from the values of others. For example, I have clients who are working toward becoming multimillionaires. Some of them will attain that wealth through mutual funds and stock investments and tell me they wouldn't do it any other way. Some believe that managing wealth through real estate is more in line with their financial strategies, so they structure various investments of commercial and residential properties. Either approach may prove successful over the long term, and neither is "wrong." However, a vast number or combination of strategies may be most appropriate. As these investors grow and are introduced to alternative investment strategies, each group may eventually realize it can be healthy to build wealth with more than one method. Sometimes you will find a "diehard" stock or real estate investor who then risks transcending the boundaries of his or her expertise.

For every investment strategy out there, you'll find those who will rave about how great it is on the one hand—or lament its very existence on the other. Everyone has either a good or bad experience with a specific investment strategy. Depending on personal experience, that particular method may then become either taboo or highly recommended. As a result, individuals form an "absolute," such as "you should never" or "you should always"—and preach that absolute to others. The more you understand the principal methods of wealth accumulation and your values around money, the more you come to understand there are few, if any, absolute strategies. Rather, you'll simply discover there are times when one method is better than another—and vice versa.

I have a client couple who thought variable annuities were the best thing out there. Jay and Lisa put $85,000 into one and let it grow for a long time. Years later, it was worth less than $10,000 because they spent most of the money to live. Then, tragically, Jay died. The variable annuity had a death benefit equal to the original deposit, so Lisa soon received a much-needed check for $85,000. Conversely, I have seen other people invest money into a variable annuity under the wrong circumstances. They needed liquidity and current income, but the investment representative failed to inform them that the illiquidity of the variable annuity would make it absolutely wrong for them. Their investment experience was quite negative since they had to fork over large surrender charges when liquidating the annuity to pay their bills. One person will tell you to *always* put your money into a variable annuity, while another person will tell you to *never* put your money into a varible annuity. For each, personal experience is the primary "variable." In reality, it comes down to your own values and goals in order to determine what is right for you.[3]

## DEFINE YOUR VALUES

As you begin to define your values, organize them into their simplest form. Which ones will help you reach the most important specific goals? One of your values might be that "Each new investment should be more appropriate than the last one." This is a very simple and logical value to help weigh the cost/benefit of repositioning your investment assets.

---

[3] Variable annuities are long-term insurance contracts designed for investing for retirement. An annuity offers options under an insurance contract, which includes mortality and expense-risk charges, as well as providing for lifetime payments. Annuities offer the opportunity to allocate premiums among fixed and variable investment options that have the potential to grow tax-deferred, with an option to receive a stream of income at a later date. Early withdrawals may be subject to a deferred sales charge and, if taken prior to age 59½, a 10 percent federal penalty may apply. Money distributed from an annuity will be taxed as ordinary income in the year the money is received.

I recently received a call from a client, Ann, asking me if it was a good idea to liquidate some of her account to help finance the purchase of a rental building for a relative. The relative was going to pay a yield of 6.5 percent back to her. Ann was having a hard time determining whether this made sense, but she felt somewhat obligated to help because she has money. So we looked at what she would have to liquidate to give him the funds. Her best option was to sell a mutual fund in her brokerage account.[4] The fund had substantial gain and would therefore create a taxable event to sell. Also, while there would be no future guarantee of returns in the next 12 months, the fund's performance was significantly greater than 6.5 percent. Based on the premise that each new investment should be more appropriate than the last one—and considering her goal was long-term accumulation—this opportunity appeared to be a financial distraction rather than an improvement. The relative, however, believed he had taken the necessary steps to guarantee Ann wouldn't lose her money. Whether or not his "guarantee" was foolproof, it did help to minimize her risk and allowed Ann to contemplate more creative financing terms. For example, Ann proposed that the terms be either 6 percent or equal to the return of the S&P 500 (Standard & Poor's).[5] This makes the investment worth considering and could be in line with the aforementioned "appropriate" value. Under those terms, had the market provided her with a higher rate of return she could still collect on that return from her relative. On the other hand, if the market declined that year, she would still receive a consistent 6 percent yield. Now it's up to the relative to see if those financing terms are in line with his values necessary to secure a profitable deal for himself. Identifying a value question to help make the decision takes much of the emotion out of the equation. Not only does Ann have a basis for making a decision to lend the money, the relative has a basis for understanding why her answer might be no.

Having an arrow aimed at financial independence as a target will help keep you from making poor financial decisions. You might establish a value of "Excess cash flows are used to create more income." I had a conversation recently with a client named Lee who received a bonus and

---

4  A mutual fund is a professionally managed investment company that invests in specific stocks, bonds, options, futures, currencies or money-market securities. The investment manager chooses which securities to invest in based on the fund's objective and its diversification requirements. An investor should assess the risk/reward potential of any investment based on his or her personal risk tolerance. Past performance is not a guarantee of future performance.

5  The financial services industry is replete with "alphabet soup" abbreviations and acronyms. This book's policy is to explain each acronym/abbreviation on first reference only. The reader also is encouraged to refer to the glossary at the back for more information.

was wondering what to do with it. Normally Lee would pay down debt. Over the past year, however, he was able to get ahead of his credit card balances. Lee's initial reaction was to go spend the money on things and sign up for treats that would create further monthly commitments, such as memberships and home electronics. It made sense for him to have fun at first—until we discussed the reason people work. We don't work just to buy things. We work to gain independence, so we aren't slaves to a job. A portion of one's earned income needs to go into other assets that also create income. Lee decided to adopt a new value: Each time he had a large influx of money, such as this bonus, he would invest at least half. This value not only helped him to become wealthier and more independent, it made the tangible purchases more fun as he knew he was making good decisions with money.

Your values help take the hundreds of complex and unforeseeable circumstances and identify a method to handle those circumstances one at a time. Often I'll have a client with a decent income who wants to buy an expensive car as a reward for achieving a promotion, degree, award or even a birthday. These personal gifts can cost upwards of $1,000 per month when you take into account taxes and insurance. The purchases are generally a lease and go for two or three years. For those who aren't focused on their target and have a loose set of monetary values, the decision to spend comes easily. Much later they realize the actual cost of their spending. Most people who buy and pay little attention to the effects of buying don't like to know the facts. They tend to neglect to add up the total cost of the purchase over the years of the contract. So they usually just look at the price of today—$2,000 down and $1,000 per month—and decide whether they can afford $3,000.

On the other hand, people who have established monetary values to help them make these decisions know the cost of spending well before any commitment is made. They add up the $2,000, plus $1,000 a month for three years, then calculate the cost as $38,000. They don't stop there. If they're 15 years away from retirement they calculate it as if they had invested the $38,000 for retirement. Depending on their interest-rate assumptions, they might come up with a future number north of $100,000. At that point they decide if the promotion treat (or whatever they're celebrating) is worth more to them than $100,000. Generally it's not, and this exercise helps them realize that.

You can change the numbers, but the concept will remain the same. A payment of $500 a month will cost more than $50,000 and so on. All level of cost has a measurable effect on your goals. As Sir Isaac Newton said—and Descartes before him regarding the two ends of a stick—"To every action there is an equal and opposite reaction." You can ignore the reality of the reaction, but you can't stop it from happening. If the effect is small or incidental to meeting your goal, then a decision to purchase may be appropriate. If the purchase takes you farther from your goal (even to the point of putting your financial security in jeopardy), the decision will be easily made to invest rather than spend. You might decide to rent the car for just a week—to satisfy your short-term desire—and invest the rest.

If financial independence means nothing to you, then nothing will stop you from buying. But when you have a goal that matters more to you than instant gratification, your values will step in and offer some advice. Simply put, "Does this decision take you closer to or farther away from your targets?" If it takes you farther away, I hope you'll have the courage to follow your values and make the right decision. *You don't have to "do without" throughout your life; you just have to discover a productive way of gaining what you want.*

With experience comes wisdom. On your path to financial independence, you might follow a hot stock tip and see your money devalue by half.

Painful as it may be, experiences like this (if you choose to learn from them) will help you make better decisions in the future. When you're considering investing in a stock, your values will cause you to question the investment: Could this stock purchase get me closer to my goal of financial independence? What are the chances I could lose all of my investment? What do I need to understand about the company in question to know what the risks are? What are the real costs of this investment? If you cannot complete your "due diligence" (research) to satisfy your values, don't invest the money.

> *You don't have to "do without" throughout your life; you just have to discover a productive way of gaining what you want.*

You're usually aiming your arrow toward one of the following targets:

- Personal development
- Philanthropic causes
- Building a successful business
- Financial independence
- Special goals, such as owning a vacation home or paying for college

You also develop values that help you determine how direct your path is to the target or targets. Here are some effective values:

- Will this opportunity make life better for my family?
- Is this investment more appropriate than the last?
- Earned income is used to create more income.
- Excess cash flows are used to create more income.
- Come to a comfortable understanding before you let the arrow fly.
- Evaluate investments if they're losing more than 10 percent.
- Invest in things you have the greatest amount of control over.
- If you have less control, is the upside potential worth the additional risk?
- Understand the costs of any investment.
- Evaluate the desired outcome of each investment.
- Don't take anything at face value.
- Own the outcome.

And the simplest value-related question to ask in all circumstances:

*How does this action take me closer to, or farther from, my end goal?*

The beauty of that simple question is that it forces you to recognize that there are two sides to every decision, and every decision has ramifications. It also helps you remember that decisions are made with a goal in mind.

Once you've identified your targets and values, see if any of them overlap so you can combine them. You don't want redundant targets or goals (that are really the same thing) cluttering your mind space or disguising what is most important. Likewise, you don't want to establish values just for the sake of having lots of them.

My former office neighbor across the hall, "Spike," was good at this. He was nearing the end of his career in financial services—and he was quite astute at reading people and understanding how things worked. For Spike, there was one value in a business transaction that was more important than anything else. When we discussed business opportunities I was pursuing, he quickly determined whether I was likely to get the deal. Spike knew that, nine times out of 10, if I didn't talk directly to the decision maker I had very little control over the decision-making process. His #1 value for predicting the outcome of my business opportunities was therefore to determine how direct my path was to the top person. As much as I liked to argue with him, ol' Spike was usually right.

If you take the time to identify and understand the values that are relevant to your pursuit of wealth, you'll capture a great deal more time and money along the way. The more you put your values to the test, the more confidence you'll have in your decisions—and your financial foundation will be more secure. Just like my bow-shooting ability, not trusting your anchor yields wild arrows. When you trust your values, you can move confidently toward your target.

## VALUE YOUR VALUES, BUT LET THEM EVOLVE

What money beliefs or values are you holding onto that you really know very little about? What money values did you get from your parents that you cling to today—but don't fully understand? For many of our parents and grandparents, retirement meant living comfortably on Social Security and a pension. For them, preparing for retirement was a matter of buying and owning most of the things you wanted to have in life before you quit work. Their goal was to pay off the mortgage, purchase the lakefront cabin, own their cars free and clear, and have a fully furnished house. They may have wanted to have some money in the bank as a cushion, but it easily could have been less than $100,000.

To what extent are their life experiences relevant to your life and financial situation? Today if you followed their strategy of putting all of your money into paying down your mortgage and retiring with even $300,000 in 401(k) savings and no pension, you would find a very short-lived retirement. You would most likely be back to work in your late 60s or early 70s. Today your parents (and especially grandparents) may not understand some of the financial decisions you make on the path toward financial independence. They may believe you should do what worked for them. If you blindly accept their monetary values of having very low fixed overhead in retirement at the expense of putting much less emphasis on building wealth, you may have failed miserably. Rather than just agreeing with their strategy, understand why that value was so important to them. It may have pertained to living through the Great Depression of the 1930s, or there may have been other factors. To what extent are their life experiences relevant to your life and financial situation?

Today financial independence is much different from one person to another. Therefore, the strategies or values that work for someone else won't necessarily work for you. Holding onto advice from someone you respect without educating yourself about the details can actually have devastating effects. Yet there are timeless values, such as *live within your means,* that transcend many generations. As a matter of fact, many of my principles get back to the basics of fundamental fiscal responsibility practiced by the Great Depression era, while still remaining flexible enough to embrace current times.

I visited the Jefferson Memorial in Washington, D.C., a couple of years ago and was deeply drawn to some of the logic written on its walls. One phrase really caught my eye:

*"I am not an advocate for frequent changes in laws and constitutions, but laws and institutions must go hand in hand with the progress of the human mind. As that becomes more developed, more enlightened, as new discoveries are made, new truths discovered and manners and opinions change, with the change of circumstances, institutions must advance also to keep pace with the times. We might as well require a man to wear still the coat which fitted him when a boy as civilized society to remain ever under the regimen of their barbarous ancestors."*

Those simple words say so much.

Early in the 21st century we are starting to see massive numbers of Baby Boomers moving from the workforce into retirement. While they were accumulating money for retirement, fluctuations in investment performance weren't all that crucial so long as the ultimate outcome of healthy positive returns was met. Now, as they enter into the next stage of spending their wealth rather than accumulating it, they will soon realize that fluctuations in investment performance matter a great deal.

When the stock market went up and down, many Boomers habitually invested each pay period into their 401(k)s. The market volatility sometimes worked to their advantage as they purchased mutual-fund shares at lower prices, then held those shares during the market's recovery. If they're now spending their money on a monthly basis and taking that income from the same fluctuating investments, volatility has the opposite negative effect. They may be liquidating mutual-fund share prices during bad economic periods and selling their investments for half the price (or twice as many shares sold) in order to meet their monthly obligations. A series of negative returns can erode their primary income source years in advance of expectations if not properly planned for.

Therefore, some of the strategies that were appropriate while they were working won't work all that well when they're retired. While evaluating their retirement investment decisions, they can begin with the same initial question: How will this action get me closer to my goal? They must realize that their primary goal has now changed. While working, their primary income source came from their job. This income also was redirected to feed their portfolio the money necessary to build to the size sufficient to cover their expenses in retirement. As they retire, they'll be taking income from their portfolio to provide for their needs.

Other life changes also may trigger adjustments in financial decisions. These could include:

- Marriage
- Children
- Owning a house
- Family dynamics, such as aging parents or health problems
- Job changes
- Unexpected good fortune
- College
- Retirement
- Deaths
- Divorce

At the very least, life changes would suggest an evaluation of your financial values and strategies.

Your set of targets and values isn't something you can simply declare—and then expect that declaration to work for you the rest of your life. Your mind is not unlike your body in that it learns, experiences and grows. The things you believed in when you were younger may have changed. Your ability to grasp the depth of your beliefs because of your learning, experiencing and growing may have become much greater. You may even find that, rather than adding more values to your list, you actually are decreasing them. As you work your way through life, you may understand that only a few things really matter, and focusing on just those few things will show you the best path toward your goals.

## TO SUMMARIZE

1. Having confidence in simple, consistent and clear values can help solidify your decision-making process.

2. The monetary decisions you make today might take years to come to fruition. This means it's even more essential that you make strong decisions today.

3. Ask clarifying questions and satisfy your values before you invest your money.

4. There is usually more than one way to get from Point A to Point B.

5. Having clear values makes saying "no" to a bad investment idea easier.

6. An effective values question is: "How does this action take me closer to, or farther from, my end goal?"

7. Each generation is faced with unique challenges. Strategies that worked for one person and generation may not work for another. Identify values that work specifically for you.

8. Let your values evolve and grow as you also evolve and grow.

9. Pay attention to triggering events that may create life changes and can call for adjustments in both your values and financial decisions.

## Principle 1
## Know That Values Determine Decisions

### Principles in Action

#### Sample: Top three values *

1. That excess income is used to create additional wealth
2. That each decision/action takes me closer to my goals
3. To own the outcome

#### Now list *your* top three values

1. _____
2. _____
3. _____

---

\* For each of the 17 Principles in Action, I have included answers from a sample couple, David and Janna, to provide some guidance in these exercises. These are intended as a guide—or rather an example of a couple sharing their situation in an effort to spark ideas for you.

## Principle 2

---
## Pursue Visionary Goals
---

Any anchors and values you have in life must be in line with your goals. Without goals—more specifically, visionary goals—your anchor points aren't tested. I once struggled with understanding what "visionary" truly meant. Was being visionary something we were born with, and those who didn't have a vision were doomed to mediocrity or failure? Or was being visionary something anyone could nurture and develop?

I pondered my dilemma one fall day walking along the edge of a ridge overlooking a tag alder swamp. If you aren't familiar with tag alder swamps, trust me, they are a nasty piece of woods. These swamps seem to have only one purpose in life: to get humans wet and lost. Animals hide in these swamps when they have nowhere else to go. The grass stands 7 feet tall with thick stands of 10-foot tag alder trees measuring 1 to 2 inches in diameter. To make matters worse, unless you're bending the trees over to walk on them, you're in knee-to-waist-deep mud and water. After you enter one of these swamps and walk about 15 feet, you no longer can see where you came from or how far the swamp extends.

The ridge I was traversing was 20 feet above a virtually impenetrable tag alder swamp in Michigan's Upper Peninsula. The swamp was skinny, only about 100 yards wide, but stretched for a mile east and west. It came to a point along a high ridge and a cedar swamp, which is usually where I would cross and then walk west along the ridge. This time, though, instead of walking along the edge of the ridge and looking down into the swamp, I was casually walking about 30 yards from the edge and was unable to see the tag alder trees. As I walked, I saw something I hadn't seen before in these woods: Beavers had recently gnawed down a large tree and had worn paths from dragging branches into the swamp.

What I was about to see redefined my personal definition of a visionary and transformed it into something I could use.

I went to the edge of the ridge and looked below to see a picture-perfect beaver pond of clear water, surrounded by noticeably fewer tag alders. My first thought was *What are beavers doing in this part of the woods, and how did they ever see the possibility of building a home here?* Then I started to think about what beavers need to survive and build a home for their families: trees of varying sizes, some moving water they can dam to create a pond, grass and mud for securing the dam, and a natural barrier to help hold water on at least one side of the pond. When I looked at the swamp again, I saw the obvious genius of it all.

A narrow creek endlessly pushed thousands of gallons of water a day through this long swamp. The small tag alder trees were ideal in size for building a home and securing the dam. The beavers didn't have to drag the trees a great distance, and they had an unlimited supply of trees for food and future repair needs. The ridge, which extended the length of the pond, functioned in two ways: a natural border to the pond that held the water without a dam and a slide for larger trees for the beavers to gnaw down and drop into the water. In fact, this area was a beaver's dream come true.

So I thought, *Are these beavers the smartest of all the beavers in the world, or did they simply know what basics were required to build a home?*

Similarly, is a visionary person someone who can dream up the impossible, or is he or she also a person who simply has established larger goals (in the case of the beavers, knows what their "home" looks like) and begins to put the pieces together?

As I contemplated this question, I realized that recognizing long-term goals made my short-term needs (goals) easier to identify. The simplicity of establishing goals as a means of accomplishing visionary life achievements was within my capabilities. From that day forward, rather than mastering the art of becoming a visionary, I've worked toward establishing visionary goals.

## WHAT ARE VISIONARY GOALS?

Visionary goals don't have to be earth-shattering. They can simply represent your longer-term aspirations. For some people, these goals may be crystal-clear. For me, long-term goals are vague visions of what I would like to have the ability to do, rather than a clear, tangible item of desire. My visionary goals then provide the framework for short-term goals I want to work toward accomplishing.

For example, while evaluating my college-internship options there were two main long-term goals I sought to achieve. First, I wanted to understand money. I came from a family of modest means and, at that time, I was doing a horrible job with my own finances. Beyond having debt to help pay for the cost of college, I carried credit card debt and had a low credit score. I knew there must be a better way to live. Second, I didn't know exactly which career would be best for me, but I did know that I wanted to be in a leadership position. When I saw an opportunity to work for a financial services firm under the direct supervision of an energetic boss who was excelling inside the industry, it was easy to recognize this as an opportunity to advance my long-term goals. When I took the internship, my vision for a sound financial future (especially given my obvious personal difficulty in that area) and developing my leadership skills were all I desired to accomplish. Finding my life's work was a definite bonus. I didn't know I'd enjoy the business so much—and that one day I would help countless people make better decisions to get them on track for a better life. I certainly didn't think I'd eventually write a book on the subject! I worked each day with great zest, seeking out opportunities to further advance toward my long-term goals.

## PEOPLE LIKE TO KNOW WHERE THEY'RE HEADED

When I was a kid my younger brother and I used to explore the woods near our house. It was a half-mile walk to the ski hill, and across the street from that was a large cedar swamp. Without seeing a map, we didn't know how big the woods were. I can still remember the first day we set foot in those woods. Joe stayed within eyesight of the road while I walked ahead through the trees. I ventured forward through the underbrush until I couldn't hear Joe yelling anymore. That was far enough, and I ran back to safety, heart racing with visions of getting hopelessly lost. Each day we returned Joe and I would explore farther, marking trees along the way with our pocket knives to help guide our direction home—not unlike Hansel and Gretel in the old fable. By the end of the summer we made a startling discovery: the other side of the woods! I can still remember crawling under a pine tree to the edge of a cattail swamp and seeing a house on the other side. Once we realized the woods weren't as large as we had first thought, we quickly explored the rest and found that a road in fact circled the entire piece of property. There was, therefore, no way for us to ever get lost.

That knowledge of boundaries and a clear understanding of where we were headed gave me an immense feeling of relief. The clarity allowed Joe and me to really discover the woods and find the treasures hidden within. In most of my experiences in life I find it reassuring to know in a general way where I'm headed—even if I don't always know the precise route to my destination. The time when I'm a little more anxious is the instant when I don't really know where I am. If, during that moment of anxiety, decisions are made, they are usually poor.

I have a friend whose 85-year-old father fell and broke his hip, after which he had surgery with, of course, a large dose of anesthesia. A few days after being brought from the hospital to a nursing home, the man was still recovering from the effects of the operation and anesthesia. He was having lunch with his adult son in the dining room of the nursing home where he had never lived before. With great sincerity the old man fixed his gaze on his son and said, "Hank, I just have one question for you: Where in the Sam Hill *am* I?" The older gentleman had always loved geography and had a good sense of direction. When driving, he was known for his ability to intuitively find his way without a map. But in the nursing home he was a fish out of water; he had no sense of place. Indeed, it's hard for any of us to keep our eyes on larger goals when we feel lost and disoriented.

Visionary goals help you establish the framework for your life and therefore the clarity you need to make solid decisions throughout life. Such goals are often large but vague in detail. Think of the type of lifestyle you want to live in retirement as a framework for one of your visionary goals. It's fine to be general with your long-term vision. The purpose is simply to get a mental picture of what you hope to achieve one day. This outline of a lifestyle gives you the framework for what level of income to shoot for, as well as how much of that income to save in order to be able to afford your chosen lifestyle. It also may help identify what career paths you need to take in order to get there. Now you can work backwards.

For example, you may desire to one day retire to a grand country retreat while maintaining a place in the city. The retreat sits near the base of a mountain or on the shore of a lake. Wildflowers and nature are as plentiful as sunsets. You can imagine spending the best times of the year doing the things you enjoy most:

- Northern time outdoors when the season is right
- Visiting the white sands of the tropics when you need some warmth
- Being there for your grandchildren wherever their parents take them
- Spending time in the city with front-row seats to the best shows

These ideas and others may become your visionary goals for financial independence. This dream involves owning a couple of homes, one in the city and one in the country. In order to help make that happen, maybe you need to learn what owning two homes is really like; be sure to try to make some money doing so. Search for manageable real estate to purchase as an income source. It's common in Michigan, for example, for vacationers to rent a northern lakefront cabin for a week or weekend, especially during the summer. In fact, *www.vrbo.com* is a Website used by people all over North America to advertise rental availability. VRBO stands for "vacation rentals by owner" and, as the name implies, most of the cabins on the Website are owned by individuals who rent out their personal vacation homes while they aren't there. Some do this as a lucrative business, and some do this to help subsidize the cost of their own vacation home. Some, I'm sure, have good intentions but lose money. Do all the necessary research and make a smart buy in a good rental location.

The place you purchase might not look anything like your dream escape, but it's a start. It's not just owning land, it's also an education and a stepping-stone toward bigger and better things. If done right, the small vacation retreat you buy today may help pay for the one you dream of down the road. It will certainly help you make better decisions when the time comes for you to purchase your dream retreat. I have a number of clients who have done this very thing in their own lives; generally they have great outcomes.

Establishing the visionary goal of owning a second home and thinking through the steps of what is needed to accomplish it forces you to do the things necessary to have it. If all you do is dream and are envious of the things you don't have, then you'll never learn what it takes for people to own what they want. Deciding how you're going to take the initial step toward accomplishing your visionary goal helps you recognize the obstacles you first need to overcome: your credit score, income, other debts, experience or simply lack of focus.

Your monetary values can help you identify the opportunities or obstacles to achieving a visionary goal. You may decide that rather than spend $10,000 a year on various vacations, it may be more worth your while to purchase a small vacation home, even if the net potential annual cost is thousands of dollars a year. Your values may help you realize that "spending money without building equity" gets you farther from your dream of owning your own place. While vacationing in a place with no room service or other amenities may not seem as appealing as a five-star hotel, this small sacrifice makes it possible for you to own the vacation home you really want. If you do things right, other doors could well open, and you might find yourself duplicating the process, buying other income-producing properties and obtaining your dream vacation home much sooner than you ever expected.

By establishing a visionary goal and figuring out the short-term needs to accomplish it, you stay true to your monetary values and learn from your experiences. Through each experience, you grow closer to reaching your goals, which gradually become much clearer. Visionary goals may change somewhat in substance as you're exposed to new ideas in life. You may even find that some of your visionary goals become bridges to something else even more inspiring. Or you may find yourself quite content with a simpler life. It's OK to change your target, so long as you always have one. Years later, while basking in your success, you'll be able to look back at the "vision" of where you started your journey with small steps.

One of the beautiful things about visionary goals is that they give you the courage to stick to your strategies. The story of Charles and Amy from the Introduction represents a couple who may not have identified clearly everything they wanted in life, but they had a good idea of where they were headed. In the beginning, when savings were small and their life experiences limited, they laid the foundation by having shared values of how to accomplish their goals. They made tough yet educated decisions, which ultimately led them to a prosperous life. Their values helped them identify what financial experiences or opportunities were appropriate in reaching their visionary goals.

> *When you look at yourself today as if it were tomorrow, it's like having a second chance to get things right.*

## MEASUREMENTS KEEP YOU GROUNDED IN REALITY

I'm a loyal Detroit Lions fan and always will be. Each year I believe they have a great shot at winning the Super Bowl. My optimism continues through the season until finally, once again, they're mathematically eliminated from the playoffs. Then I lose interest in football and wait for the next season. Even when the Lions have lost almost all their games, why do I hold onto hope until the very last second? My expectations for the Lions are based on hope, dreams and potential, rather than facts. My fantasy of Detroit's Super Bowl victory can last just a few months. The league has the ultimate measurement in place to bring me back to reality: winning games. Luckily I'm doing no harm to myself by wishing the Lions made it big. As surely as day follows night, the next time football season starts I will expect nothing but the best for my team. Go, Lions!

In life, on the other hand, the ultimate measurement generally doesn't appear for many years. Unfortunately, this can allow people to live in "fantasyland" for a long time. Through establishing your vision and identifying some of the steps in realizing your larger dreams, you also will be establishing measurements to help you stay the course. If you see retirement only as something to achieve 15 or 25 years from now, the likelihood is slim that you'll be prepared for it. Just like anything else you succeed in at work or play, when you have a timetable and method of evaluating your progress, you're more likely to succeed and get the job done. Visionary goals become your framework.

*The most common statement I hear from people in their 60s is "I should've started sooner."* What lies ahead is no great surprise to anyone. If you're going to retire without a pension, ask someone who is already retired without a pension what it's like. It's no great surprise. They'll tell you they don't get a paycheck anymore, but they still need to pay their bills. Don't look back 20 years from now and ask, "What might I have done differently?" *Look ahead as if it already is 20 years from now and see if you're doing what you need to do today to get there. When you look at yourself today as if it were tomorrow, it's like having a second chance to get things right.* If you want to change what you see, don't wait! Take action immediately. *Time is something you cannot get back. Today is sooner than tomorrow.*

Detroit has been going through heavy layoffs through much of the early 21$^{st}$ century. Many people who expected to have jobs into their 60s are finding themselves out of work in their 40s. I read of a man who recently lost his job in the automotive industry. This wasn't his first experience of being laid off. Back then he wasn't prepared for it. Those were difficult times as he struggled to provide for his family. From that time on, he decided to save his money and never be in that helpless position again. He made a special effort to save when times were good, because he never knew how long they would last. He also pursued other interests in order to have career options in the event his job changed or was lost. He cultivated relationships in related industries to establish a client base for a consulting business. So when layoffs once again came his way, he had the savings accumulated to handle the adjustment and had the contacts ready to go into business. Today he is making more money than he used to make as a full-time employee and is an inspiration to others.

Life will provide plenty of opportunities and plenty of hits. You don't need to have gone through tough times in order to be prepared for them. As you work toward your visionary goals, you'll identify many potential obstacles and overcome them before they block your progress. There are plenty of knowledgeable, seasoned men and women in the world, like Spike across the hall from me, to share their life experiences (including their failures) so that we don't have to make the same mistakes they did. It's sad but true: Many others around you will feel the pain of being unprepared and lacking options. Remain in control over your destiny by having a clear understanding of what you desire in life, thereby helping you avoid many of life's potential hardships—and reaching your dreams. Take a long look into the vision of your future for the answer to the question "What can you be doing today?" If you know where you're headed, you'll soon figure out how to get there.

Look in the mirror every day. This is your ultimate measurement. It helps you understand that you own your actions, decisions and position in life. While you're paying attention to financial goals, relationships, and business or social achievements, continue to look at *you*. Your life may not be perfect today, but it's the pursuit of improvement that yields a prosperous, happy, healthy life—and inspires others to do the same.

## TO SUMMARIZE

1. Without visionary goals, your anchors aren't tested.

2. Long-term needs and goals build your visionary framework.

3. Most people make better decisions when they understand their boundaries and know where they're going.

4. Once you have your visionary framework in place, work backwards to discover what you need to accomplish today. "Begin with the end in mind," says Stephen Covey in *The 7 Habits of Highly Effective People.*

5. Measure progress made toward your goals, as this will keep you grounded in reality.

6. Don't look back and say, "If only I had done things differently ..." Look ahead to your visionary goals as an opportunity to get it right the first time.

7. Learn from the failures and successes of others.

# Principle 2
## Pursue Visionary Goals

### Principles in Action

**Sample: Top three visionary goals**

1. To retire with a house on water and surrounded by woods where we spend half the year during wonderful weather. To then spend the other half of the year in an apartment or condo in a great city where we eat out, take in shows, and are exposed to lots of people and diverse culture.

2. To have a family that is financially secure, allowing us to have great family time together and not always chasing our tails keeping up with bills.

3. To have a profitable business selling wildlife photographs, taking trips to exotic places to get the right "shot."

## NOW LIST *YOUR* TOP THREE VISIONARY GOALS

1. _____
   _____
   _____

2. _____
   _____
   _____

3. _____
   _____
   _____

# Principle 3

## Take Ownership in Your Future: 'My Word Is Good'

After interviewing hundreds of clients, I've realized there's a very common behavior that shows why some people are more productive with money than others. By and large, the successful people I interview aren't relying on anyone or anything else to take care of them. They embrace money and take control. "My word is good" carries weight only if the person saying it takes ownership and responsibility for his or her life. Dreams sometimes do materialize in life. However, if you are risking your financial independence on a wish (a crutch), you'll tend to find yourself always dreaming and never having.

A crutch is something one depends on for support. After I had knee surgery, I used a crutch to help me walk around. Without it, I may not have been able to get myself to work. After the first couple of weeks, I had to start moving around without my crutch in order to advance the healing process. If I had become totally dependent on the crutch, I likely wouldn't have recovered as well as I did. While the crutch was absolutely necessary for me in the early stages of my healing process, a good crutch can become a "rogue" crutch if one depends too heavily on it. Kids are quite adept at using their parents as a primary crutch. Little children are smarter than we generally give them credit for—and if you do everything for them, they'll soon learn they don't have to grow up and take responsibility anytime soon.

## HERE ARE THE MOST COMMON FINANCIAL (sometimes termed "rogue") CRUTCHES:

- **A pension.** Many believe that someday they'll receive a respectable retirement pension income from their respective employers.

- **A future job change.** Some believe that eventually they'll advance into a career that pays them outstanding sums of money.

- **A business idea.** They believe they're one step away from hitting it big with their great invention or business idea.

- **A "plan" to never retire because they love their job.** They believe they'll work until they no longer wish to—and that this will be their choice. They don't consider that the company might eventually replace them.

- **A dream of winning the lottery.** They believe that someday their number will actually come up.

- **The most common crutch of all?** The ever-faithful parents!

Yes, I've found that even people in their 50s who are making large six-figure incomes still believe that when they're older and haven't quite finished saving for the future, Mom and Dad will come through. Right now, Mom and Dad are healthy and doing great. Although these individuals hope their parents live for a long time and become wonderful grandparents for their children, they believe that Mom and Dad have lots of money. They also believe that eventually most of that money will be theirs. So they continue working into their 60s and act like they love their job and wouldn't know what to do if they didn't work anymore. All the while, they're starting to wonder to what extent their parents' suddenly emerging healthcare costs are taking away from their eventual inheritance. Such things aren't often talked about, but people sometimes think about them.

I recently met a couple, Tony and Jill, who were deeply dependent on their parents' money. They were very well-dressed, wore expensive jewelry and pulled up to my office in a luxury car. From outward appearances they looked much richer than some of my wealthier clients. They were in their 50s and wanted to retire soon. Both were excited at the prospect of an active early retirement. They wanted to do a lot of traveling to different countries and return home to a nice place down south on the Gulf Coast. They have been spending a lot of money and want to keep that lifestyle going though retirement. They had become accustomed to dining out often, taking in top shows and receiving preferential treatment wherever they went. They believed that all four of their parents, who had grown up during the Great Depression, did too much scrimping and saving most of their married lives. Jill and Tony both felt they had been deprived of many of the finer things during their respective childhoods and definitely didn't deprive their own kids.

By now I was getting a little nervous about their financial stability. Unless they made an amazing income, my fear was that they didn't have enough money to their name. Unfortunately, I was right. They were in debt up to their ears and had minimal savings in 401(k)s. I started reviewing other numbers with them. Neither would receive a pension, Social Security estimates were well below their expenses, and they didn't want to work part time in retirement. I asked them why, if they wanted to do all these wonderful things in life, hadn't they saved more money? It was almost as if they were negotiating with me to share a magical secret that would instantly create hundreds of thousands of dollars.

Finally, I saw the problem. Both of their parents were well-to-do. Her side of the family was older and not in the best of health, and his side wasn't far behind. They didn't know for sure how much money they'd inherit, but years ago both of them had seen some of their parents' statements and knew there was a lot there. Those same parents who chose not to give their children a lavish upbringing now, 40 years later, had become a crutch for their adult kids' financial existence, even survival.

> *"Do YOU want to be responsible for your own future, and are you ready to learn how to do that, or are you going to continue to rely on something or somebody else to support you?"*

When I meet people in this situation, I have to stop the meeting and ask a rather pointed question: *"Do YOU want to be responsible for your own future, and are you ready to learn how to do that, or are you going to continue to rely on something or somebody else to support you?"*

Alternatively, a virtually opposite trait exists in families that are doing a good job regarding their future. Contrary to what many people believe, not only can you enjoy the money you make, you can do much more throughout your life when you achieve financial independence rather than simply live for the moment.

The United States is a country where people who start with nothing can become very rich, famous and even powerful. Frequently, the fact that they had nothing to start with is one of the reasons they achieve such success. Some people need their backs up against the wall before they finally drop their crutches and take matters into their own hands. While I hold a tremendous amount of respect for those who can rise from nothing, I have an equal amount of respect for those who have something and achieve the greatness they desire. The latter group also has what might seem to be a surprising burden to bear—the crutch of current success. As I mentioned earlier, college was one of my first experiences of seeing and getting to know people from affluent families. Some of the students were very well taken care of by their parents, even spoiled. It's interesting to see years later that some of those wealthier college students are now struggling to make ends meet on their own, while others have taken ownership in their future and are quite successful today by any standard. Others of us students from more modest beginnings have had similar outcomes.[6]

I want to make it clear that I believe we all have crutches in life. In every strategy put forth, there's something that we're counting on. If there was nothing you relied on—such as your 401(k), Roth IRA (individual retirement account) or other investment strategy—that may mean you had totally given up. The crutch I *don't* recommend having is the one where we wait for something to happen, rather than taking positive action for the stability of our own future. This is a close cousin to the crutch of believing we'll make it big, and because of that belief we don't do the day-to-day things necessary to be secure in case the breakthrough doesn't actually transpire. So some crutches are healthy, and some are not. Like fire and water, our crutches need to be kept in check.

## BOTTLENECKS AND CRUTCH MANAGEMENT

Back in my early years as a financial advisor, I used to eat lunch with Dusky, a friend and associate. We began our career on the same week and consequently went through many similar struggles and successes in tandem. One of our favorite places to unwind for lunch was the fast-food joint across the street. We didn't go because we thought the food was good (though it wasn't bad), we went because this particular establishment was managed horribly. After an intense week of making a number of rookie mistakes on the job, we found a peculiar satisfaction in critiquing someone else's flaws. Management at this restaurant was so poor in maintaining a productive flow of services—and the staff so vocal about it—that we could have been charged extra just for the "pleasure" of watching. It was reality TV ahead of its time.

---

[6] I attended Siena Heights University in Adrian, Michigan, but I didn't obtain a degree. A series of events—including a life-threatening and expensive accident in my junior year—eventually led to my decision to leave school. Working full time appeared to be the best solution at the time. As is often the case with big decisions in life, there were many factors: some within my control, some out of my control, some logical, some having to do with being a young college student with unclear and shifting priorities. I've been fortunate in life, even with my unfinished college experience, and I encourage the pursuit and completion of a higher-education degree.

During our time standing in line and eating, Dusky and I would solve all the restaurant's problems by eliminating the areas that produced the biggest bottlenecks, thereby allowing for a more efficient business flow.

A consistent bottleneck was a vocal worker, Kathy, who seemed to have no concern for the customers or management and what impression she was making on them. I specifically recall one afternoon when the line at the counter was excessively long. Kathy was a small, slender, chain-smoking woman in her 40s who had a hard time coping with stress. Kathy took her frustration out on the rest of the restaurant—staff and customers alike—as if it were their fault she was slow. She couldn't have weighed more than 110 pounds, and yet she fronted such a fierce "affect" that she scared everyone else who worked there. Not to mention the customers! Kathy was a bottleneck because she slowed and sometimes stopped the flow of business.

Bottlenecks in business are areas where the least amount of "stuff" can flow through or is temporarily stopped up. Practically speaking, you'll never eliminate all the bottlenecks. Once you have fixed the largest problem, the second-largest problem becomes Enemy #1. Firing Kathy would have eliminated a major bottleneck, and it would have been a start to dealing with the other problems in the restaurant. Reducing bottlenecks in business is an effective yet continuous improvement exercise.

Identifying and then working to reduce the dependence on our crutches is not that much different from strategies used to minimize bottlenecks in business. If you take an outsider's perspective while evaluating your financial strategies, you can pick out strategies or events that you're relying too heavily on—just as easily as Dusky and I could point out the bottlenecks we saw at the fast-food restaurant. Even in a nearly perfect system where you have a great amount of control over the process and outcome, you rarely have perfect control and are therefore dependent on *something* going your way. You can be consistently working to identify potential problems that could impede your desired outcome. So, just as some bottlenecks in any system are practically inevitable, you can never eliminate every financial crutch. You can, however, protect against rogue ones, five of which are identified earlier in this principle.

As noted above, not all crutches must be eliminated or minimized. *"Crutch management" is the process of identifying, even safeguarding, a few of your crutches.* For some, this is like a strategic game of football. You line up your players on one side of the field, your opponent on the other. The goal is to hang on to the football and eventually make it to the end zone—total financial independence. Having the football represents control, which is something you want in your possession as much as possible. As your pot of wealth grows, there will be others who will find creative ways of trying to *take* it. You may have the 401(k)s and IRAs invested in equity mutual funds all lined up like players on your team and not know that they're vulnerable to the same opponent, such as stock-market volatility. The fact that you have a crutch—401(k) and IRA invested identically—is easily disguised, and you go about life not keeping it in place. For every crutch, even a productive one, there are just as many if not more opposing players on the other side of the line of scrimmage who can ruin your game plan.

Maybe your crutches are your advisors. There are numerous Hollywood "Where are they now?" stories in which financial advisors get the blame for a fortune lost while the star was out playing. The story is the same with all too many professional athletes. Or perhaps your crutch (or delusion) is health-related—your inability to believe that, in an instant, things could change, and you could suddenly have to pay hundreds of thousands of dollars in medical expenses. It could also be your 401(k), as you invest money dutifully yet don't compare performance or value against what your actual needs are.

To help ensure a comfortable life, discover what your potential obstacles could be and safeguard against them. For most people who don't have an excess of wealth to build a fortress around, identifying your crutch (or crutches) is a process of seeing your future from a pessimistic point of view. Try to imagine all the things that could go wrong, developments that would disable your current wealth-building strategy. This will help you identify your points of vulnerability, as well as safeguard your current resources.

Try not to rely on anything too heavily, especially things that are beyond your control. This is a recipe for disaster. Some soon-to-be retirees who are expecting 100 percent of their income to come from a pension or Social Security are a good example. They worked for years earning a living, raising a family, having some fun and keeping out of trouble without concerning themselves too much about building large amounts of capital. They believed that when they put in enough time the company would provide for them. Many of those same people are currently nearing retirement and now see things quite differently.

Their perception of the quality of the pension may have come from the retiring worker they replaced when they first took the job. The old-timer may have told them a story about how he or she was retiring in a couple of months and would have an income even larger than what the newcomer was making. Words of wisdom may have been to work hard and pay your bills so that someday the newcomer would also be able to stop working while still bringing home a pension check. Therefore, the strategy that may (or may not) have worked for the retiree 25 to 40 years ago stuck, and the newcomer's crutch became the belief that he or she would receive an adequate pension during retirement.

Things change over time, and the newcomer from our story would have done well to change also. People live longer, competition is fiercer, markets are more demanding and "the clothes that fit the child" don't fit the adult (see the quote from Thomas Jefferson in PRINCIPLE 1). But the crutch never left. All through his or her working years, the newcomer expected someday to receive this large payoff that would provide for the future. That dependency allowed the newcomer to take care of only today as if tomorrow were somebody else's concern.

Now the once-far-distant retirement is here, and you suddenly realize it's actually nobody else's concern but your own. For the company, today is what matters as it is trying to stay competitive in the ever-changing global economy. Pension retirees can complain about what they expected or what they were promised. But company officials will say, "None of that matters if we go out of business tomorrow; you should have planned." And the cold, hard truth of the matter is yes, you should have planned better. While you can't go back and retrieve time, you can start doing a better job today. People often ask me if it's worth it for people, later in their career or even retired, to learn more about money—or if it's just too late for them. *I believe it's never too late.* While there might not be a miracle strategy that could elevate their financial position overnight, they can at least improve their situation relative to what it is today. Small changes today can have a large impact tomorrow, no matter how old you are.

If the newcomer would've had a different conversation with the old-timer, things might have been different. For example, a few old-timers might have done the newcomers a favor by saying, "This is a great place to work, but no matter what you think of the company's good nature or intentions, the economy might stick a knife in your back and twist the blade just when you're least expecting it. So do your family a favor, and never count on anything from the company long term. Take care of yourself and your family first by building a fortress of resources so you always have options."

While the words of wisdom may have been a blow to the optimistic joy in starting a new job ... if the newcomer had heeded the advice, today he or she wouldn't have to worry about money. Retiring with a pension of 25 to 30 percent of current income would be more than expected. For as long as the income lasts, it's just icing on the cake.

## **IDENTIFY YOUR CRUTCH**

So how do you identify your crutch? It's simple. Just write it down. From what source(s) do you believe your financial freedom will come? If you said "401(k)," check your math. How much are you intending to live on in the future? How much money do you need to have accumulated to grow that income?

Next, take a look at the amount of money you currently have saved. How much per year will you continue to save, and what rate of return can you expect to earn? For example, let's say someone is 45 years old and expects to live on $100,000 ($198,000 indexed for 3.5 percent inflation) at age 65. Then he or she needs to maintain that income with inflation for the next 30 years. I know 95 may be a long time to plan on living, but expecting to die by age 80 isn't realistic either. If this person earns 7 percent on the money during retirement, he or she would need to have $3,571,239 saved by age 65 (assuming no pension or Social Security). Then, assuming $200,000 in a 401(k) and an investment of $15,000 per year, earning 9 percent return will accumulate to $2,042,950 by the time he or she turns 65. This is still less than what is actually needed by more than *$1.5 million.*[7]

> *For any of you who are starting to get lost in the numbers, it only proves my point. That is, we often count on things too heavily before we've even made the calculations to see if they will work!*

For any of you who are starting to get lost in the numbers, it only proves my point. That is, we often count on things too heavily before we've even made the calculations to see if they will work!

If you do the math, it's easy to see how your 401(k) has become your crutch. The $200,000 may seem like a lot of money, and so might the $2 million it may be worth later. Those amounts aren't enough for the individual in question, however, based on his or her personal goal of $100,000 income at age 65.

"I'm sure Social Security will be there in some form" may become the next crutch. Even inputting $20,000 per year of Social Security income with a 1.25 percent cost-of-living adjustment, the pot of gold needed at age 65 is $3,289,741—*still short $1.2 million!*

---

7 The hypothetical investment results are for illustrative purposes only and should not be deemed a representation of past or future results. This example does not represent any specific product, nor does it reflect sales charges or other expenses that may be required for some investments.

Then one might ask, "Can't someone get by on $2 million?" And I'm sure they could—up until age 79, at which time they'd be flat broke. Or one may say they don't really need to live on an income of $100,000. That's fine, but if they're accustomed to living on more than that amount today, they need to know how they'll reduce their expenses in the future. For many people, the house is currently financed at 80 percent, and the kids are getting ready for college (that they haven't saved for yet). And although their current household income is well in excess of their retirement goal, they still carry balances on credit cards. It might be possible for someone to spend much less than what they make today in retirement but, if they're like many people, they'll have to make some major spending changes. The desired income and future numbers are relative. Some people spend $50,000 a year and are on pace to achieve an annual retirement income of $33,000, only they don't know it because they haven't yet run the numbers.

## NUMBERS DON'T LIE

The nice thing about numbers is that they don't lie. My dad used to tell me the same thing about my compass. My first real lesson was at age 13, coming out of the woods at night alone. My dad was about a quarter mile away on the other side of a trail where we were to meet at dark. I had followed him in and out of this area numerous times and thought I could get out on my own. But everything looks different at night ... and sounds different. Your mind starts to play tricks as shadows creep, leaves rustle and branches snap around you.

After walking a short distance, I came to a low swamp area with ankle-deep water. Never before had I crossed water on the way to or from my spot, so I began to panic. I knew that a quick look at my compass would get me back on track. I shined my flashlight on the twirling ball and waited for the arrow to point positively north. I needed to head due west, left of the north arrow. To my surprise, west was straight ahead, right through the water. I didn't believe this was possible, so I shook the compass and checked again. Once more, west was straight ahead. Now panic really set in. Coyotes yelped, owls hooted and critters scurried in the black of night. I had visions of being lost for days or attacked by large hungry animals. I wasn't sure which way to go and believed my compass was broken. The next "logical" thing to do was ... scream my head off! So I did, until finally I heard a distant call from my dad, right in the direction my compass was telling me to go.

For many people their crutch is "not believing the numbers." Until you're satisfied with the accuracy of your numbers, your personal compass, you'll have a difficult time doing what is necessary to reach your goals. As I said, numbers don't lie. Our assumptions, expectations and knowledge will change. But if you tell me "X" is what you want to live on and "Y" represents the assumptions of inflation, rate of return and life expectancy, the answer will be quite accurate based on those factors.

> *Let the gifts that come your way in life be just that: gifts. The minute you start depending on them will be when things go bad.*

Eliminating your unhealthy crutches helps put you in reality. I have seen people who are expecting a large amount of money in the future, such as $500,000. *In my experience I've seen that if they actually ever do receive the money, it will likely be a lot less than the expected $500,000.* Since they believe such a large amount of money is coming, they start buying things they otherwise would not, well in advance of receiving the money. They also stop saving their own money. They intend on catching up with their savings once the large check comes. The money is supposed to be here in July, then August, then October, and so on. Suddenly it's not $500,000, but closer to $400,000. That figure doesn't include some expenses or taxes, so it actually might be more like $300,000.

Time drifts by, yet still no money. Many of those anticipatory purchases are on credit, so they have to start making payments. Because the monthly costs are greater than their income, they need to sell some investments to help cover bills. Still more time goes by, costing them more money. If they finally do receive the infusion, what's left may be enough to get them back on their feet in the same financial position they were in before news of the windfall. Or the money may never come through, and what once could have been great fortune turns out to be a demolition derby, even bankruptcy.

Most people are generally optimistic. This in itself is not a bad trait. But being *overly* optimistic *and* depending on your rogue crutches can cause great harm. *Let the gifts that come your way in life be just that: gifts. The minute you start depending on them will be when things go bad.* If you live your life knowing that you are ultimately responsible for your future and plan accordingly—using the knowledge and resources available—your life will go much more smoothly. The same is true with the windfalls. When you have the bases covered, it's much easier to capitalize on the opportunities.

## PUT YOUR STRATEGIES TO THE TEST

Take a look at your situation. If you aren't retired yet and have time to accumulate wealth, identify your primary investment. Most likely, it's your 401(k). Evaluate your strategy, and be sure to think through how to get the most out of that investment. Then ask yourself a question: *If my 401(k) doesn't work, what do I have next?* What is Plan B? Maybe your answer is a Roth IRA. Great backup! You probably have more flexibility with investment choices in the Roth IRA than you have in your 401(k). So evaluate the investment used in the Roth and determine if you're duplicating your primary strategy or diversifying from it. Now ask yourself what you would do next if the Roth didn't work. Plan C. Do you have other alternative sources of income? Do you look for ways to diversify your income away from your job? Are you investing in real estate for future positive cash flows? What about other income sources, such as a small business?[8]

If you're already retired or nearing retirement, take a look at your income sources. If the primary source is a pension, then ask yourself what you would do if the pension were no longer there. The answer might be a combination of strategies to cut overhead. Or maybe you've accumulated a significant amount of money in a 401(k) and are relying on that as your primary income source. Is all the 401(k) money invested in the market in the same kinds of mutual funds or company stock? If all your income is coming from stock market investments, what are you planning to do when the markets go through a significant decline? Is there a portion of your investment you could diversify to provide some levels of guaranteed income or downside market protection?

What these exercises encourage is preparation for the "what if" scenarios. While discovering alternatives, you're also learning more about

---

8   Using diversification/asset allocation as part of your investment strategy neither ensures nor guarantees better performance and cannot protect against loss in declining markets.

money and what your options are. This exercise may appear to be pessimistic, but soon you'll realize it's liberating. You'll feel more in control as you've identified alternatives and backup plans, rather than living in fear of the unknown. I've seen more than one initially ideal retirement come crashing down financially because a couple didn't properly anticipate possible future events. When you aren't prepared, problems have a way of happening all at once. One of the most common problems is getting stuck with two mortgages. People precipitously purchase their retirement home, expecting to sell their primary house quickly. Years later the mortgage payments and eventual taxes on the property have eaten a significant portion of their retirement nest egg, forcing a permanent reduction in standard of living. Sometimes it's healthcare and nursing home expenses that erode an otherwise good retirement. These healthcare costs could've potentially been avoided by purchasing the proper insurance policies ahead of time. Such situations and many others stand as a lesson for other retirees to learn from and respond to proactively.

## **DO YOU REALLY OWN THE OUTCOME?**

You might win the lottery, you may receive a large amount of money from an inheritance, maybe your company will go public and you'll make millions. It's more likely, though, that none of those things will happen. I believe in being optimistic and find myself often expecting the best possible outcomes. I would not want to live any other way. However, I also believe in balancing that optimism with doing what's right today. Being in control has a great deal to do with taking responsibility. *My word is good.* Say it out loud and ponder if you believe it's true that you own your financial independence. Do you really own it? *My word is good.* Do you just have some savings going on the side for your retirement or a rainy day? Or do you actually have an investment plan established and know what income level it will provide you in retirement? *My word is good.* Are you just putting a few dollars away in a college fund? Or will you be able to tell your children that their education is assured? (By the way, a lot of wise parents tell their children they'll take care of half of all undergraduate college/university expenses if the son or daughter takes care of the other half.) *My word is good.* Do you just have some mutual funds invested "aggressively" for the future? Or do you know exactly how your mutual funds are invested and have chosen those funds strategically to meet your needs and expectations? *My word is good.* Have you signed up for some insurance at work and have a will "somewhere"? Or have you run the numbers and had the conversations to make sure your family will be OK if you die unexpectedly?

Identify what you need, then decide how you'll take care of that need through your individual efforts today, not from what you hope to receive in the future. In so doing, not only will you most likely reach your goals, you'll alleviate stress along the way. It's such a liberating feeling to know that you aren't dependent on things out of your control—and that you're actively working to create a secure future. *My word is good.* Say it as many times as you need to in order to fully comprehend the power of the statement.

*Now own your independence!*

## TO SUMMARIZE

1. Believe in your ability to plan for and implement your own financial independence. Take ownership and say, *"My word is good"* with conviction.

2. Elderly parents are a very common crutch. Too many people anticipate a large inheritance, which may or may not be forthcoming, to solve their retirement problems.

3. People also put too much emphasis on pensions and Social Security, although those crutches are decreasing as we become aware of the inherent problems with these programs.

4. Some people need to have their backs against the wall (no other options) before they finally believe in themselves and succeed financially.

5. Some crutches are healthy; like fire and water, they just need to be kept in check.

6. Crutch management is a process of identifying your major dependencies, then safeguarding against their failure.

7. Put your crutch to the test and crunch the numbers. Like a compass, your numbers don't lie, so believe them.

8. Each time you take the weight off a crutch, you gain more *control*. And that's the bottom line here.

# Principle 3

## Take Ownership in Your Future

### Principles in Action

**Sample: Three crutches**

1. Pension: We're counting on 40% of our retirement income to come from a pension.

2. Inheritance: Our parents are wealthy, and they said there would be quite a bit of money for us. I don't like to admit it, but I realize now that I've been somewhat counting on that.

3. The 401(k): We're saving 15% into it currently and should have more than 1 million dollars in it by the time we retire.

**Now list *your* top three crutches**

1. 

2. 

3.

## Principle 4

---

### Play Both Offense *and* Defense

---

Most people believe that they could finally get rich if only they made more money. I have seen people, however, who have never made more than $80,000 a year become millionaires and others who have made more than $200,000 annually be worth only a few hundred thousand dollars. Time and again it's proven that how much money you earn doesn't determine your wealth. It's what you decide to *do* with your income that determines how wealthy you will become.

If you want to get rich, you need to gain control over your expenses and maintain plenty of free and clear cash flow. There are two major components of cash flow: what goes in as income and what comes out as savings or expenses. Financial offense is focusing on income, while defense focuses on how efficiently you use existing income to create additional positive cash flow.

Offense gets all the glamour. People chase incomes and dream of the day when they might make hundreds of thousands or millions of dollars. Great offense is a skill, and some people are masters at it. But having a strong offense will not necessarily determine whether someday you'll be financially independent.

Defense focuses on using your existing resources to the best of your ability. A strong defense captures all the available income and uses it effectively for creating more wealth. It keeps committed expenses to a minimum, resulting in flexible cash flow, which makes you able to "pounce" on investment opportunities.

## FIRST FOCUS ON DEFENSE

If you desire control and a lifetime of wealth, defense is ultimately the most efficient method to master. I know if you're in the middle of the rat race you might think I'm wrong, but here's why I'm a firm believer that a strong defense is more valuable than focusing on offense. If you are inefficient with your income level today, you'll probably be even less efficient with a higher income in the future. If, however, you become adept at managing your income today, when it grows (and if you continue with your good habits) you will realize more wealth from the higher income. I can't tell you how many people I've interviewed whose income has increased 70 percent or even 100 percent in the past few years, yet they feel as if they can't pay their bills. It's because they have never understood how to spend within their means and build wealth. Until you learn to maximize the resources available to you, increasing income may be an exercise in futility. So while you're taking normal measures to advance your earnings, you'll also want to immediately take measures to improve positive working cash flow with the income you're already handling.

Spending within limits or boundaries can elevate your position indefinitely, while having no boundaries can lead to financial hardship and many more years of difficulty. Living modestly in the early stages of your career helps keep you from being "strapped" by payments and debt while allowing you to save extra money toward a secure future. Reallocating income to other income- or growth-producing assets creates wealth. If you live beyond your means, you have no leftover resources available to grow wealth. It's that simple.

I recently met Bill, who had suddenly experienced an unexpected pay raise and felt it was time for some material satisfaction. His annual income was substantial, especially for someone in his 20s, at just over $100,000. Many of his friends were older and wealthier, so even though his income was good by most standards, it was well below that of most of his social network. Bill felt the need to keep up with them in purchases and spent money as if he earned twice the amount he did. Spending money before you earn it isn't a good idea, particularly if your income doesn't increase substantially to help you catch up to the purchasing and interest charges. Bill believed that, in the next few years, his income would be three times what it was today.

Just as suddenly as Bill's income had escalated, he got hit with the "perfect storm," some of which was his own doing. His income was cut by 60 percent. At the same time, interest charges on his accounts increased, with the biggest blow being his mortgage. On top of that, the housing market declined, and he owed more than his house was worth, making it impossible for him to refinance into a program that could lower his monthly payment. You can do the math for someone who was already strapped (spent):

> *I've always had the philosophy that it's wise to save your money when things are going well ... because there will probably be periods of life when it won't be as good.*

*Lower income + Higher interest rates = Bankruptcy*

For a while Bill felt he was on top of the world as he lived his dream life, but it was just a "house of cards," not substantiated with real financial means. For him, the next chapter of his story is going to be difficult as he deals with the collapse of his assets and tries to dig out of his massive hole of debt and get back to basics, leaving the plush life behind.

I've always had the philosophy that it's wise to save your money when things are going well ("make hay while the sun shines") because there will probably be periods of life when it won't be as good. If you have accumulated some wealth, you'll be able to ride out the stormy seas and still prosper. Like so many other people I meet, Bill thought the good times would continue indefinitely and that he could save later. That might be the case for some people, but in many of the cases I've seen, high income comes with high volatility. Those who have planned ahead for the volatility seem to do just fine. Those who think they're invincible end up being crippled by that kryptonite.

## IT'S ALL ABOUT CASH FLOW

The first step to having a strong defense is to analyze where you are. I don't want to tell you to do a budget. That sounds boring, and most people don't want to feel hamstrung by a nickels-and-dimes budget. So think bigger and prepare a cash-flow analysis instead. *Imagine your personal finances as a business, and organize your fixed and variable overhead.* Separate things into the two columns, starting with fixed expenses. Itemize all consistent or committed expenses, such as utilities, debt service and other payments. Then list out the variable (or discretionary) expenses, such as travel, entertainment and gifts. Use your checkbook, credit card statements, and debit card statements as resources to go back and track your spending. Be sure to include your federal and state taxes, as well as Social Security. If you don't have an outline for a cash-flow analysis (budget), you can download a spreadsheet from our Website at *www.jpstudinger.com.*

Once you have everything listed, categorize items into groups, such as:

- What it takes to run your house.
- How much money you spend on transportation, food, entertainment and debt.
- Your wealth accumulation (the most important of the three).

Then compare your totals with your gross income and see what's left over. This is where you may get disappointed, especially if your analysis shows you to be in the red. That's OK though. Knowing where you stand today is one of the first steps toward improving your situation tomorrow. The work you just did will help you identify where to begin cutting. You can't fix what you don't know is broken.

My stories sometimes portray a grim picture of people who are having a tough time with money, but that doesn't have to be the norm. I hope you're inspired by the challenge of gaining control over your money and the pursuit of wealth. The principle here is simple: You will be wealthier if you have control over your cash flow. If you keep waiting for "the big break" before you change your spending habits, stop waiting. Making more money as a solution to your high expenses seems logical, but until you master the discipline of managing the money you have it's possible that no amount of income will get you on track. Just look at all the examples of people winning the lottery, then going bankrupt. Understand and practice the principles of growing money, and you will have money forever. Otherwise, you're just a participant in the big rat race, with a tightening stranglehold on your life.

Picture your cash flow like your arteries. Clogged arteries can stop the blood flow to your heart, leading to a heart attack or even death. Are your financial arteries clogged with overhead, leading you to eventual bankruptcy or even poverty?

Or are your arteries clear with minimal overhead and a strong free-and-clear cash flow, positioning you for a long, healthy financial life?

I often meet with people who are evaluating a buyout, early retirement or layoff. They may have minimal fixed overhead and are able to take advantage of good opportunities to advance their financial position. On the other hand, those people who have expenses close to or even exceeding their income have very little choice in the matter and end up with more stress and negative financial consequences.

> *In reality, lenders are institutions that are trying to capture as much of your future earned income as possible. You're only stealing from yourself if you borrow more than you make.*

Wealth accumulation is a process that includes an understanding of where you are, what habits keep getting you there, and how to break them or capitalize on what you're doing well. The greater the expectations of future income, the more tendency people have to spend and borrow. Some doctors or other high-wage earners can be great examples. Their future generally holds a high level of annual income. It also takes them many years to realize it. Lenders know this and see a doctor (or med student) as a great borrower. Lenders position themselves as those who help you buy something you really need or want today. Debt may be helpful when purchasing appreciating assets—but not for buying things that go down in value. *In reality, lenders are institutions that are trying to capture as much of your future earned income as possible. You're only stealing from yourself if you borrow more than you make.*

Sometimes a quite well-educated doctor will spend earnings many times over, with expectations to get even when the big payday comes. Unfortunately, interest charges and lack of awareness can lead to years of financial catch-up. Instead of being quite wealthy shortly after finally becoming a high-wage earner, some have a negative net worth lower than vocations that make a fraction of the doctor's income. If a physician's threshold for debt remains high, he or she may never break the cycle. It's difficult for someone who has sacrificed as much as doctors routinely do (in med school) to finally make it, then sacrifice further by applying most of their income toward debt or savings. More commonly, if you were already spending money before you had it, when you finally make the great income, you just spend more of it. The lenders infiltrate even deeper, not wanting to be paid off, rather trying to capture as much as they can of the now-much-greater income. Certainly not all doctors spend prematurely, but I've seen a number who have, and it's a debilitating experience for them. I also have seen a number of doctors and other high-wage earners who took a different path and experienced significant growth as their income increased. Where you end up tomorrow is determined largely by the choices you make today. After all, wealth *is* a choice.

Rather than purchasing material assets and increasing finance charges, pursue increasing free-and-clear cash flow with defense. Any measure you can take to minimize your committed overhead—and allocate that money toward good assets—will help ensure your financial stability and growth. Pre-committed assets choke your cash flow and your ability to reach goals. If your expenses have clogged your financial arteries, then you need to find ways to reduce those expenses.

## ANTICIPATE CASH-FLOW CHANGES, AND STAY AHEAD OF THE CHANGES

I have a client, Colleen, whose income went from over $200,000 a year to $70,000. She knew this was going to happen in advance and prepared gracefully for the change. Rather than spend the higher income, Colleen immediately checked her budget and made sure she was able to live within the $70,000 income. As she began adjusting to that lifestyle, she saved the difference. She moved into another house, bought investment real estate (while her income was higher to help qualify for a mortgage), minimized fixed monthly financial commitments and saved every dollar available. As a result, her net worth quickly doubled, and today she is in an amazing financial position. Colleen is in control financially and doing things that are important to her. What she did was both logical and practical. It was also brilliant. Most people, however, would not have responded that way.

Ask yourself if you would've been as proactive as Colleen was. One of the reasons most people get into trouble during personal economic changes is because most people don't attempt to reduce their lifestyle until *after* the income change takes place. The outcome from following Colleen's lead by cutting early and investing versus cutting after the income change and not investing can be measured in hundreds of thousands—or even millions—of dollars. If Colleen had waited, not only would she not have the investment accounts she has today (worth hundreds of thousands of dollars), she also would've had to rely on credit cards to fill the income voids. She wasn't able to reduce her living expenses overnight. It took time and planning, which included the selling and buying of homes.

Another couple, Rex and Melissa, also had advance warning that Rex might lose his job. They lived in fear of the potential cut, not altering their lifestyle one bit during the anxious months that followed. Sure enough, one day the hammer came down. Thankfully, Rex was given a full six months' pay as severance. Unlike my proactive client above, they didn't start looking for another job until after Rex got his pink slip. Even then, rather than reduce their lifestyle and use the severance as a means of accelerating their financial position (as they were behind on college and retirement savings), they used it to keep up with their current lifestyle and took their time finding a new job. By the time Rex found another job, the severance pay was used up, and they had built up credit card debt they couldn't pay off. A few short years later, their kids were in college, and since Rex and Melissa didn't have money to pay for tuition and expenses, they racked up even more credit card debt that will take them years to recover from. In the meantime, because Rex and Melissa pay for their expenses with high interest rates, they save only a minimal amount into their retirement plans. They are realistically worth well over $100,000 *less* (and under a great deal more stress) because of being reactive rather than proactive. They would've been better off if they adjusted before they were forced into it.

I've often realized in my own life—and in witnessing the lives and actions of many others—that productivity is a wonderful cure-all. Life can get pretty enjoyable when you identify something worth working for and know you're taking strides to reach your goal. On the other side of the equation, life can become pretty frustrating if working long and hard hours is keeping you away from the things you enjoy but still not gaining much positive financial ground: all sacrifice and little gain. If the latter is you, there's an easier way. While spontaneously spending money may offer fleeting moments of great joy, it's small in comparison to the fulfillment that comes from realizing and taking control over your destiny. When you have control, even if you haven't yet accumulated wealth, the pressure to own material items once viewed as a necessity are replaced with satisfaction in other more organic experiences. You may still make those material purchases sometime in the future. If you do, it could well be at a time when you feel the outlay isn't at the expense of the stability of your foundation. Practicing that sort of discipline toward defense is more fulfilling than those who haven't yet discovered that truth can imagine. *The person who utilizes defense is consciously buying freedom and opportunity. Those who buy material depreciating assets (especially on credit), expecting to offset the purchases through a future higher income, are purchasing their own shackles.*

An analogy from the game of chess might be *apropos* here. Those who try to attack too quickly—with insufficient preparation, piece development and defense of their own King—often have their willy-nilly attack fizzle out, and they subsequently get rebuffed by a counterattack. But those who first set their defenses, *then* attack, usually are more successful in achieving their goal: checkmating the opposing King.

Advertisers and marketing firms do a great job of making you believe that you deserve all the good things in life—*right now*. But remember what your parents used to tell you as you lay in bed scared by a movie you had just watched? "It was just a movie; it wasn't real." Now tell yourself the same thing after you get sucked into the world of desire: "It's just a commercial; it's not *real*." Or: "If it seems too good to be true, it probably is." Get yourself back to your own present reality and build on what you need for *your* gain, not what other people need you to buy from them for *their* gain. It's the job of business, of course, to make products easier for people to purchase. No matter what the sign at the store says, though, something isn't really on sale if it will cost you 20 percent interest charges over the next year to pay it off. But for the retailers, it's a home run. Not only did they move their inventory, they will receive payment on that inventory for months while you pay exorbitant interest. Don't be on the consumer side of the equation, getting lured into "easy" credit to buy, then needing to pay for months (or years). In that scenario there is only one loser—and you can look in the mirror to see who it is.

As you work through discovering and improving on your free cash flow, don't ever forget what the struggle felt like before. Use the memory of the anxiety and uncertainty in your life as a catalyst to get really good at defense. This is the starting point to becoming wealthy. Once you have freed up cash, you can begin to create wealth. And while you're going through these exercises, pay attention to the number of people, companies or organizations you owe money to every month. Then take a look at all the ways you create income and wealth each month. If your only income source is your job, then it's time for you to learn how wealth is created. *Be an equity partner in the world rather than a debtor of the world.*

## TO SUMMARIZE

1. How much money you earn doesn't determine your wealth. It's what you decide to do with your income that determines how wealthy you'll become.

2. Financial offense focuses on increasing income. Financial defense utilizes existing income and creates more wealth and income from that base.

3. If you're inefficient with your income today, you'll most likely be even less efficient with more income in the future—unless you have finally taken control of your money by developing a strong defense.

4. Prepare a cash-flow analysis. Split expenses between committed/ongoing overhead expenses (usually monthly) and variable/discretionary expenses. Also list your sources of income or wealth.

5. Visualize cash flow like the arteries feeding your heart. Are they clear and open, or are they clogged, leading to eventual heart failure?

6. Anticipate income changes and adjust well in advance.

7. If you aren't focusing on defense, you're working too hard for the same results. In other words, strong defense will help you reach a million dollars much more quickly and on less income than having a poor defense would.

8. Lenders want your income for their gain. Don't feed their insatiable appetite for your money. You're only stealing from yourself when you spend beyond your means.

9. Benefit from the spenders of the world by having a strong defense and owning equity in what they buy, rather than simply being one of the spenders committing your hard-earned income for other people's gain.

## PRINCIPLE 4
# PLAY BOTH OFFENSE *AND* DEFENSE

### PRINCIPLES IN ACTION

**SAMPLE: CASH FLOW**

| | | | |
|---|---|---|---|
| David's Income | $60,000 | Janna's Income | $60,000 |

| FIXED OVERHEAD | | VARIABLE OVERHEAD | |
|---|---|---|---|
| **Investing** | | **Discretionary Overhead** | |
| 401(k) | 18,000 | Dining out | 3,000 |
| Roth IRA | 5,000 | Vacations | 2,000 |
| Brokerage account | 3,000 | Tickets, events | 1,000 |
| TOTAL INVESTING | 26,000 | Hobbies, sports | 2,000 |
| **Utilities** | | Subscriptions | 1,000 |
| Home utilities | 2,800 | TOTAL DISCRETIONARY | 9,000 |
| Phones | 960 | **Other** | |
| Cable/Internet | 900 | Grocery food | 4,200 |
| TOTAL UTILITIES | 4,660 | Dry cleaning | 700 |
| **Debts** | | Housecleaning | 1,800 |
| Home mortgage | 11,000 | Gas, oil | 3,800 |
| Car loan | 3,600 | Daycare | 6,000 |
| Lease | 3,000 | Babysitting | 1,700 |
| TOTAL DEBT | 17,600 | Monthly memberships | 3,000 |
| **Insurance** | | TOTAL OTHER OVERHEAD | 21,200 |
| Homeowners | 1,000 | TOTAL VARIABLE OVERHEAD | 30,200 |
| Car insurance | 2,000 | | |
| Medical insurance | 6,000 | | |
| Life insurance | 1,800 | **TOTALS** | |
| Disability insurance | 900 | INCOME | 120,000 |
| TOTAL INSURANCE | 11,700 | TOTAL FIXED OVERHEAD | −89,460 |
| **Taxes** | | TOTAL VARIABLE OVERHEAD | −30,200 |
| State taxes | 4,000 | FREE AND CLEAR CASH FLOW | 340 |
| Federal taxes | 12,000 | | |
| FICA | 9,000 | | |
| Real estate taxes | 4,500 | | |
| TOTAL TAXES | 29,500 | | |
| TOTAL FIXED OVERHEAD | 89,460 | | |

# Principle 4

## Play Both Offense *and* Defense

### Principles in Action

### Know Your Defense

#### INCOME

| | |
|---|---|
| $120,000 | 100% |

#### PERCENTAGE OF INCOME DEDICATED TO:

FIXED OVERHEAD (LESS INVESTING)

| | |
|---|---|
| 63,460 | 52.8% |

VARIABLE (FUN) OVERHEAD

| | |
|---|---|
| 30,200 | 25.2% |

INVESTING

| | |
|---|---|
| 26,000 | 21.7% |

FREE AND CLEAR CASH FLOW

| | |
|---|---|
| 340 | 0.3% |
| | 100% |

# PRINCIPLE 4
## PLAY BOTH OFFENSE *AND* DEFENSE

### PRINCIPLES IN ACTION

**CASH FLOW**

#### FIXED OVERHEAD
**Investing**

TOTAL INVESTING

**Utilities**

TOTAL UTILITIES

**Debts**

TOTAL DEBT

**Insurance**

TOTAL INSURANCE

**Taxes**

TOTAL TAXES

TOTAL FIXED OVERHEAD

#### VARIABLE OVERHEAD
**Discretionary Overhead**

TOTAL DISCRETIONARY

**Other**

TOTAL OTHER OVERHEAD

TOTAL VARIABLE OVERHEAD

### TOTALS

INCOME

TOTAL FIXED OVERHEAD

TOTAL VARIABLE OVERHEAD

FREE AND CLEAR CASH FLOW

## Principle 4
## Play Both Offense *and* Defense

Principles in Action

**Know Your Defense**

INCOME
_____

**PERCENTAGE OF *YOUR* INCOME DEDICATED TO:**
FIXED OVERHEAD (LESS INVESTING)
_____

VARIABLE (FUN) OVERHEAD
_____

INVESTING
_____

FREE AND CLEAR CASH FLOW
_____

## Principle 5

# Buy Things That Go Up in Value

*This principle encompasses the one critical element that will, more than any other principle, determine the amount of wealth you create.*

Almost everyone has heard the saying, "The rich get richer, and the poor get poorer." Is it true? Do the rich get richer, and *therefore* the poor get poorer? Or do the rich keep getting richer because they continue to buy what got them rich in the first place? And do the poor keep getting poorer because they continue to buy what got them poor in the first place?

### DOES MONEY GROW ON TREES?

In many ways, accumulating wealth is like planting trees. My wife and I enjoy three trees (one peach, one nectarine, one cherry) that were planted in our backyard a few years before we moved in. With some tender loving care by Kris and me, followed by patience, the trees gradually started to flourish. Throughout the years, they have blossomed into great fruit bearers, especially the peach tree. Each small branch holds so many peaches that the tree loses at least 6 feet in height around picking time.

While some of our fruit trees have been more successful than others, we never would've had even one peach if an elm tree had been planted instead. I don't know of an actual tree that grows money, but I believe you *can* grow wealth, just as a farmer or orchardist grows fruit, by planting the right seeds.

Today we have a financial epidemic in America. Small companies are popping up all over that don't have the resources to provide future pensions for their employees. The large companies (and governments) are trying to get out of the pension business. Even if companies did provide a pension, workers change jobs so often their benefits would be minimal. So the shift in responsibility of accumulating wealth is moving at warp speed to the individual, and most people are standing around wondering what to do.

I see this shift not as a problem but as an incredible opportunity for just about everyone. Pension or not, life is much better when people create their own prosperity and grow their own wealth. Having sufficient financial resources, rather than relying on an institution to provide you with income, is actually liberating.

The principles that help generate individual wealth have been around for ages, but most people haven't taken the time to learn them. Now ordinary people need to have wealth, the amount of money commonly associated with being "rich," just to survive. Everyone needs to take initiative and learn what only the wealthy people knew in years past. So what have wealthy people always known? They know to plant apple seeds if they want to grow an apple tree. They also know that if you want to grow wealth, then you need to plant the seeds that create wealth. After the planting, of course, come the watering, cultivating and nurturing.

Logic tells you that if you want an orchard of trees that bear fruit, you'd be advised to plant fruit-bearing trees. I've met with too many people who go through their working years spending money on depreciating assets rather than productive growth assets, then wonder why they don't have much money for retirement. It's as if I'm in the Bill Murray movie "Groundhog Day"; I keep seeing the same story over and over and over again. They want income for life but have spent most of their money on things that produce little or no future income (and are in fact a financial drain). Before I even look at their assets, people tell me of all the wonderful things they want to do in life and all the fun they have had over the years. They are in their early 60s now, ready to retire, and are seeking advice for a successful plan. When I look at their assets I see all the non-fruit-bearing trees they planted. Then, when I find some fruit-bearing trees in the mix, they generally account for only 10 to 30 percent of the portfolio needed to retire.

Sometimes I don't know if these people are praying for a miracle—or if they really don't understand that it takes much more than they have accumulated. They put the investment statements in front of me, lean back in their chairs and ask, "What do you think?" Then before I answer, they add, "We really don't feel we should have to save very much more than we already have." They're suggesting, of course, the idea that years worked (rather than dollars saved) equates directly to a secure retirement.

If you were to stroll through their "orchard," you would find boats, electronics, clothes, furniture, expensive homes, luxury cars, snowmobiles, jet skis, and other things that go down in value or don't provide for their future. If you want to build wealth, though, you need to acquire things that appreciate, not depreciate, in value.

Does this mean you have to live like a miser without the enjoyable things of life? By no means! *You just have to find a balance based on both your financial resources and your ambitions.* If you want to spend your early years traveling, going through money and being carefree, go ahead. Just know that when you're done having fun, you're going to have to buckle down more than the person who started saving money right away.

Why do you work? Is it to make an income? What do you buy with your income? Do you purchase more depreciating assets, thereby tightening the stranglehold that endless payments and bills have on your life? To put it differently, do you work primarily so you will have to work longer?

*Or ...*

Do you work in order to make even more money and gain more long-term security? Do you buy assets that produce more income? Do you then take your multiple income sources and buy more assets that will eventually allow you to live in total independence? In short, do you work today so that someday you can be free?

Consider the difference between earning an income to spend on assets that drain you financially and investing in assets that elevate your financial position and spending capability. (Can you imagine going to work for fun, not needing the income because you have individual wealth?) When you understand the dynamics and simplicity of this principle, I think the choice for most people is obvious.

## THE SECRET TO BECOMING WEALTHY

That's enough talk about the problem; here's a solution. One way to become wealthy is really not much of a secret at all. *You just have to buy things (assets) that appreciate—or have the ability to go up in value.* Of course, there's a science to investment decision making and income creation that elevates some to higher levels of wealth. For most people, however, the fundamental principle of having money and being considered rich is quite logical. *You just have to buy things (assets) that appreciate—or have the ability to go up in value.* Or think of it as *not* buying things that are virtually guaranteed to lose money. You might not know the perfect things to own, and that's OK. You might start out overly conservative or overly aggressive. You might miss out on growth potential or lose some of your investment in the market. Some mistakes are inevitable—and reversible. The important thing is to involve yourself in the pursuit of acquiring wealth with a thirst for learning and understanding of what investments work well for you. Funnel your resources—time, income or property—into a column on your balance sheet that has the potential to create more time, income and property. Do this habitually, and you almost can't help but get rich.

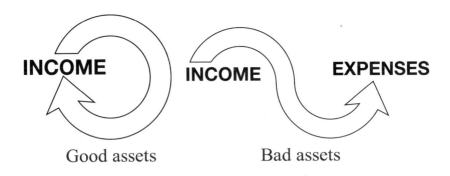

Realize that becoming wealthy seldom results from a windfall or winning the lottery. You don't achieve wealth with "occasional behaviors"—acting on a good tip or following a budget once in a while—just like you can't get in great shape by working out just once a month. When you start working out, you have a tendency to also improve other areas of your life. You want to eat a little better because you don't want all those tough workouts at the gym getting used up by eating too much cheesecake. Your mind and body get into a zone, and soon you're experiencing great physical (and mental) improvements. I started running not too long ago. If you had told me when I started—when I wasn't able to run more than a half-mile—that in just a few months I'd be running a half-marathon, I would've said you were crazy. But that's exactly what happened.

Buying appreciating assets is a similar experience. The more positive assets you start to build, the more you realize the power and simplicity of it. The more effort you make toward establishing your good-asset column, the less you desire the things that take away from your success. So go ahead, get in the financial zone!

As you pursue good assets, be careful not to mislead yourself into making "investments" that are really nothing more than bad assets in disguise. A number of years ago I was talking to a couple, Amir and Lena, about their investment strategy and the steps they were taking to make sure they had enough money for their children's college, as well as their own future retirement. I quickly realized they were going to be short on funds.

As I delved deeper to understand where their income was going, they explained their philosophy of, in effect, pampering their children with "toys" and having the place where all the other kids wanted to hang out. Their idea was that if their kids were home then they couldn't get into trouble—and this would give them more quality family time.

Now don't get me wrong, parents need to spend quality time with their children and build a fun family atmosphere. You can and need to do both: Have quality time and prepare for the future. But when their children reached college age, neither the parents nor their teens had the money to pay for it. They believed they needed to entice their children through money and material possessions in order to keep the family together. Inadvertently, they taught their offspring to spend now and not plan for the future, showing little concern for financial responsibility. As their children are now young adults and establishing families of their own, Amir and Lena are continually reminded that most of those material investments weren't investments at all; instead they were teaching their kids that Mom and Dad were cash machines that always got them what they wanted. Even now, the young-adult children keep coming back for more. It's a treadmill that Amir and Lena are having trouble getting off.

There isn't a single purchase to blame for the struggles they have with money today. Rather it was the pattern of believing that material purchases would somehow bring more stability to their family than showing unconditional love and collectively building a strong financial foundation. Amir and Lena still buy depreciating assets and consider them an investment. Similarly, I have had people tell me they recently made a $15,000 "investment" in a home-entertainment system or got a great (lease) deal on a luxury car. Deals are great to get, and these items are fun to own—if you have the money and aren't sacrificing income. And, to be sure, money and material things can never replace healthy relationships.

## GOOD VS. BAD

So … what things should you buy to become rich? To learn the answer to that question, you have to understand what your good and bad assets are. Look around your house. Almost everything you own or lease is likely a bad asset. Almost all bad assets depreciate in value immediately. Perhaps the best/worst example of a bad asset is a new car, which loses nearly a third of its value the moment you drive it off the lot. Bad assets are usually the things that are the most fun to have, yet they drain the cash out of your pocketbook. I generally place even your home in the bad-asset category. Yes, I know that most homes do go up in value. However, you'll need to have a place to live for the rest of your life. Even though your home usually appreciates, most people don't turn that equity into income for their future. Most people instead use that equity to buy another house. Some sell their home to pay for an apartment or another living arrangement, while others own their home free and clear. So while some may not be paying a mortgage to live in their home, their home is also not creating income and, therefore, remains in the bad-asset column. In my experience I've seen situations where people sold their home and downsized, or used a reverse mortgage to generate income from their house. I see those strategies as a last resort and possible safety net, rather than as a primary strategy to accomplish financial independence. If you put your primary residence in the good-asset column, it can give you a false sense of security.

Here are some other bad assets: furniture, electronics, cars, clothes, boats, jet skis, fancy pens, pets, jewelry, books, magazines and toys. Now factor in other expenses, such as debt payments, dining out, vacations, lease payments, club memberships, cable TV, cell phones, taxes, gambling and the many other ways people spend their money.

Take a look at your personal finances and calculate how much of your monthly cash flow goes toward the items just mentioned. How much do you have left over? If you're like most people, the answer is *not enough*.

Now here are some good assets: investment real estate, small businesses, stocks, mutual funds, annuities, CDs (not compact disks but certificates of deposit), bonds, education, retirement plans and various other assets that have the potential to make money.[9] Some of these assets are designed for capital appreciation, while others are structured for income. Stocks are generally viewed as an investment for appreciation, whereas most real estate and business ventures are pursued for income purposes. It's important to develop both types of assets.

| APPRECIATING (GOOD) ASSETS | DEPRECIATING (BAD) ASSETS |
| --- | --- |
| INVESTMENT REAL ESTATE | FURNITURE |
| SMALL BUSINESSES | ELECTRONICS |
| STOCKS | CARS |
| MUTUAL FUNDS | CLOTHES |
| ANNUITIES | BOATS |
| CD'S | JET SKIS |
| BONDS | JEWELRY |
| EDUCATION | MAGAZINES |
| RETIREMENT PLANS | TOYS |

[9] Investments are not guaranteed and are subject to investment risk, including the possible loss of principal. The investment return and principal value of the security will fluctuate, so that a redeemed security may be worth more or less than the original investment.

The growth assets will compound in value. The income assets will help purchase other good assets—and may even allow you to quit your day job![10] How much of your money currently goes into the good asset categories? Again, if you're like most people, the answer is *not enough.*

If you aren't investing in good assets, then you'll forever be a slave to your income. You will constantly need to produce revenue and will be in the proverbial "rat race" with the rest of the world. *If you aren't "partnering" up with good assets, then you have nobody else trying to make money for you.* This means that all your purchasing of bad assets has to come from your earned income, leaving *not enough* money to purchase good assets. I recently was having a conversation with a lady who was explaining how, in her business, she has the ideas, then hires others to do the "grunt work," thereby allowing her more time and energy to come up with other great ideas and make more money. If she didn't employ others as part of her team, her potential would be limited by her need to do 100 percent of the work.

The same concept applies to investing money. Investing in good assets is like hiring employees to do the work, thereby allowing you to do what you do best (or enjoy most). By committing the majority of your resources toward assets that have the ability to create income and opportunity, you create additional resources that in turn will help you create more income and opportunities. Alternatively, when you buy things that cause only further drain on your cash flow, you are, in effect, just flushing all of your hard work down the commode.

Consider the struggle your money has on either side of the T-chart. Your good assets and bad assets are constantly battling over resources. The good assets are trying to achieve financial independence, whereas the bad assets are fighting for destruction and unlimited expenses. If this were an actual battle in real terms, involving soldiers with lives at stake, imagine the irony of which side most people provide resources to. We declare that financial security is important and raise our flag to independence, but we give most of the resources to the soldiers who take that

---

10 The phrase "good assets" is not meant to imply that all the assets listed are good; it's a term I'm using to indicate that some assets are purchased with the intention of growing their value and creating income. When I'm describing bad assets, I'm also not suggesting that all those assets are bad to own, especially in the case of a personal residence. Rather, I'm trying to make a distinction that there are assets purchased where one has no intention of converting their value into income, especially assets that depreciate in value, such as retail-product purchases. Throughout the book I'll describe "good" assets as those from which you intend to grow and create income and "bad" assets as those that aren't intended to produce income.

security and independence away from us. We tell our good assets to fight and work hard on our behalf, but then they watch us give the majority of the money to the opposing side.

Imagine the frustration. The good-asset soldiers are provided minimal time and resources, while the bad assets are on a spending spree. It's a war that has been going on for centuries. Those families who decide to provide resources to the right soldiers finally win the war and live in financial independence for the rest of their lives—and often set up a good pattern for their family's lives. That's what rich people do. Those families who give most of their money to the bad soldiers have little or no wealth and wonder why they can't win the war. All the while it was their self-destructive actions that determined the outcome. That's what poor people do.

If you are in this circular cycle of feeding your bad assets and further deteriorating your chances of success, then you have to break out of it with a strong defense. When you're able to provide the good assets with sufficient resources, you'll experience growth and independence like you've never seen before.

*Greater income = More resources and opportunities*

*Income + Good assets = Greater income*

*Income + Bad-asset spending = No resources or opportunities*

This reminds me of another story of my rookie associate, Dusky. We joined a fitness club for some late-night exercise after another grueling day at the office. We were fresh out of college, and neither of us had been to an expensive exercise facility before. Dusky and I were both from small, rural Michigan towns where a gym consisted of some weight benches, barbells, dumbbells and maybe a jump rope. Upon entering this gym, Dusky and I knew we "were not in Kansas" anymore. Before us stood three stories of high-tech machines. To say we were intimidated—even awestruck—would be an understatement.

Using machines instead of weights was a new concept for us. Dusky and I turned more than a few heads as we strolled through the rooms. Not because we were the best-looking, buff people there. On the contrary. We wore ragged T-shirts and cotton shorts, expecting to sweat in them. Everyone else wore clothes that looked more conducive to attracting a mate than working out, complete with jewelry. It was like we had walked into the pages of a fitness magazine—not to mention that we stood baffled by the machines for minutes before attempting to exercise. Only then we'd bend in unnatural positions until a reasonably tactful person next to us said (ahem) we were using the equipment backwards.

After enduring more than enough embarrassment, Dusky decided to strut his stuff on the treadmill. He was a self-proclaimed runner and thought he could save face with his effortless stride. I stood next to him as he began showing off his skills. The machine started at a slow walk speed. So Dusky held the button down for a long time and brought it up past a brisk trot. He glanced at me and smirked, as if to say, *See, these machines can't even make me break a sweat.* Dusky then tapped the "up" arrow button 20 or 30 more times to try to find a speed worthy of his advanced ability. It took about 20 seconds, which was 10 seconds after Dusky had taken his finger off the button, for the treadmill to catch up to his request. Suddenly Dusky's legs and feet started moving at speeds most humans wouldn't think possible, nor would I if I hadn't seen it with my own eyes. I think his body was actually parallel to the floor with the tips of his toes just making it to the end of the treadmill before coming back to the rapidly spinning surface of the machine.

I wasn't sure what to do. I wanted to help him, but he had so many body parts moving in so many directions I couldn't reach in past his flailing arms to hit the speed control. I considered ramming into him as if he were being electrocuted by a downed wire and needed the current broken. Everyone in the rest of the gym stopped and stared in amazement, even disbelief. This tall skinny blonde kid was giving everything he had just to stay on the treadmill and not be thrown, violently, back into the row of treadmills behind him. With each flailing cycle of his arms, however, Dusky managed to hit the "down" speed button so that after a half-minute he finally regained control of his body and brought the machine to a full stop. I was in too much shock to laugh, and he was too exhausted to say anything. So we just turned around and left the building. I don't think we ever went back.

What does all this have to do with buying good assets? In the beginning, it can seem like you're starting small and that what you're doing isn't even worth the effort. Then when you aren't looking, things begin to take on a life of their own. You reach a point when your money may actually reach critical mass and grow at levels well beyond what you contribute to it. The appropriate good assets can gain momentum and reach very large levels of wealth. One day you may look back and recall that it all began with one simple action that seemed so small and irrelevant. The one place where the analogy with Dusky (appropriately) breaks down is that he was soon out of control, whereas people who invest wisely gain even more control over their lives.

I have clients whose net worth has absolutely mushroomed, going from having just a few hundred thousand dollars to becoming millionaires in a very short period of time once they grasped this very basic concept. When they stopped buying depreciating or bad assets that eroded wealth and began purchasing appreciating or good assets, the numbers moved in the right direction—and fast.

## FIND OPPORTUNITIES INSTEAD OF EXPENSES

In a perfect world, people would enter into their career living well below their means and would have the ability to put 30 to 50 percent of their earned income into good assets. In that perfect world, they would do without some of the extra amenities for a period of their lives. In doing so, they would have the ability to do much more financially for the rest of their lives. Sometimes this approach is referred to as short-term pain for long-term gain.

But most people don't do that. And most people have expenses that are very close to their earned income—or even exceed it. These people now have the difficult task of gradually balancing their budget, either by increasing their income or decreasing their expenses to allow for enough freedom to invest in themselves and their future.

Let's go back to the maxim that the rich keep getting richer. The rich have learned that they need help to have and sustain a wealthy lifestyle. They have "partners" on their side to make life a little easier. Their partners are the good assets that they or someone in their family took careful time, sacrifice and dedication to buy, instead of splurging on all the many depreciating assets this world has to offer beyond current earning capabilities.

They planted the fruit trees in their backyard. As a result, they now have fruit to eat or sell instead of having to go to the market. They are equity partners and benefit from the spenders and debtors of the world. You too can profit from the spenders and plant a fruit tree in your backyard; you just have to plant fruit-bearing seeds. Later I will talk about also partnering up with good advisors.

If you wish to spend money on something that won't produce a return, use your head and try to discover a way of actually making money for that purpose. For example, if you desire vacation property … buy some.

But purchase a property you can rent and make money on in the meantime. Or find an intermediate property you can purchase, make alterations or developments on, then sell for a gain. Maybe you can find a property with a large lot that allows you to subdivide it and build a second home on part of it. Now you can keep one for yourself and rent or sell the other one.

Maybe you desire to travel to the nicest locations in the world. Maybe you're also an accomplished photographer. Figure out how to sell photos of your excursions. Create a legitimate business and, besides creating another revenue source, much of your travel and equipment will now be tax-deductible (see PRINCIPLE 6 for more on this idea). If you have a specialized interest and are quite talented at doing it, publish your findings. Put them on the Internet, write a handbook or make a video. Turn that talent into income and the cost of your hobby into a business expense.

This is when wealth accumulation is a lot of fun and, as you will realize, allows you to have many more of the experiences you long for—much more than if you only pursued those adventures through your earned income.

## FOCUS

If becoming rich is such an easy and obvious thing, why don't more people do it? A big reason has to do with the "instant gratification" theory of human beings. People want things now. What fun is it to wait to buy a mid-level car in a few years when you can lease a Porsche today?

Then there's the "I might die tomorrow" theory. People reason, "Why shouldn't I buy this giant house and make it look like a showcase home? If I died tomorrow, all my money would be useless anyway. So I might as well enjoy it now." This attitude also can be summed up as: "Eat, drink and be merry, for tomorrow you die."

Well, if you lease the car today (before you can afford it), then you'll probably never be able to afford the car you want. You likely *won't* die tomorrow, so spending all your money on your house in effect guarantees you won't have money left over to live where you want when you're older.

And, as I said in Principle 3, you have to *own* your own outcome. The concept of becoming wealthy is very simple. But the reality of being wealthy does require action and often, behavioral changes, to make it happen. It takes time to accumulate wealth, and it often starts with very small numbers. You have to find some satisfaction in the saving and the accumulating of money. People love to buy fun, tangible things, and a line item on a brokerage statement isn't usually as exciting as driving a new off-road vehicle. In fact, many people are a little confused by mutual funds and other investments and feel far removed from their assets. Therefore, they continue to migrate to things they understand and can touch, like large-screen, high-definition TVs.

To accumulate wealth you need to understand your investments and make them a tangible entity you can put your arms around. Things become more tangible when you realize their relevance. Everyone needs to know how much money he or she needs to accumulate in life. Too many people don't know that answer until it's very late in the game. Here's a fun exercise: Walk around and ask people how much money they need to have saved to put their children through college. Ask them how much money their family would need in case the main breadwinner passed away. Ask them how much money they need to successfully retire. Some people need to have $500,000 saved in order to supplement their pension and Social Security income in order to live comfortably. Others who don't have a pension and aren't counting on Social Security may need to have saved millions of dollars to retire. Identify the amount you need, then you'll know your "number." These are things everyone needs to know, but few people do. In fact, I'll bet if you asked 10 people those questions, you'd be lucky to find one who could give you a halfway intelligent answer. The amazing thing is … they really aren't very hard questions.

Giving your financial independence a "number" helps make it become a reality. If you don't have a clue how much money you need to save, then who is telling you not to buy that depreciating asset, which you really don't need anyway? No one. Giving it a number helps make your financial statements more tangible.

## GIVE YOUR CONSCIENCE A CHANCE

Remember those old cartoons where the character had an internal debate—and an angel would appear on one shoulder and a devil on the other? The angel conscience was usually portrayed as a softy, and the devil conscience used to beat up the angel. Every now and then, the angel would muster up enough courage and anger and knock the devil into a cloud of "poof." In those cartoons, the angel usually had the best answer.

If you don't know the answer to how much money you need to save (your number), in effect you're keeping your angel in the dark. Your angel conscience won't even have a good argument when it's battling with the devil. Given those circumstances, nine times out of 10 the devil is going to win. Give your angel a chance. *Figure out how much money you need to accumulate and how much money you need to invest every year. Then put away a little more than that.* That's what the rich do.

Create milestones on your road to wealth; have some fun with it. If you need to have $1,000,000 and are just getting started, be proud of the $10,000 saved so far. When you have $100,000 of good assets accumulated, you'll start to see the effects. Keep working and build your assets up to the halfway mark of $500,000. Sure, it's a long and challenging journey. But without focus, you're pretending the road isn't even there. Denial makes it more difficult to accumulate the wealth you ultimately desire, whereas embracing the challenge empowers you to excel even beyond your expectations.

Use the rule of 72 to help you understand the power of compound interest. If you divide a number into 72, you discover how many years it will take for your investment to double. For example, if you earn 10 percent (72/10), your money doubles every 7.2 years. $125,000 becomes $1,000,000 in just three cycles. Continuously buying additional good assets with your income only speeds up the process! One more cycle, and it becomes $2,000,000.

## TO SUMMARIZE

1. The rich keep getting richer because they keep buying the things that got them rich in the first place. The poor keep getting poorer because they keep buying the things that got them poor in the first place.

2. Here's the secret to becoming wealthy: Buy things that have the ability to go up in value or create income. Focus on mastering this behavior until it becomes habitual.

3. You can't get rich on occasional behaviors, just like you can't get in great shape working out once a month. Get in the financial zone!

4. List your good and bad assets, then list how much money you spend on each type of asset. If you don't invest in good assets, you'll forever be a slave to your income.

5. Partner up with good assets so that you have other people making money for you also. Bad assets fight good assets. If most of your money goes toward bad assets, how can you expect to win the financial war?

6. If you give your good assets enough nourishment, they'll reach a point of perpetual growth.

7. If you desire a bad asset, like a vacation home, be creative in discovering how you can make a good asset buy it for you.

8. Wealth starts with small numbers. Remember that saving early lets you save much less for the same results. Be patient and celebrate the milestones.

# Principle 5
## Buy Things That Go Up in Value

### Principles in Action
### Sample: What do you own in good assets?

| | |
|---|---|
| Cash assets | $15,000 |
| Investment assets | 175,000 |
| Business assets | 0 |
| Other appreciating assets (antiques) | 15,000 |
| Investment real estate | 45,000 |
| **Total good assets** | 250,000 |

### What are your bad assets?

| | |
|---|---|
| Home equity | 150,000 |
| Auto equity | 5,000 |
| Vacation property | 0 |
| Other personal property | 50,000 |
| **Total bad assets** | 205,000 |
| Unsecured debt | 9,000 |
| **Total unsecured debt** | 9,000 |

### How much money do you allocate toward good assets per year?

| | |
|---|---|
| Business investments | 0 |
| Roth IRAs | 5,000 |
| Brokerage account | 3,000 |
| SEP/401(k) | 18,000 |
| **Total** | 26,000 |

### Totals

| | |
|---|---|
| Good assets | 250,000 |
| Bad assets (less unsecured debt) | 196,000 |
| Income allocated to good assets | 26,000 |

### What % of income produces what % of good assets?

21.7% of income is allocated toward good assets, which are 56% of total net assets.

# Principle 5
## Buy Things That Go Up in Value

### Principles in Action

**What do *you* own in good assets?**

___
___
___
___

Total good assets

**What are *your* bad assets?**

___
___
___
___

Total bad assets

Total unsecured debt

**How much money do *you* allocate toward good assets per year?**

___
___
___

Total

### Totals

___
___
___

**What % of income produces what % of good assets?**

___

## Principle 6

---

## Ask Yourself, 'Am I Spent?'

---

In high school I worked at Norden's Foodland in Manistique, Michigan. I remember receiving my first two weeks' paycheck for more than $100 when I was 15. From my paper route before that, I was lucky to clear $25 in two weeks. That day I felt like a rich man—and proceeded to spend as if there were no tomorrow. It took only a couple of days before my hundred dollars were in merchants' pockets rather than mine.

### THE MONEY TRAP

Most people get used to living on their entire paycheck. Like many, I learned this bad habit while living with my parents. I'll give credit to my mother for trying very hard to persuade me to save my income and manage a budget, but I just wouldn't do it. As a teenager, I had no overhead and could spend everything I made. If I ran out of money before my next paycheck, it was no big deal. Mom and Dad still provided me with all the necessities of life; I just had to do without the "extras" for a few days.

Going to college or leaving the nest is most young people's first introduction to some degree of fiscal responsibility. Most students have to cover rent, food and social life. To "help," credit card companies approach vulnerable students and provide a high-interest line of credit to anyone with a pulse. While most student bank accounts don't have a comma on the balance sheet, their debt certainly does. No matter what their age, many people make the mistake of believing that their credit limit is synonymous with a cash reserve. It has become a learned behavior: Spend everything you earn—and sometimes even more than that. Don't face the reality that you have any overhead. If things get bad enough, you can always find someone to bail you out. Right?

## DEEPER AND DEEPER INTO THE TRAP WE GO

The cycle continues. People spend money before they start making a good salary, and from that moment on they play a seemingly endless game of catch-up. Just when there appears to be a glimmer of financial respite on the horizon, we revert to the old bad habits and purchase something we've been dreaming about. Even financial windfalls, such as a bonus or large tax refund, all too often must go toward debt balances rather than being available for something more useful.

If you're living paycheck to paycheck, it's probably because you didn't calculate your living expenses from the beginning and have spent more than you make. Many people have a misconception that their $70,000 salary means they'll take $70,000 home with them. It's easy to forget about the taxes and insurance payments that come directly out of their check. No matter how much money is made, they'll likely always live from paycheck to paycheck until they manage their money with a strong defense. They're in the all-too-familiar cycle of living beyond their means and still not measuring up to their most important expense: investing in their future.

## INCREASE POSITIVE CASH FLOW

You can avoid that nasty cycle by looking for ways to reduce your overhead. Just as businesses may need to lay off employees, restructure their debt or cut unprofitable product lines, you also will need to make tough decisions. Start with the easiest things. *What do you not have a contractual obligation to that isn't a necessity?* Some of the obvious things are the small-dollar purchases like the daily coffee, mid-day snacks or convenience charges. List all of these items that (though you rather enjoy them) don't add significantly to your life. You aren't necessarily *deleting* them just yet, but you need to know how much they total. If need be, they could be the first to go. You'd be amazed how all those small purchases can add up.

It's easy to spend $4.50 on something. It can really add up though, especially if you're married and your spouse is also spending $4.50 a day on insignificant items. Nine bucks a day equals $3,285 per year. Spending an extra $9 a day on miscellaneous items can equate to $623,965 in your retirement.

Next, look for smart strategies for restructuring your debt. Here you aren't necessarily looking for ways to make the lowest payment. Some short-term financing options, such as interest-only programs or home-equity loans, may seem fine at first blush. However, perpetual debt that doesn't reduce in amount tends to increase dramatically. So making headway toward paying your principal balances on your debt is generally a good idea. You may find ways to refinance your car, transfer credit card balances, consolidate loans or lower your primary mortgage rates, while at the same time lowering the balances. Debt tends to be a relatively easy place to free up monthly cash flow. Just remember that every dollar freed up, especially through a consolidation or longer amortization strategy, must be allocated either toward paying down principal balances or toward good assets (investments). People too often get consolidation loans and start out with proper intentions but end up incurring more debt—and then borrow again, thereby digging an even deeper hole.

Next take a look at your taxes. If you aren't having a strategy meeting in September or October with the person who prepares your taxes (even if that person is you), you're probably paying more than you need to in taxes. Most people don't look at their tax situation until March or April. Even then, all they tend to look at is the refund or how much they owe rather than evaluate Line 39 to understand what got them there. A normal tax return really isn't that complex and is something everyone serious about becoming wealthy will want to try to understand. But if you're attempting to get any kind of valuable information or education from your accountant in April, when he or she is working into the wee hours of the morning just to keep up with the returns, don't expect to get a great deal of personal attention.

There's only a limited amount you can do to reduce your tax liability after December 31. But you can make a significant difference if you evaluate your tax situation before year end by having a strategy to identify methods of lowering your tax bracket, increasing your investments and putting more of your hard-earned income into your own hands. *One simple strategy is to evaluate your tax withholdings in October against your total projected tax liability for the year.* Especially if you're accustomed to receiving a refund, you may find that federal taxes have been adequately funded months before year end. If that's the case, then opportunities open up, such as increasing the contributions to your 401(k) or other pre-tax savings by withholding less in taxes. Not only will this further reduce your tax liability, it also will support much-needed retirement savings that otherwise wouldn't have been allocated. Depending on how young you are, with compound interest that could mean having six or even seven figures more in your retirement portfolio by the time you retire—all by merely being proactive with your own money.

Most of the changes to your cash flow haven't yet affected your actual standard of living. If you still need to free up more money, look deeper. Take a hard look at your entertainment spending and determine what "entertainment" was really worth it. I know we all need to have a little fun in life, but at what expense? Look through the previous year and recall the things that were fun and/or deeply meaningful—and you know will be remembered for a long time. Those may be things you don't want to sacrifice. Then sift out the other stuff that really wasn't worth its salt. After that, take a look at your monthly credit card statements and try to recollect all

> *If you borrow the lifestyle for too long, it's no longer a sneak peek at your future but an increasingly distressing glimpse of a life you'll never own.*

the things you purchased. I'm guessing you'll have a hard time remembering what you bought—or if all the dinners at the upscale restaurants tasted that great. Also look at the material items around your house and see what you really like, as well as what you really need. Look at all your kids' toys that are still sitting around not being played with. How many of those toys could have been replaced with some "at home" creativity? Cardboard boxes make great forts! Avoid expensive experiences and purchases that you can do without. If you can return little-used newer purchases, by all means do so.

## DIG DEEPER

Finally, if you still need to find more money to save for your future, don't forget about the large items—and be bold. It may be much more worth your while to take a step back for a year or two now in order to live comfortably for the rest of your life. Consider whether you really need to live in such a large house. Do you have to drive such an expensive car? Do you pay attention to how efficient your car is in miles per gallon and repairs? What kinds of vacations do you take?

Dropping memberships, selling the car for a more practical model or canceling the premium channels on television may feel like you're giving up too much. Indeed, for some people this may seem incredibly difficult. According to my principles for becoming wealthy, however, some of these extra pleasures or bad (material) assets are intended to come after a person has satisfied his or her savings goals and covered overhead, not before. *Therefore, is it really giving something up, or simply returning a "borrowed" life that, in effect, you visited early for a preview of the future?!* Just because creative financing makes it possible to buy things doesn't necessarily mean it's best to do so. Perhaps you were just test-driving that lifestyle for a short period to see if it was worth working for. If you borrow the lifestyle for too long, it's no longer a sneak peek at your future but an increasingly distressing glimpse of a life you'll never own. Be proactive with the cuts rather than postponing the inevitable. The longer you put it off, the tougher it gets.

I know for many people giving up material purchases seems painful. Some focus on the pain of sacrifice rather than the accomplishment of taking positive financial action steps. It can be difficult to say no when others (and even you) are used to hearing yes. To their surprise, though, what they experienced was the satisfaction of finally getting ahead. They used to slave at their job without gaining financial freedom as they scraped by to keep up with increasing bills. After gaining control and actually having discretionary income, they finally saw some light at the end of the tunnel, and their job became a positive part of their growth experience.

If the hard part of cutting back for you isn't so much giving up things you borrowed early and enjoyed, then it might be in what others will think of you. If you see someone having garage sales, dropping their memberships, or turning in the lease for a used, economical car, do you assume troubled times, gross overspending and falling behind on payments? Maybe so. On the other hand, they might not be behind on anything. Maybe they've simply decided that they desire more financial stability and wealth than they have currently—and are cutting the fat to achieve that objective. If you have to take some of those measures in order to get back in line with your goals, lead by example, instead of worrying about what people will think of your actions. Tell them you're heading down the homestretch of retirement savings and want to make sure you do it right. Let them know you don't want to tap into the retirement fund in order to send your child or children to college. And if you don't get a chance to communicate directly with some people about what you're doing, so be it. You're just a blur on their radar screen, as they are on yours. You can share your experiences with those who care, but don't let the (perceived) negativity of others stop you from reaching your personal goals.

The Joneses had it all wrong. You don't need to keep up with *anyone* by spending furiously on material things. At the end of the day what matters is that you are in control of your life, not how many material items you can show off. Live a good life and enjoy the things that are really important to you. Having more or less "stuff" than someone else won't mean much the day after your last one on earth. It will mean a lot, though, in this life to know that while you drew breath you did what you thought best for your family and yourself.

Besides, wealthy appearances often aren't accurate, and other people generally have much less stability than you might think. Most people assume their neighbors have more, earn a higher income and manage their money better than they actually do. I am here to tell you ... I have seen the "neighbor's" finances, and frequently those perceptions are wrong. In fact, it's often the people whom you would never expect to have money who are the wealthiest. If cutting back via financial defense isn't socially acceptable today, it will be soon. You can thank the "fashionably unprepared" for that. As many of them are nearing retirement and starting to recognize what lies ahead, the vast numbers of people cutting back may actually create a new trend!

## TURN EXPENSE INTO INCOME

Along with cutting back, don't forget that through a little creativity you can discover ways of keeping what you want by creating more income. Yes, it's possible to make money on a vacation and still have a good time. While vacationing with my family on Sanibel Island in Florida, we were asked if it was OK to be photographed. An elderly married couple (who were about to take a guided kayak tour with us) were on vacation, and they were taking pictures to sell to magazines and to post on their Internet site. They had been doing this for years: traveling all over the world taking wonderful pictures wherever they went and selling those pictures for some income. At the very least, it helped make their vacations partially tax-deductible.

There are many areas of your life where you can pursue a passion and still create income. I had a great conversation with a young lady working her way through college. She loves horses and has become quite good at training them. She's also rather successful at *trading* them. She buys horses at a reasonable price, trains them to be great show horses, then sells them at a premium. I asked her what her best trade was. One horse purchased for $6,000 was later sold for $20,000!

Think outside the box with things you would like to do or have and see if you can find a way to get your hobby to pay for itself—or even become a viable, successful business!

## EASY STEPS

If you're attempting to really cut back hard, I would caution you not to go overboard. Despite all my aforementioned "frugal" advice, I'm a firm believer in balance, which means enjoying your life by spending *some* of your hard-earned cash today while simultaneously saving for your future. If you set too strict a regimen in order to reach your goals in a very short time, it may prove too tough to handle and eventually result in excessive splurging—simply as a reaction to undue asceticism. I once tried an extremely disciplined diet for a few weeks, only to throw it all away one evening as I gorged on all the things I had been craving the entire time. I would have been better off to eat some occasional treats to satisfy my taste buds. That may have helped me stick to the diet long enough to actually reach my goals. After all, life can get pretty boring, even desperate, if you don't factor in some fun. So satisfy your "angel," but also give your "devil" his due. Work out a reasonable budget that allows you to enjoy yourself while still investing in your future. When push comes to shove, though, opt for the angel. You'll be glad you did, especially down the road a few years.

If the amount you must save looks so daunting that you fear the lifestyle change, then take manageable steps. Rather than cutting out all the enjoyable stuff throughout an entire year, try it for just 30 days.

Here's how it works: For one "normal" month (because one needs a frame of reference) keep track of *everything* you (and your spouse) spend, then for a second month don't waste a penny more than you need for paying your expenses and eating. Save all the rest, or use it to pay down debt. For one month, don't go out to eat for breakfast, lunch or dinner. Bring a sandwich or leftovers to work every day that month. Instead of spending $5 or $10 each day on miscellaneous items, like coffee or magazines, keep all that money in your pocket. You might even want to cut out subscriptions for the month. Don't buy junk food, soda pop or expensive extras. Don't go golfing or to the movies. Don't take any vacations or weekend trips. Keep track of all the extra money you don't spend—and squirrel it away. At the end of the month fund your Roth IRA or your children's college education—or simply apply the extra cash toward your credit card bill.

During the same month look for ways to increase your income. This could be an opportunity for you to un-clutter your house and have a garage or eBay sale. Maybe you could put creative thought into a hobby that could turn into business income—like the couple I met on Sanibel Island taking pictures or the college student training and trading horses. Search the Internet for ideas to catapult your dreams into opportunities. Get together with friends and brainstorm about side jobs, or ride a bike around neighborhoods looking for good real estate opportunities. There are plenty of ways to start residual income streams if you just take the time to seek them out.

If you're married and have children, make sure everyone knows what you're doing. Teach your children at a young age that in order to provide for the future, one has to make a few healthy sacrifices along the way.

Here's the most important part of this strategy: Have a "blast" doing it! Yes. Have fun. Who knows … you may even realize you don't have to spend a lot of money in order to have a good time, and you might even decide to make some of the "cuts" permanent. If you have family or friends in the area, take this month to visit them. Go for walks through your neighborhood. Surf the Web for free local events. Volunteer. Do community service or work with religious organizations. Especially if you find it tough mentally to live on less, volunteer at organizations that help people in poverty. It will remind you how blessed you are to have what you have. Jog, clean your house, weed the garden, play a board game with your kids or do some other activity that costs nothing. Don't get trapped into just watching TV. You want to be creative during this month and look for ways you can make permanent improvements in your life. Above all, you don't want to just "survive" the experience only to spend twice as much the following month. You want to be developing habits you can use moving forward.

You just might discover that you can get in better shape, take care of your house, have some great family bonding time and have increased financial prosperity at the same time. Stay positive with the exercise. Don't see it as drudgery but as a chance to live life in control over your money and your future. Choose to be both wealthier and healthier that month!

## TO SUMMARIZE

1. Increase cash flow by cutting expenses or creating income from your hobbies.
2. If you consolidate debt, make sure you're improving your financial position, not just lowering your payments by extending the terms of your loans.
3. Be proactive with taxes and review them well before year end.
4. If needed, be bold and cut back your big-ticket items, such as vehicles, memberships and even your home. Put everything on the table.
5. Don't be concerned about what other people might think of you as they see you cutting back on your spending and establishing a thriftier lifestyle. Lead by example, as it's likely that most of those same onlookers need to be taking similar action.
6. Take it a month at a time. Go hard for a month or two, then moderate for the rest of the year in order to create a healthy balance for your family. But continue the new practices that the family had fun doing.
7. Be up front with your family about your strategies so everyone can learn from the experience. This will show your children that you

don't have an infinite amount of money, and it will instill good habits for their future.

8. Take pleasure in the fact that you're making amazing strides to improve your finances in ways that will make you wealthier—and happier—for the rest of your life.

# Principle 6

## Ask Yourself, 'Am I Spent?'

### Principles in Action

**Sample: Where could you cut back, and how much money would that free up?**

| | |
|---|---:|
| Possible debt refinance | $1,100 |
| Turn in lease, buy used with cash | 3,000 |
| Eat out less | 1,500 |
| Convenience purchases (gas station, party store, small-package food) | 1,000 |
| More fuel-efficient car | 1,000 |
| **Total cut-back money** | 7,600 |

**Where could you create income?**

| | |
|---|---:|
| Pictures sold from vacations | 2,000 |
| Photography lessons | 5,000 |
| Photography book | 5,000 |
| **Total potential income** | 12,000 |

**Net increase to free and clear cash flow**

| | |
|---|---:|
| Total cut-back money | 7,600 |
| Total potential income | 12,000 |
| **Increase to positive cash flow** | 19,600 |

## Principle 6
# Ask Yourself, 'Am I Spent?'

### Principles in Action

**Where could *you* cut back, and how much money would that free up?**

_____
_____
_____
_____
_____
_____

**Total cut-back money**
_____

**Where could *you* create income?**

_____
_____

**Total potential income**
_____

**Net increase to free and clear cash flow**

_____

**Increase to positive cash flow**
_____

## Principle 7

### Leverage Others' Expertise for Personal Gain

*The Socratic maxim that the recognition of our ignorance is the beginning of wisdom has profound significance for our understanding of society. The first requisite for this is that we become aware of men's necessary ignorance of much that helps him to achieve his aims. Most of the advantages of social life, especially in its more advanced forms which we call "Civilization," rest on the fact that the individual benefits from more knowledge than he is aware of. It might be said that civilization begins when the individual in the pursuit of his ends can make use of more knowledge than he has himself acquired and when he can transcend the boundaries of his ignorance by profiting from knowledge he does not himself possess.*
    –Friedrich A. Hayek, *The Constitution of Liberty* © 1960

Aren't you glad I don't write like Mr. Hayek?! But go ahead and read it a few more times. But what he says is profoundly important in understanding how to advance in society. He encourages us to prosper from, rather than be fearful of, what we don't fully understand. It is a skill—just as important as the ability to dream up a new idea or invention—to be able to leverage and advance someone else's idea into other realms of production. Recognize and seek talent around you to advance your own aims. Welcome diversity and those with intellectual gifts rather than be intimidated by them. All of us have different strengths (and weaknesses). Celebrate the way in which others' abilities complement your own.

## GAIN FROM OTHERS' EXPERIENCES

This brings us to *leverage*. People are generally more familiar with this concept as a method of purchasing items and going into debt. That more common method of leverage is generally not in your financial best interest. There are, however, other very positive methods of leverage. When you consciously learn how to leverage resources in pursuit of accumulating wealth, your road to riches can be significantly reduced in length. One of the most powerful resources available to leverage is another person's expertise.

There are mentors in life, and there are trusted advisors. Successful people often have both, sometimes in the same relationship. Many successful individuals have built a whole team of others they leverage in order to consistently make great decisions. Indeed, a sign of strength is surrounding yourself with strong people who will at times challenge your own presuppositions rather than "yes men" who unthinkingly, even obsequiously, go along with whatever you say.

> *Mentors generally are a few steps ahead of where you are today in a certain area—and share their own successes and failures in the hope that their experiences will improve your future prospects.*

Mentors generally are a few steps ahead of where you are today in a certain area—and share their own successes *and* failures in the hope that their experiences will improve your future prospects. A mentor can provide wonderful, unbiased insight. Treasure a true mentoring relationship because great ones can be very difficult to find.

I've had some outstanding mentors in the wealth-management business. One of my longest-term mentors is the same person who initially hired me into the industry, Frank Mossett. In the early part of my career, Frank made sure I received the resources I needed in order to stay on the right track. He used to meet with me weekly for breakfast to go through general questions and what he called "management education." When I eventually started my own company, Frank provided insight and support, which helped me make better decisions. Although distance, families and jobs have cut down on our communication, Frank has always been there for me, willing to lend his time-tested perspective to help shed light on my quandaries.

One of the reasons I've been so lucky to have people like Frank in my life is that I ask questions. If it were more important to me to mask my ignorance on a topic than to learn something new, then I wouldn't get the full benefit of great mentoring relationships. Thankfully, I've always understood and accepted the fact that there are subjects I don't fully understand and that other people know quite a bit about. Then I ask them for their input and advice.

## **FIND YOUR TRUSTED ADVISORS**

A professional advisor can be just as valuable as a mentor, although this service usually isn't free. Such individuals become more involved than a mentor and earn the title "trusted advisor" when they prove to you that they have your best interests at heart. A trusted advisor offers consultation, guidance and professional expertise to help light the way of your path toward success. These advisors are usually compensated, either directly or through commissions. As paid professionals they help you navigate the maze of opportunities, decisions, rules, and laws regarding finances and the pursuit of wealth.

When I first got into this business my impression was that the average American thought he or she wasn't rich enough to need (or pay for) the services of a wealth manager. Many people didn't believe that they would need to retire with hundreds of thousands of dollars if they would be receiving a pension—or that they would need *millions* of dollars if they retired without one. Therefore, the average American wasn't inclined or motivated to accumulate massive portfolios. I remember back in my cold-calling days, people reasoned they were going to receive a pension and were thus all set and in no need of financial advice. Back then I didn't test the argument. Today that belief has changed. Most people now realize that wealth is no longer a luxury for the extravagant few but a necessity for most. Today it's clear that just having a pension doesn't make a person "all set."

As we in the United States trudge forward with balancing budgets, with private personal retirement savings plans, and with trouble over pensions and Social (in)Security, the financial services industry will continue to flood the marketplace with possible solutions. This flood of information may eventually lead to less dependence on paid professionals to show you the basics. Someday, if/when children consistently learn about investment strategies in grade school or middle school from those qualified to teach the art of managing one's finances with control and growth, it may become second nature to do so—and most consumers will be financially savvy. In this future, the Internet or remote consultations may provide many of the necessary search functions to answer technical questions better than the massive entry-level advisor sales force of today. It is my personal hope that the concepts of investing in Roth, 403(b)s, mutual funds or REITs (real estate investment trusts) will one day be much more clearly understood and be as commonplace as operating a personal computer. At that time, technology may help millions make prudent, independent financial decisions. Advice through personal face-to-face meetings may be reserved to cover only very complex financial transactions.

But for *today*, when we see some of the largest consumer debt in our nation's history and TV commercials encouraging consumers to buy stock in a company based on flashy images rather than fundamental valuation, a good and trusted advisor is of vital importance. I have far too many meetings where my role is to convince someone to stop racking up debt and start building wealth, let alone educate on the specific functions of investments. All this indicates to me that most Americans aren't ready (or able) to succeed financially without some one-on-one help.

The financial services industry, like any other fast-moving enterprise, is constantly changing. Therefore it can behoove you to gain from an advisor's perspective to determine which strategies work best for you. An advisor can help you see and understand the numbers behind your goals. He or she also can use appropriate software and research to determine how much money you need to support your future, using inflation and growth-rate assumptions. An advisor also will show you what your future fixed-income flows will look like—and help you establish the best strategy to manage your debts to prepare for your future. Further, advisors can play a key role in helping you make rational financial choices and defeat the emotional devil on your (and everyone's) shoulder regarding those monetary decisions.

A good advisor also has the experience to offer you a broader perspective than you may have on your own. Advisors often consult with many other people; this allows them to see more clearly where you are headed and what you must do to get there. An advisor can provide you with the strength and courage to take the appropriate steps to attain your long-term goals. Once trust has (legitimately) been established, he or she can be your North Star and provide you with the point of reference for a system that maximizes your odds of success ... or, just as importantly, minimizes your odds of failure.

If you need to build a $4.5 million dollar portfolio, your advisor's insights can direct you in the most efficient methods possible with less waste and greater insulation of your nest egg. If done right, you'll be able to build wealth faster and keep it longer than you could have on your own. Finding the right team of people with the intellect, expertise and integrity to help point you in the right direction will likely prove to be one of your most financially rewarding decisions.

## TO SUMMARIZE

1. Recognize what you don't know and pursue insights from others who do. This is an essential step toward realizing your goals.

2. Leverage the knowledge and resources of others around you to mutually advance to a higher position.

3. Seek out one or more mentoring relationships. A good mentor provides unbiased free advice by sharing his or her successes and failures.

4. Professional advisors are generally paid and earn the title of "trusted advisor" when they prove to you that they have your best interests at heart.

5. As the financial services industry becomes more efficient at sharing strategies and information with the general public, individual consultation with advisors may be reserved for more complex situations.

6. Leverage an advisor's professional experiences to learn what strategies have worked or failed for others.

7. Use an advisor's insight and software to help make projections of your numbers so you can feel comfortable with what is required for you to attain your goals.

# Principle 7

# Leverage Others' Expertise for Personal Gain

## Principles in Action

### Sample: List your top three mentors and why

1. *My next-door neighbors: They are retired and quite successful. I like the way they saved their money and didn't overspend. They vacation around the world and really seem to enjoy themselves. They have always been very willing to share their personal experiences and learnings with me.*

2. *My college professor: I've stayed in close touch with a college professor. She gave me great advice back when I was in school and making difficult decisions. She continues to be there for me today. She has helped me with numerous career decisions.*

3. *My older brother: He has done some things really well and also made a few mistakes, but I really like where he has ended up in life. He's so willing to share his life's story and is there for me whenever I want to run something by him. His personal finances are an open book for me to learn from.*

## Principle 7
# Leverage Others' Expertise for Personal Gain

### Principles in Action

**Now list *your* top three mentors and why**

1. _____

2. _____

3. _____

# Principle 8

## Choose Your Team Wisely

Taking advice from someone means you need to have trust at some level. Certain people trust others too freely. Others don't trust people at all. When building your team, you will have to decide whom you trust and whom you don't. While it's best to trust yourself the most, there are ways of figuring out which advisors are giving you good (as opposed to self-serving) advice. In this principle I'll share with you the methods I use to determine if I can trust, and take advice from, an advisor. If you don't learn to trust anyone, then you had better be doing a boatload of self-education on financial planning, estate planning, tax planning, insurance-policy planning and investing. The amount of information you need in order to learn to replace what you could receive from others is overwhelming, if not impossible. I utilize the expertise of others regularly to round out not only my own planning needs but also the needs of my clients.

Remember, nobody cares more about your money than you do. Or at least nobody should. The more resolute you are in your financial values and decision-making abilities with regard to money, the easier it will be for you to find and receive good advice from good people.

I used to manage a financial planning office in Marquette, Michigan, and would sit in on meetings with other advisors. One of the major employers in Marquette is a prison. After meeting with a number of prison workers, I know that the life of a prison guard is not for me. Prison guards stay alive by expecting the worst of the criminals and not trusting anyone. If they let their defenses down, an inmate can take physical control and harm them or others. That job skill at times overlaps with life outside the prison, all too often to the workers' detriment.

I'll never forget a meeting I was in with a couple, both of whom worked at the prison. While the advisor, Wade, was talking, the husband stared into my eyes with an angry face. His wife wasn't much better. She sat there with her arms tightly crossed over her chest. They didn't listen to what we said, but they apparently were paying great attention to how we were saying it. It was a study in body language—both directions. During the meeting they told us some of the things they wanted to do in life, but they left out a lot of details. The more I probed their financial strategies, the more they clammed up. From what I did see, they were doing many things wrong, which was costing them a lot of money—and would cost them even more in their future. Needless to say, our firm and this couple didn't end up working together; there was no way of establishing a relationship.

I believe they *wanted* to trust, but until they were able to, they would have a difficult time working with anyone. Unfortunately for them, their investment mistakes were causing unnecessary strain on their lives. In short, their job experiences interfered with their ability to find a trusted advisor.

Not all of us are immediately trusting of others, nor should we be. I have undergone some personal situations that led me to question facts first and trust later. A few of the bad experiences were simple, such as a boss twisting the truth to get a desired result out of me. Other times it has been much more elaborate, such as someone posing as a rich venture capitalist and tying up my time for two weeks, as well as the time of some of my respected friends and colleagues. Usually (but not always) if my "gut" is telling me something is wrong, there probably is. I have a policy of not making decision *only* based on my gut-level feelings, but such visceral reactions can be a strong indicator that I need to look deeper into the situation to try to discover what doesn't measure up. Maybe the investment strategy is foreign to me—and I'm uncomfortable because I don't fully understand the terms and language. If I can't relate to a strategy in a manner with which I'm familiar, it's tough for me to evaluate its

> *You'll find it's not entirely necessary that you understand all the details of a situation before you act. It is, however, very important to at least understand the framework and the major moving parts.*

effectiveness. The more questions I ask, the more dots I can connect. Eventually I can tell if I can trust the source enough to move forward, or if I would be better off backing away. If you're having difficulty knowing whom to take advice from, continue your research on the matter. You'll find it's not entirely necessary that you understand all the details of a situation before you act. It is, however, very important to at least understand the framework and the major moving parts.

## COMPENSATION FACTORS AND OTHER INTERNAL MOTIVATIONS

I once met with a real estate developer in Michigan, along with one of my clients, Ralph, to determine whether the developer was offering him a good investment opportunity. Ralph had a long relationship with this developer and was about to sell a large piece of property. The meeting started out well with some idle chitchat. Then the developer began bragging about all of his successful real estate ventures. He made a point of saying more than once that he didn't need Ralph's money and was just doing this as a favor to him. His numbers looked interesting, and his stories were compelling. However, there was something missing, something that didn't feel right. So I asked him what he was trying to do long term. The developer elaborated on a grand goal of establishing a billion-dollar, publicly traded REIT.

As I asked more questions on the subject, it was clear he was a long way from accomplishing his objective. There's nothing wrong, of course, with working hard to accomplish a grand goal, but understanding this motivation made it clear why he wanted my client's money. Not only did he really need Ralph's money, he needed just about everyone else's in town in order to make his REIT dream a reality. So the problem I had with the developer right away was that he wanted us to believe he had little interest in having Ralph take part in his investments, when in fact it was actually essential for him to raise a great deal of money. In fact, it was much more important for the developer to have Ralph's money than it was for Ralph to invest with the developer. After uncovering that spin, I was able to see the other things he was trying to hide. His flamboyant stories became less interesting and were seen for what they really were: a sales pitch attempting to distort the truth. Not surprisingly, I counseled Ralph *not* to invest his money with the developer, and he heeded my advice.

While interviewing prospective financial advisors, you'll find that people have many different reasons for being in the industry. Understanding the motives of the person who sits across the table from you is one of your first tasks in determining whether to move forward in an advisory relationship. You may interview people who:

- Like the job for the flexibility of their work schedule and good compensation.
- Enjoy the work because they're extremely analytical.
- Just want to make money from you.
- Like understanding money and want to teach others how to accumulate it as well.

A common debate in the industry is whether it's better to hire a salaried or fee-based advisor versus a commission-based advisor. The argument is that a non-commissioned advisor has your best interests at heart because he or she isn't swayed to recommend something based on a commission. It needs to be noted, though, that there are other factors besides just commissions that may sway advisors with regard to their recommendations. Additionally, many salaried or fee-based advisors are still working at a for-profit company that's determining which products that advisor offers.

Just about everyone is in this business to make a living. That is a given—and a goal I don't quibble with. One way or the other, investment advisors are making money, and they have a responsibility to generate revenue for themselves or their company. If someone is making a living by telling you what to do with your money (including the people who don't call themselves financial advisors), they're getting paid by you or someone. This includes insurance sales people, mortgage brokers, accountants, real estate developers, speakers at investment seminars and, yes, even authors on personal finance!

One day I received a call from a young lady, Diane, who said a fee-based advisor was recommending that she sell all her mutual funds and move the proceeds to his firm. She explained that he didn't receive a commission on the investment, and therefore he was looking out for her best interests. She wondered what to do. What he failed to tell Diane, however, was that she had a 3 percent surrender charge to sell her existing mutual funds. He also ignored the fact that the mutual account had grown substantially, producing a phenomenal return. Nor did he mention that while he wasn't receiving a "commission," he was charging a 2 percent fee on the entire account, thus raising the internal operating expense of her investments substantially. So his advice was to pay more than $2,000 of surrender fees, move into something that hadn't done as well over the same time frame and increase her annual costs for doing so. It hardly seemed that his recommendation was in Diane's best interests!

Another example: I became aware that a commission-based advisor was recommending that another person, Mark, move a very large IRA into an expensive insurance vehicle. The new investment offered fewer fund choices with more cost and less liquidity for no benefit. I recommended against it. The advisor was hoping Mark would do it though, to the tune of a very high commission!

As these examples illustrate, the financial services industry is a for-profit enterprise, and financial advisors and the companies they work for will receive compensation one way or another. Whether they earn it through "commissions" or "fees," this compensation is what establishes their interest in you as their client. Even if advisors are paid a salary and it appears there's no direct financial benefit to them, they're still employed by someone and want to keep their job. They might not be receiving compensation directly at that moment for selling you a strategy, but they will receive performance reviews and are compared with other employees in the company who may bring in more revenue. Bottom line: Their job security depends on their ability to effectively convince clients to take their advice.

Therefore, the most important decision-making criterion for you is *not* how the advisor gets compensated, but *whether you believe he or she has the highest standard of ethics and how seriously he or she takes your interests*. For the record: You won't be able to entirely remove financial interest from a relationship with an advisor you hire, nor do I believe you want to. Whether someone is paid in fees or by commission, understand what their motivation is for providing you with advice. Look for clues regarding their business ethics and level of greed. Because discerning these kinds of things is neither simple nor automatic, I'll outline some clues for you.

## ETHICAL CONSIDERATIONS

It has been said that the 1980s and 1990s constituted the decades of greed. Even now in the new century there appears to be no end to the incessant drumbeat of corporate fraud, deceit and investment mismanagement. In some financial organizations, advisors who believed they were recommending something good for clients later discovered that company officials and policy misled them.

I once worked for a firm that had its sales force convinced that upper management performed an extensive amount of due diligence (research) on product companies, then hand-selected the best ones for our clients. Later I learned that was hardly the case. Management did due diligence all right—but not to find the best companies. Rather, the goal was to line up the ones that would provide a sizable kickback to the home office. Generally the sales force doesn't understand the extent of the kickbacks. Even consultants with years of experience in a firm have only limited knowledge as to why one mutual-fund company versus another is being pushed through the system. Some companies' practices have been exposed. The corporate and investment firm scandals help bring to light some of the fundamental problems with the industry. Awareness of how the industry makes money will help protect the future integrity of the industry, along with the financial success of Americans.

Make no mistake ... virtually everyone has some degree of greed. I believe that most of what we do in life, even the noblest of actions, is to satisfy some internal need or desire. So greed or self-interest isn't what's at issue here. The point of differentiation I'm concerned with is the persons who are solely focused on short-term maximizing of gain versus those who are focused more on the long-term results for themselves *and* others. The good advisors know that to accomplish their personal, financial and career goals, they must first satisfy the needs and desires of the people who trust them. So yes, they are helping others for personal gain. But they also are looking at the long-term benefits, not just the short-term possibilities of their personal income aggrandizement. By looking at the long-term benefits for themselves and clients, they can make the most judicious recommendations to retain client relationships, build trust, gain referrals and experience *mutual* success.

> *At that moment the focus for the advisor tends to change from what he or she needs to stay in business for the long term to what the advisor wants and needs today for the short term ... sometimes at the client's expense.*

An advisor who looks at personal short-term possibilities—such as "keeping up with the Joneses," staying current with excessive bills, meeting corporate sales goals or handling social pressures—might recommend something to a client that isn't in the client's best interests. At that moment the focus for the advisor tends to change from what he or she needs to stay in business for the long term to what the advisor wants and needs today for the short term ... sometimes at the client's expense.

When interviewing prospective advisors, try to recognize signs indicating who is more short-term-focused than long-term-focused. Here are some clues to look for:

*1. How much is the other person getting to know your needs or educating you versus trying to sell you?*

Is the advisor's recommendation based on a solution that meets *your* needs, or is he or she trying to make your needs fit his or her solution?

Just because advisors ask a lot of personal questions about you (such as where you are from or if you have a dog) doesn't mean they care. But if they start selling right away *without* asking questions, that may be a good indication they're more focused on the sale than they are on finding a solution appropriate to your situation.

Watch for too many stories and bragging about life experiences. Some of the biggest cons I met had the most amazing life—or at least that's what they wanted me to believe. One guy in particular really had me going. It took me a few weeks to connect the dots, especially because he was so good at representing his trade. I finally realized he was full of you know what.

Do they have only a few options to offer, or can they also explain what your other possibilities might be and why their suggestions might not work? Then test their reasons. I recently asked an advisor what options he had proposed to a client besides an expensive insurance policy. He told me about three other strategies but quickly added that they wouldn't be as effective. I then asked him for the break-even point on all the strategies in order to determine which one was truly the most effective for the client. He said there was no comparison. What he didn't know was that I had already run the numbers and knew that two of the other three strategies were much better. So I told him some of my data, then asked again why he was so sure he had the best strategy. He immediately began backpedaling. *Ask for numbers—not theory*—and you're more likely to discover when advice could be bad. Sometimes it's also a good idea to ask questions you already know the answers to!

*2. Don't be fooled by their appearance.*

Physical appearance can sometimes mask the fact that advisors aren't good with money themselves. I've met quite a few people who advise clients on what to do with money, but their own spending habits are atrocious. They are big-time spenders living a fictitious life, hoping for an eventual payoff. In my experience, it's usually the desperate ones who feel they need to overcompensate by presenting themselves as being rich. In a similar vein Shakespeare said, "Methinks the lady doth protest too much."

I've also seen a number of people who live simple lives yet have tremendous wealth. Try not to judge too much by what it appears they have or don't have.

Attempt to find someone who shares your philosophies and values around building wealth. Ideally, you want to receive advice from someone who has personal experience with his or her own money that you would like to model yourself after. To illustrate: If I'm going to take advice from someone on how to be healthy, I want him or her to also be healthy. So I try to find family physicians who share my values of eating well and exercising—and who are in good shape themselves.

*3. Do the advisors have a healthy self-awareness about what they're good at and what they're not good at?*

Usually the better you are at something the more comfortable you are in saying what you don't do well. It would be impossible to work with "the" expert in every field all wrapped up in one person.

If they're good at something, ask them why. If they aren't as good at something, ask them why. Note: Their first responses are generally rehearsed. Then ask the questions a different way. Asking people to expand beyond their initial answers can produce valuable information. Testing technical knowledge in this way can provide clues regarding their abilities—beyond a slick sales pitch.

## THE QUALITY OF THE PERSON, NOT THE SIZE OF THE FIRM

I have worked at large firms, and I have worked at small firms. It is my belief that when looking for an advisor, the size of the firm is not very important. You want to make sure anyone you're dealing with has access to a wide variety of resources, which includes investment selection. These days there are very few exclusive investment vehicles that are better in one established firm than what may be available in another. It's also easy enough to ask what the firm is *not* able to offer as a way of determining the company's scope of coverage. In my experience, the larger something is the more systematized it needs to become in order to be profitable. In the very personal relationship between advisor and client, that "system" isn't always the best thing for the client. In some large firms, the home office dictates what the advisor offers because it's receiving a large commission based on volume sales of certain products.

> *When I was interviewing photographers for our wedding, the best question I asked was how late they had to stay to do the job right.*

When it comes right down to it, the most significant decision will be *who* you are working with, not (as stated above) the size of the firm. Whether the advisor works in a large or small firm, *challenge* his or her advice from time to time to make sure you have a full understanding as to why he or she recommends specific vehicles. Ask what other *options* are available. Ask what is *wrong* with the proposed solution. This will help you understand if the advisor is just passing advice on down the line, as you will be looking for evidence of personal analysis rather than regurgitated or "stock" responses.

Your goals during a first meeting could be to explain your situation, determine how well the advisor listens, and ask questions to understand if the advisor fits your profile as someone who is qualified and looking out for your best interests. You also want to make sure your personalities "click," especially if the objective is to establish a long-term relationship. If you're looking for a short-term consultation rather than a long-term relationship, then test the prospective advisor's technical abilities. You'll want to be able to pull as much strategic information as you can from him or her in a short period of time.

Listen for clues that tell you how excited the individuals are about their job and what their motivation is to do the job well. When I was interviewing photographers for our wedding, the best question I asked was how late they had to stay to do the job right. I said "had" to stay rather than "would" stay because I wanted to give the impression that the question wasn't important to me. Little did they know, it was the most important answer they would give during the entire interview. Their answer to that question told me how dedicated they were in their job. Most photographers hinted they didn't want to stay any longer than they had to. Some didn't want to stay past the first dance. One response stood out from the rest. In describing a wedding he had just shot, he excitedly described his favorite picture of the bride and groom walking barefoot toward their room at the very end of the night. As I continued to ask probing questions into his motivation for being in business, it was clear that this person loved what he did and took great pride in the outcome. Needless to say, we hired him—and our wedding pictures are fantastic!

Most articles describing what to ask a financial advisor pose questions that don't tell you much about them as a person or their quality of counsel. To really understand someone's motivations, you might ask such questions as:

- Why did you get into this business?
- What do you see as the most important steps to becoming wealthy?
- What are some things you practice in your own life to help you accumulate wealth?
- What are the things you see most often that keep people from achieving the wealth they desire?
- What do you believe are the most effective investment vehicles?
- What were some of the mistakes you have made that you have learned from?

## 'ONE SIZE' DOES NOT FIT ALL

After you know something about the advisor, talking about yourself and what you're looking for can be difficult. To help people open up, my initial meeting with a married couple often involves questions that lead to a more thorough conversation regarding their present and future finances than they've had with each other in a long while. I find that potential clients usually come to the first meeting prepared with numbers and facts but aren't always thinking about their dreams, fears, motivations and emotions. If we don't discuss those intangibles, however, decisions based strictly on numbers can run counter to their deeper needs.

There's no *one* "right" investing strategy that fits everyone. In fact, even though something may make sense numbers-wise, it might not make sense emotionally for the client. A perfect example is your house. Many people have an emotional attachment to owning their home and don't like to increase mortgage balances to use for consolidating debt or reinvesting into other opportunities. Even though someone may have thousands of dollars in credit card debt, with eternally high interest rates, these same people may have a very difficult time taking the money out in a home-equity loan or refinancing their property to reduce their cost of debt and increase their savings rate.

Numbers may show that the overall debt level will be lower in 10 years with an increase in the balance of the mortgage; however, some people still don't feel good about it. They would rather look for alternate strategies that will help them sleep more soundly at night. For certain individuals, consolidation strategies work well. For others, such approaches only get them deeper in the hole and take away from their future options of relief, giving good reason for staying away from the strategy.

People sometimes make decisions about their money that traditional advisors often don't understand or wouldn't have made themselves, but that doesn't mean the decisions are wrong. Owning investment real estate can be a good example of this. In some financial planning firms, advisors steer customers away from owning rental properties. Clients enter the office to discuss their future, and halfway through the meeting they mention that they own a few rentals. They might be clearing a few hundred dollars a month in profit and have a decent amount of appreciation on the house. They usually have equity in the property and may have a small stockpile of cash lined up for buying another rental. They also may have been paying down the debt and creating enough cash flow to purchase other properties—all signs of a good solid investment. While not yet real estate tycoons, they were at least making money.

No matter the internal rate of return on the property (if it's even calculated) or what level of sophistication the property owner has, some advisors' recommendations to the client will always be the same: Refinance the properties to the max and take the cash out to invest in the market. Or sell the properties outright and invest the proceeds in the market.

The reason to sell isn't because the properties were a poor investment. Rather, the advisors didn't understand the concept of owning real estate or being a landlord. The advisor could tell the client what to do with his or her 401(k) or Roth IRA—but felt clueless and unable to offer counsel in terms of rental property. Or the advisor might see the rental property as competition for managing your money. Therefore, the easy answer is to sell it or pull the cash out with debt. Now, many of those same advisors recommend that their clients invest in real estate investment trusts because it's an asset category that generally fared well during the bear market of 2000–02. Financial advisors can relate to a REIT because it represents a "normal" financial investment.[11]

Likewise, some mutual-fund advisors will almost always recommend selling every individual stock you own and replacing them with mutual funds, regardless of how well the stock may perform. On the flip side, many stock traders would say that owning a mutual fund is a mistake. Sometimes advisors recommend a complete overhaul because of their own compensation structure, sometimes because of upper management, sometimes because of poor ethics, sometimes because of what has

---

[11] Real estate investing involves risks, such as refinancing in the real estate industry, interest-rate risk, lease terminations, and potential economic and regulatory changes. The value of the shares in the trust will fluctuate with the portfolio of the underlying real estate-related investments. There can be no assurance that a secondary market for the REIT will be maintained by the issuer. The investment may be illiquid. The redemption price of a REIT may be worth more or less than the original price paid for units of the trust.

worked for them recently, and sometimes because they don't grasp the variety of ways people can become wealthy.

The more I worked with landlords and other small-business owners, the more I welcomed them into the room and understood that I could learn much from them. I realized that many of these people were already doing the right thing, namely following Principle 5 and *buying good assets*.

## ASK QUESTIONS

One of your major ongoing "assignments" when developing the relationship with your advisor is to ask questions, including challenging questions as to why certain strategies are being recommended to you in the first place. Some clients have an easier time entering this stage of the relationship than others. It's important to feel comfortable and understand what you're doing. If you don't, then that's a clear sign you must ask more questions and possibly do some individual research before you implement the proposed plan.

I met with a client, Kim, who was a teacher at a local school. She had multiple 403(b)s, with the largest one inside a very expensive insurance vehicle. The money had been there for only a year, so I asked where it was before then. She said it was with Fidelity, a no-load mutual-fund company available through her work. When I asked her why she moved the money into the insurance vehicle, she said, "Because the advisor said I should." Perhaps because of a facial expression I had at the moment, Kim immediately said, "What, did I do something wrong?" She sensed in her gut that the advice might have been bad but felt uncomfortable questioning the advisor's motives. Unfortunately, the advisor took Kim's money from the best plan available through her work (which the advisor would not have been paid on) and moved it into one of the worst plans (that paid the advisor a very large commission). Even more unfortunate, the new plan had a 10-year surrender charge starting at 9 percent, so Kim's money was going to be there for a very long time.

Throughout your professional relationships, it's important to do everything in your power to make sure you're receiving good advice. Do your own research. If something doesn't look (or feel) right to you, it might not be. If the strategies recommended don't seem logical, continue to ask probing questions to understand how these strategies serve your best interests. As noted before, if you feel you're being *sold* rather than *educated*, that could be a useful clue—or cue—that it's time to say, "No thank you." If your advisor gives you a positive quick spin to every question or objection you bring up, ask about the possible negative effects of the strategy. When you need to get to the bottom of something, don't shy away from asking questions because you fear what the other person will think. If the prospective advisor is impatient with you and causes you to feel uncomfortable about asking clarifying questions, that could be an indicator right there that something is wrong.

Good advisors welcome questions—the more the better. After asking a series of questions, you could discover that your concerns were unfounded, and you just needed more information to feel comfortable about the strategies. Either way, it's important to look out for yourself. At the very least, you won't be second-guessing yourself afterward if you've made a full attempt to understand the information. At the very most, you are the one who has to retire on your money, so you had better do what's needed to have enough of it. Gut feeling and emotion may help you recognize that you need to ask clarifying questions, but they aren't the most reliable determinants for making your final decisions. Strive to arrive at a logical conclusion as to why you do or don't move forward with an investment plan. Always look at the numbers.

By the way, if you're married it can be very helpful to have your spouse's perspective both during and after sessions with prospective advisors. If you're single, you might want to find a trusted friend to go with you to a session or two as a working relationship with an advisor is being considered. Then checking one's perceptions with a spouse or trusted friend can be an excellent safeguard in such situations.

If you're the type of person who has a hard time dealing with conflict, address that fact early. Tell your advisor during the first interview that you sometimes need to take time to understand things—that you sometimes need to ask questions, review prospectuses and research material before you can feel comfortable making decisions. At that time, ask for his or her permission for you to pose tough questions about the advice being given. Make sure your advisor is comfortable with your decision-making process and would always welcome your inquiries. When someone is uncomfortable answering questions, it can mean any of three things:

- They don't know the answers.
- They think you won't like the answers.
- They're impatient to sell you something.

Though it may feel a bit uncomfortable, you also have the right to ask your advisor if he or she will be compensated better should you choose one option over another. After a while, you'll become pretty familiar with different investments and know which ones reward the firm more than others. Remember, compensation in itself is not a bad thing, so long as it isn't skewing the direction of the advice from *your* best interests to the advisor's best interests. If advisors didn't get paid for their services, they wouldn't be in business at all. One way to look at it: We prosper by allowing others to prosper as well.

Educate yourself. Read books, publications and trade journals. Attend seminars, watch videos and use the Internet. Don't hesitate to take extra time whenever necessary to feel comfortable with both advisor and advice before acting on it. Take responsibility for the advice you receive because, in the final analysis, you can only look to yourself for your successes and your failures.

One word of caution: If you're taking time to research and educate yourself, make sure you aren't being overly complacent in relation to your future. You need to be able to make decisions in life, and time goes by fast. Every day you do the wrong thing (or nothing) is another day you'll have to work harder to gain back the same positive desired result. While you're checking things out, stay productive by saving into money markets, paying down your debt or buying temporary insurance policies. These steps will help you keep moving in a positive direction while you're taking the time to discover the best direction *for you*.

## TO SUMMARIZE

1. Whether an advisor is fee-based or commission-based, try to evaluate his or her ethics and level of greed.

2. Look for clues that might indicate an advisor's motivation, particularly if he or she is short- or long-term-focused.

3. The firm an advisor works for is important, but even more important may be the individual. Be sure you're evaluating the person who

will be giving you advice. Look for his or her ability to make independent decisions and analysis rather than give robotic advice. Ask your advisor why a certain investment company is being recommended over another—and how broad his or her ability is to choose the investment products.

4. If your goal it to build a long-term relationship with your advisor, make sure this is someone you're compatible with. But if you're looking for specific advice for a short-term problem or opportunity, then test his or her technical skills in the area in question.

5. Ask your advisor thought-provoking questions to help evaluate competency levels.

6. There is no one-size-fits-all investment that is perfect for everyone.

7. Question why someone might want you to abandon investment strategies that have worked for you in the past. It might be that the advisor doesn't understand the strategies—or that he or she wants to manage your money.

8. A gut feeling might help you identify when you have to ask more questions, but don't make your final decision based on a feeling. Strive to arrive at logical, rational decisions with regard to managing your money.

9. Address concerns up front rather than waiting until things get really uncomfortable.

10. Take ownership by being responsible with the decisions you make with your money. Take the time to educate yourself and understand what you're doing with your money—because you are the one who will have to live on it in retirement. One would assume that nobody cares more about your money than you do.

11. Don't sit idly by while you research. Constantly improve your financial position, even if you don't know all the perfect places to be investing your money or whom to hire at the moment—and why.

## Principle 8

## Choose Your Team Wisely

### Principles in Action

**Sample: List your top three advisors and what you perceive their motivations might be**

1. *My accountant: I know she wants my fee revenue. But beyond that, client retention is very important to her, and she responds quickly and accurately.*

2. *My wealth manager: He's interested in helping others succeed. He lives well, so I know he's doing well for himself, but I've never gotten the impression that he gave advice for his interests over mine.*

3. *My estate attorney: She has helped me get my financial house in order and make sure that my family will be protected if anything were to happen to me. She also has helped protect me from liability in the small rental house I own by setting it up in a limited liability company. I think her main motivation, however, is protecting her good reputation.*

# Principle 8
## Choose Your Team Wisely

### Principles in Action

**Now list *your* top three advisors and what *you* perceive their motivations might be**

1. _____

2. _____

3. _____

## Principle 9

## Decide What Motivates You, Then Pursue It

I believe that people make a change in their lives for one main reason: They don't like some aspect of their current situation. This dissatisfaction is due to one of two things:

People either feel *pain* in their current circumstance and want to alleviate it, or they see the possibility for *pleasure* and want to move toward that better place.

I had some great firsthand experience in being a parent by previously training our dog. Granted, children are quite a bit more complex, and so far I may have done a better job with the dog! The chief strategy we used with our dog was to train through pleasure. We gave him treats for good behavior. Sometimes he also got into trouble, and he learned that there were some behaviors he did not want to repeat. For the most part, he was a very well-behaved animal and made good decisions with few commands. I think his great attitude was mostly due to his positive training experience. Rather than being reprimanded for doing everything wrong, he was rewarded for doing things right. I'm learning that children are much more complex than dogs, and life doesn't appear quite as black and white with them. Still, with each good decision my kids make, they act either because they have to or because they want to.

Adults are more complex than kids or dogs, so understanding everyone's personal motivations is difficult if not impossible. Still, if you pay attention to your actions throughout the day you will notice that you do things either because you feel you *have* to or because you *choose* to. *Choosing* to do something is generally out of desire for pleasure, while *having* to do something is generally avoidance of pain. For instance, we tell our kids that we either have to go to the doctors often because we don't take good care of our body and are frequently sick. Or we choose to exercise and eat good food to improve our health.

Here's another one. You might feel that you have to invest into your 401(k), so you regretfully part with your money. Or if you choose to become wealthy, you manage the 401(k) opportunities with zest and invest with conviction. Whom do you think will end up with more money in retirement?

## ARE YOU A PLEASURE SEEKER OR PAIN AVOIDER?

I see lots of people who don't want to get caught off guard, so they plan for wealth accordingly and proactively. Rarely do they have to make tough decisions to avoid pain. They act before the deadlines, save their money early and look for ways to increase their income. I have a client, Mandy, who realized a long time ago she didn't want to count on Social Security. She saved her money into her 401(k) as soon as she was eligible, then saved even more money into Roth IRAs and other investments. She took time throughout the year to read books and understand financial strategies to remain a step ahead of her goals—and well ahead of the pain.

I have another client, Ronnie, who came to see me because he couldn't sleep at night. He was quite stressed out about money after realizing in his 50s that he was far from being able to retire. Even though he remains worried, he doesn't read books to self-educate. He relies on other people to figure out his problems instead of taking control of his own life and learning how to manage his income. There's no mystery why Mandy has considerably more money now than Ronnie. She is proactive and taking action toward a pleasurable future, while he is reactionary and taking action only when he has little choice and few options.

Fortunately, we have such motivators in life. Whether it's the pursuit of happiness or the desire to flee from pain, we have reasons to change our situation and improve our lives.

Ronnie tends to have a high pain threshold. In other words, he can allow things to go wrong for quite a while before seeking change and eventually (one hopes) getting on track. Part of Ronnie's problem is that he is, well, lazy—at least in relation to wealth creation. What this man will learn later is that he'll have to do much more work if he allows the pain to get unbearable, which it eventually will. Although his outward demeanor (and inaction) would suggest he isn't concerned, Ronnie lives a very nervous and stressed life. The TV ad of the mechanic talking to the car owner is *apropos*: "You can pay me now—or pay me later." At a certain point the chickens *do* come home to roost.

On the other hand, Mandy tends to have a great deal of initiative and drive. She knows what she wants and sets out to achieve it. In fact, find someone motivated by pleasure rather than pain and you'll usually see someone who's very successful—or at least dies trying to be!

Compare the difference in those who save for retirement, such as Mandy and Ronnie. Ronnie has put everything else before his financial security. He may have been having fun spending his money, but eventually all his actions will be controlled by pain avoidance. Even though he has finally recognized he needs to have more money, right now the biggest problem is getting control of his debt to free up some cash flow. In his 60s, Ronnie will have sacrificed plenty to amass a few hundred thousand dollars. Mandy, on the other hand, has enough foresight to have fun today and get ready for the future. She beats her annual goals and therefore will hardly ever find herself in a reactive position. She's much younger than Ronnie but already has hundreds of thousands of dollars. Even on a similar income as Ronnie, she could have millions by the time she's in her 60s. Mandy is ready for opportunities and has been able to capitalize on a number of them while Ronnie just pours his hard-earned money down the drain.

If your motivator is pain, you wait until the pain is overwhelming before you get started. You keep right on buying bad assets, ignoring the inevitable until you can hardly make the debt payments anymore. Even though you have a nagging sense that you are self-destructing, you wait until you can't sleep at night before you decide it's time to start planning. Virtually all the individuals in financial trouble I meet tell me they wish they had done something productive sooner.

## WHAT ARE THEY WAITING FOR?

I see more wealth accumulated by the people who are proactive and building wealth for their own pleasure. So when it comes to building riches, let pleasure (not pain) be your prime motivator. Know the future you want to live (the pleasure you want to experience), then do what you must to make that pleasurable future a reality.

There are also many people in this world who are motivated by pleasure yet don't have a lot of money. They may be doing a fantastic job of staying ahead in many other important areas, but they haven't yet prioritized money as one of those important areas. If that's you, then recognize the truth of how much money you personally will need to have—and give as much energy as you do to other parts of your life to understand how to grow wealth at the same time.

The good news is that it's not that difficult and, with some minor tweaks to your financial habits, you'll most probably get on track quickly. One business owner, Izzy, had a wonderful, thriving business that was generating steady cash flow and hitting the aggressive milestones he had set for the company. You'd look at him and be reasonably sure he was motivated by pleasure. The only problem was Izzy didn't take the same proactive approach to building his personal finances. Instead, he spent his money freely, saying he could make up for it later when his income really skyrocketed. The only problem was ... it didn't skyrocket. His poor financial decisions caught up with him and devastated not only his personal finances but also his business.

So whether or not you're good at managing money, most of your financial actions will be motivated by either pleasure or pain. Have foresight, then make decisions that are in your best interests rather than being reactive after you've found yourself in a peck of financial trouble, forcing you into decisions you don't like. You don't want to personify the aphorism that "Beggars can't be choosers," nor do you want to have to "pay the piper" after you've exhausted all other options.

## TO SUMMARIZE

1. Virtually all of our actions are motivated by either pain or pleasure.

2. You will have to take responsibility for your future at some point. Your chances for success are much greater if you start early rather than wait till the last minute.

3. It may be fun to spend all your income today, but avoiding future financial responsibilities can cause great pain.

4. Just about everyone who is behind the eight ball in building wealth has told me, "I've waited too long." If it's so obvious, then what were they waiting for?

5. Some people are motivated by pleasure, but they don't take the same approach with their money. In today's environment it's essential that people are productive with their money. Apply the productive habits from other parts of your life to increase your wealth.

## Principle 9

# Decide What Motivates You, Then Pursue It

### Principles in Action

**Sample: Are you motivated more by pain or pleasure?**

*Pleasure, most of the time.*

**List your last three financial actions: Were they induced by pain or pleasure?**

1. *Taxes – pain: I didn't get them done until near the deadline. My accountant explained to me some of the opportunities I missed and is working with me earlier this year in order to be ahead of the game.*

2. *Buying the rental house – pleasure: I wanted to experience a side business and found a good property to cut my teeth on. My goal is to create a predictable income source to further increase my wealth.*

3. *401(k) reallocation – pleasure: I met with my wealth manager and determined that I was overexposed in some areas, especially my own company stock. We put together a much more diversified portfolio that should help my returns.*

# Principle 9
## Decide What Motivates You, Then Pursue It

### Principles in Action

**Are *you* motivated more by pain or pleasure?**

---
---

**Now list *your* last three financial actions: Were they induced by pain or pleasure?**

1. 

2. 

3.

## Principle 10

---
### Play the Game and Execute the Plan
---

If you want to increase the odds of success, then build a good *game plan*. How many times have you read that before? Since we all know it's one of the first key steps toward accomplishing something great, why doesn't everyone do it? Whether you're in business, trying to reach physical milestones or striving for financial success, having a well-thought-out game plan is essential to reaching a great outcome. While warming up for a 5.6-mile trail race recently, I told some other more experienced runners that I was thinking about running a marathon (26.2 miles) later in the year. The first question they asked me was: "What training program are you following?" They also followed it up with words to this effect: "You need to go online and read Hal Higdon's training guide, then do it!"

"Game plan" is often said as one word: gameplan. Said together, it sounds like a lot of work. It reminds me of lima beans—a vegetable I was told was healthy for me as a kid and that I had to eat, but I certainly didn't want to. Limabeans … yuk! Let's break our first couplet back into two words, "game" and "plan," and first focus on the pleasure of the first word: game.

## THE DREAM GAME

When it comes to envisioning your financial future, you don't have to know all the answers and have specific details to be able to rough out a good game plan. Think about and envision what types of things you want in life. Go ahead and let yourself dream. Don't be afraid to think big!

As I've mentioned before, I grew up in Michigan's Upper Peninsula. For those of you who don't know much about that area, it's a long ways from city lights. There's still no stoplight in my hometown. "Yoopers" know right away if someone isn't from the area and have some choice names for tourists that describe the season in which they're visiting. Then there's the famous Trenary Outhouse Races. Every February, Yoopers race outhouses from downtown Trenary across the snow and ice. Don't think it's true? It's even on YouTube! The U.P. is a wonderful place. At night you can see an intense Milky Way while northern lights dance green and red streaks across the midnight sky. My grandparents were fond of teaching us constellations and gazing for planets. On many a clear night I still look for the Big Dipper, pointing me to the ever-true North Star.

Grandparents see the limitless potential in you and tell you to reach for the stars because you can have anything you set your heart to doing. Staring into space with my grandparents made those promises seem like reality. That time in your life when you looked up at the sky and dreamed the wildest of dreams, you were playing the game. You probably hadn't yet experienced the hard knocks of life that have come to make it seem as if your dreams and reality are on different planets.

I love a great daydream. Dreaming is the main ingredient in any game and gets you on the path to where you want to be. So take some time to dream. At night drive into the country or walk to a park, look up at the sky and gaze at the stars. If you're married or have a significant other, go hand in hand. Talk about your wildest dreams. Be bold; get them all out there. Let the information flow freely and without judgment of how big or small the dreams might seem. The world is your stage. What role do you want to play on it?

It doesn't matter what age you are or if you think you're behind in relation to where you thought you might be by now. Keep dreaming. Think long and hard about all the good things you want to do, the impact you want to make on the world, the things you want to have, the places you want to go. This may be a tough task for some, especially if you're a little rusty at dreaming and believing you deserve good things. I know, I know. You're too busy to just sit down and daydream for an hour. But this is something I really recommend in order to build a great game plan. Knowing what you want is a big part of gaining financial freedom. Don't worry if you don't know how to get there; that's where the planning comes in. Now is the time to gear up with pleasurable imaginings about the things you want—and why they're important to you. Enjoy this game, and play it more than once. After all, if you want to win, you must know *why* you're playing the game. One of the key elements of sticking to anything stems from understanding the *why*. Indeed, parents who explain the *why* of things to their children give them a great gift.

Viktor Frankl wrote *Man's Search for Meaning,* which details many of his experiences in World War II and his survival of the Nazi concentration camps. In this book Mr. Frankl shares his intimate understanding of what it takes to endure, to have the courage to keep going.

> *This uniqueness and singleness which distinguishes each individual and gives a meaning to his existence has a bearing on creative work as much as it does on human love. When the impossibility of replacing a person is realized, it allows the responsibility which a man has for his existence and its continuance to appear in all its magnitude. A man who becomes conscious of the responsibility he bears toward a human being who affectionately waits for him, or to an unfinished work, will never be able to throw away his life. He knows the "why" for his existence, and will be able to bear almost any "how."*
> –Viktor E. Frankl, *Man's Search for Meaning* © 1959, 1962, 1984

There are vast numbers of people who have had to fight through challenges that make my daily struggles seem insignificant. I often reflect on Mr. Frankl's insights when I need the courage to complete a task before me. As he says, when we know *why* we're doing something, we can usually discover almost any *how* to accomplish it.

Like Mr. Frankl, legendary architect, inventor and futurist Buckminster Fuller went through a difficult time in his life. In his early 30s he was penniless, with a wife and baby, and he considered suicide. But then, as Fuller sometimes described it, he heard a "voice" telling him he didn't have the *right* to do himself in—that he belonged to the universe. Practically overnight Mr. Fuller decided to devote himself, through his work, to helping humanity. The rest, as they say, is history.

## MAKE DREAMS TANGIBLE

From the big important things to the lesser material desires, find your personal *why* in all aspects of life. This will help make the long-term results of your efforts more tangible. If you want to provide a secure haven for your beloved family, keep a picture of them close by as you sweat through the daily grind to earn a paycheck. Keep your family close to your heart as a reminder of their love, as well as their dependence on you to keep them safe.

Dreaming about what you want is part of the game. Find ways to have fun making the dreams tangible. If you want to own a new home, go visit some open houses. See what it's like to walk through the doors of your dream home. Smell the wood, open the oven doors and take in the views of the floor-to-ceiling windows. If you want to own a sports car, go rent one and drive it along a winding road, top down and full of fire. Play the stereo or just listen to the engine purr. Fill yourself with the motivation you need to keep on going. If you want to be financially self-sufficient to donate a third of your time helping others through charitable work, then go work somewhere for a week or even just a weekend. Get a taste of what it would be like to live that life.

The game is about going in the direction you choose to go. If you know where you're headed and think positively, you will find creative ways to accomplish what you desire—and will be poised to take advantage of life's opportunities.

Once we had our children we thought it would be important to feed them mostly organic foods. Soon my wife and I also were eating more organic food—and noticing a hefty increase in our food bill. I researched some stocks in the organic-foods industry and found a few that I thought were well-positioned to grow. We've made good money on those stocks to help offset the increased cost of the groceries. We also bought a large freezer for our garage and started buying in bulk. We eat much better products now and pay less for most of it. In addition, I've purchased stocks in restaurants I frequent and companies that produce products I use. It's certainly not an ironclad rule, but it can be a rule of thumb or a starting point. If I like a product, then I sometimes look into the company to see if the stock is worth buying. Some of the gains on these stocks have been strong enough to cover a lifetime supply of the product.

I hesitate to give actual examples, as by the time you read this what specifically has worked for me might not be a good investment anymore. But, for example, we signed up for a monthly subscription for movies and bought stock in the company. I've paid a few hundred dollars now for the monthly subscription, but I've already realized thousands of dollars in profit from owning the stock. I use this discipline of trying to make money by buying stock in the product's company, then purchasing the product as a way of (1) buying what I want and (2) growing wealth at the same time. While some people just fill their home with fun stuff, I also fill my portfolio with good investments.

Think about what I'm saying. If you buy products on credit, you're often still paying for them years later. Instead of paying high interest fees, I let the company's stock growth pay for the purchase of its product! This game feeds the angel on your shoulder as both your conscience and rational mind face choices between short-term satisfaction and long-term results. The game gives your angel the confidence to show up and help you make the good, though sometimes tough, decisions.[12]

A serious word of caution: You must do your homework on each investment and not purchase it just because you like the product. Even if the product is great, and the business will be around for a long time, that doesn't necessarily mean it's the right time to buy the company's stock. Bottom line: Making good investments involves research beyond basic interest in a certain product; it also involves understanding the numbers behind the company!

The game is fun, but it's only half the equation. The game gives you encouragement to press forward, but building and executing the plan are what turns dreams into realities.

---

[12] Investments are not guaranteed and are subject to investment risk, including the possible loss of principal. The investment return and principal value of the security will fluctuate so that, when redeemed, may be worth more or less than the original investment.

## PLAN TO WIN

The word "plan" has an uncanny ability to scare people. They think it's time to break out the calculators, do research and figure out all the ways you *can't* have the things you just finished dreaming about. If you're too depressed and put off the *plan* part of the game-plan process for more than a week, pull out the picture of your family, or go rent that sports car again!

Realize that planning can be as much fun as the game itself. In reality, your planning will become the catalyst that takes you from just being a dreamer to actually having what you want. As you work through the planning, you'll soon realize this is an exhilarating part of the equation! As an analogy, some people I know enjoy planning trips almost as much as taking them.

I have some clients who dreamed for years of owning a beautiful retirement home overlooking the sunset on an inland lake. So they bought a small one-room cabin on desirable lakefront property and spent summer vacations there. Throughout the years, they took good care of their property and made small improvements. In the meantime, they moved their primary mortgage from a 30-year loan to a 15-year loan and aggressively paid the principal down. They also began saving money into a cabin fund, which they will use to construct another building on the lakefront property.

Today they still have five more years of their plan, but they're more than prepared to finish it. The house where they live now is almost paid in full. They will sell their house when they retire, then rent an apartment and tear down the existing cabin to build their new home on the lake. When it's completed, they will have a beautiful home on a large secluded inland lakefront property. They also saved more into their retirement plans than many people and will likely have ample resources to provide a lifetime of retirement relaxation. Was the planning more difficult than doing nothing at all? You bet it was. But now they're reaching the point in their lives where it's all coming together. They also realize that some of their best memories as a family happened right there in that small one-room cabin.

> *One thing successful people understand is that there will be many times you fail, but never to have tried* **guarantees** *you won't succeed.*

Other people may not have specific dreams, such as lakefront property. But they dream of retiring some day, living comfortably, and visiting friends and family. For them the plan may not be quite as complex. They began saving early through work retirement plans or in other investments outside of work, such as IRAs. Throughout their working years, they decided they needed to save a certain amount of their income and earn a certain amount of return on their investments. Year after year, they tried hard to make good choices to save money—and they evaluated investment performance to help minimize poor choices. As they matured with experience, so did their portfolio. One day they reached a point where their good assets produced (and will continue to produce) more income than their employer provided. By their choice, they retired and began their next journey.

In either situation, the common theme is to have an idea of what you want and why, then execute a good plan to achieve it. Playing the game gives you spirit and motivation; planning how to accomplish and *win* the game is what actually carries you over the finish line. If you dare to tell people your goals, they might call you a dreamer. But if you tell them your plan—and it's a good one—they'll wonder why they didn't think of it themselves, and they may even seek your advice.

## PLANNING YIELDS RESULTS

The truth is that planning will make or break you. When you look back 20 years later and think of the things you thought you'd have or accomplished, don't let a simple lack of planning be the only reason you failed. You don't want to be saying, "I wish I would have." Having what you want is almost entirely within your control if you plan and take action to get it. You've probably heard the saying, "It's better to have loved and lost than never to have loved at all." I agree with that. Crushes and desires come from playing the game. Love, passion and the real flavor of life come from planning—then doing. One thing successful people understand is that there will be many times you fail, but never to have tried *guarantees* you won't succeed.

You won't experience the thrill of success while you're dreaming the dream. The thrill comes with accomplishment, with the execution of your plans. Playing the game by merely dreaming requires very little risk on your part; there's no agony of defeat *or* thrill of victory. But when you're planning and working the details, sweating and taking chances … it's then that you reap *and deserve* the rewards.

The doers get things going and take the lead into the future. These are the people we aspire to be like once they achieve success. We see them for what they are today, but seldom do we realize what it took for them to get there. Doctors, athletes, movie stars and other wealthy people are often gawked at for what they have, as if it all came very easily. It's astonishing to really understand the sacrifices and planning that many of these people have undergone to live the lives they have today.

## THINK *HOW*

Playing the game helps you understand what in life is important for you to aim for. If you play the game well, you will develop clear, tangible goals or milestones and have the motivation to do what it takes to reach them. After you list your goals, figure out *how* you're going to accomplish them. Prioritize your goals in terms of your values, as well as on a timetable. There are many ways to get from Point A to Point B. Brainstorm for any number of ideas or combinations of strategies to reach your goals. Identify a path that works within your framework of values as discussed in PRINCIPLE 1 and your visionary goals as discussed in PRINCIPLE 2. Then study what short-term accomplishment will take you one step closer to reaching the next goal.

This planning stage is often an area where others can provide priceless insight. Leverage their experiences and learn from their perspective as they share stories of how they've accomplished what you desire to have in your own life. Learn from the failures of the countless people who have dreamt of what you want, yet made poor decisions or had unfortunate experiences, so that you may minimize the obstacles in your path. Learn also from successful people who are a few steps ahead of where you'd like to be. Ask them what worked well and what opportunities they took advantage of along the way.

From now on, when you hear the words "game" and "plan," don't think about the boredom of taking out your paper and pencil, sketching out a budget and deciding where you need to cut back. Think instead of the excitement of winning—and of getting what you want and need.

Play the *game* of life and *plan* to win!

## TO SUMMARIZE

1. Build a great game plan by beginning with the "game" of dreaming. Think big and literally look to the stars to remember the endless possibilities in life.

2. Write your dreams down—especially *why* they're important to you.

3. Make your dreams tangible. Keep a picture of the ones you love close at hand, rent your dream car or visit an open house. This will "feed your angel" to help you make good decisions.

4. Be creative and open-minded about accomplishing your dreams.

5. Don't let lack of planning be the sole reason you fail. Remember, the thrill of success is not just in the destination but in the journey. The *process* of executing your plan can be deeply satisfying.

6. Successful people know they will experience failure—but also that they will never succeed if they don't at least try. Don't assume suc-

cessful people always had it easy. If you look into the life stories of many of these people, you'll realize that many of them overcame great obstacles to get where they are today.

7. Think *how* you will accomplish your plan. Prioritize your goals and brainstorm ways to reach each one.

## Principle 10

# Play the Game
# and Execute the Game Plan

### Principles in Action

**Sample: Top three short-term goals you want to accomplish (in pursuit of your visionary goal) and how you will reach them**

1. Sell some of my photos: Open a website and link it to some of the photography clubs I'm a member of.

2. Generate consulting revenue: Schedule and advertise for photography classes through clubs I'm a member of and the photography stores I purchase from.
   [Both of these goals (selling pictures and teaching) serve a multiple purpose. Not only am I starting a business, I'm also teaching my family how to have fun and spend money on hobbies by thinking outside the box and learning how to generate income from the hobby.]

3. Get my committed expenses down to only 50% of my income (currently at 70%): I want to enjoy my income not have it all go out in fixed expenses. I'm going to accomplish this by increasing my income sources and cutting back on unnecessary overhead at the same time. By creating income from hobbies, I don't have to sacrifice what I love doing. I'm going to pay great attention to what I spend money on and determine whether it adds value to life or is just bad spending.

# Principle 10
## Play the Game and Execute the Game Plan

### Principles in Action

**Now list *your* top three short-term goals *you* want to accomplish (in pursuit of your visionary goal) and how *you* will reach them**

1. _____

2. _____

3. _____

## Principle 11

## Ask Three Telling Questions

I recently met a guy, Steve, and we got into a conversation about money and investing. Steve and his wife talk often about investing, specifically that they know they need to save more money. They don't want to make any mistakes with their money and feel they don't know what questions to ask. So they end up spinning their wheels and really not getting anywhere. I meet people all the time who acknowledge the importance of investing more aggressively, but they don't know where and how. Opportunities are difficult to evaluate and, without knowing all the details, it's easier to just walk away. The problem is … sticking your head in the sand only makes things worse in the long run.

Don and Alicia met with me for financial counsel. They had taken bad advice from someone that ended up costing them almost $100,000. Their advisor had suggested converting a paid-in-full, guaranteed life insurance (survivors' aid) policy,[13] with substantial cash value, into a non-guaranteed life insurance policy, with significantly higher insurance costs. The bull stock market turned into a bear market, and the policy soon afterward lapsed due to insufficient funds.

---

13 Guarantees are subject to the claims-paying ability of the issuing insurance company.

In 20/20 hindsight, they could see that the transaction didn't make much sense. Frustrated by the experience—and with a justifiably tainted opinion of financial advisors—they were hesitant to take advice from anyone else. "We wish we would have done more research," Don said, "and learned more about what we were doing, but we just didn't know what to ask."

The challenge for the Don and Alicias of the world is that there's a mind-boggling array of options for investing in good assets and account types:[14]

- Stocks
- Mutual funds
- Variable and fixed annuities
- Index annuities
- Immediate annuities
- IRAs (individual retirement accounts)
- Roth IRAs
- 401(k)s
- 403(b)s
- 457s
- SEPs (simplified employee pensions)
- SIMPLE (savings incentive match plan for employees) plans
- Life insurance (survivors' aid)
- Bonds
- CDs (certificates of deposit)
- Residential and commercial real estate
- REITs (real estate investment trusts)
- Tax credits
- Hedge funds
- IPOs (initial public offerings)
- Futures
- Commodities
- Precious metals
- Small-business start-ups
- Private equity funds
- Personal loans

… The list goes on! What's more, thousands of specific individual investments stem from this group. With so many options—and more developing constantly—how can you possibly know what's best for you?

---

14 Different investment types come with their own inherent set of risks and potential benefits. Please research any investment carefully before purchasing.

## THREE GREAT QUESTIONS

Most investment choices will be purchased through an intermediary, such as an advisor or other professional who (in a perfect world) determines the suitability of the investment for you. But don't just take their word for it—and at the same time don't become debilitated because you can't blindly trust them. With a little practice, determining if most investments are right for you is actually surprisingly easy. You need to ask the source three key questions, then compare the results with other options.

- What is my potential *return*?
- What is my *risk*?
- What will this *cost* me (including liquidity)?

With each investing experience the results from your questioning will become more clearly defined, and your ability *to tell the difference between a desperate salesman and a good investment opportunity by a reputable advisor* will increase. Soon you'll be viewed as a "sophisticated investor," even if you don't have the net worth to show it yet. Your ability to minimize poor choices and to increase the number of positive decisions (and to do so in a timely fashion) will directly affect your ability to create and grow wealth.

The great news is that you don't have to be a guru in order to ask excellent clarifying questions. Don and Alicia from the above example didn't ask enough questions because both the life insurance and advisor intimidated them. This led them to blindly put their faith in the advisor, which turned out to be a big mistake. After that bad experience, they avoided working with financial advisors due to fear of the unknown and not having confidence in the industry to provide unbiased, objective counsel.

It's difficult to find truly objective advice in any situation, let alone the financial services industry. That doesn't mean, however, you can put your investment life on hold. It just means you have to understand the basics of investing and continue to build on your own knowledge base.

## WHAT IS MY POTENTIAL *RETURN*?

People invest their money in order to earn a rate of return. So discovering the potential rate of return is one of the essential steps in evaluating an investment. There can be anomalies in an individual opportunity—or during a certain period of time when an aggressive investment can produce an exceptional short-term return. It's easy to get caught up in the moment and forecast an indefinite, high-flying positive return. This extreme optimism may look great on paper, but it probably won't be the end result. Time is a great equalizer, and most great runs usually collide head-on with poor decisions or deteriorating conditions. The extraordinary rate of return often finds itself back in line with the masses. Nonetheless, discovering the potential upside of an investment is exciting and important.

### ACTIVE INVESTING

How close you are to the source of the investment also might dictate what your potential upside return may be and how long it may last. Direct active ownership—such as with real estate, small business and inventions—may provide you with some legitimate inside information and control over the investment's success. Using good information to increase your return is a wonderful advantage (when legal). If you take an active role in time and education—given the right circumstances and, importantly, your skill set—you may find niche markets where your returns far exceed the norm. I view this type of investing as active investing (versus passive investing) and a legitimate job. If done well, it's very rewarding. In those circumstances where you actively understand the market you're in and what your roles in it are, you could walk away from more deals than you participate in to find opportunities that work within your model. Patience and calculated discipline could yield high returns for your efforts. Generally, the greater an investment's possible reward over time, the greater its level of price volatility or risk.

In the Greater Detroit area where I live there are some highly successful, active real estate developers. Rather than invest their money with conventional REITs, they studied the local real estate markets and devised strategies to build their own real estate partnerships with other local investors. The good ones succeeded, and some have done amazingly well. I have friends who have developed millions of dollars' worth of good income-producing commercial real estate. Some do it as a full-time job, while others take just a part-time approach. In recent years, of course, Detroit has experienced major financial hardships with the automotive industry. What the next 10 years will bring is anyone's guess. The smart (or lucky) ones may have secured their positions and will ride out the storm just fine—or even advance nicely. Some of the others are going out of business. If you've been blessed with great investment experiences through active investing, be careful not to believe that you're invincible. As noted above, time has a way of leveling the playing field, and some strategies suddenly lose their advantage. Search for ways you can continue to capitalize on your core expertise while still diversifying into other areas.

**PASSIVE INVESTING**
Although active investing has and will continue to create tremendous wealth for a relatively small minority of persons, most Americans won't build their wealth through active investing. It's possible, however (especially in light of the decreasing number of pension plans provided retirees), that active investing could become much more commonplace in the form of real estate rentals (both residential and business), through Internet business and/or through other income-producing investments. Some people will take an active role, but most others will passively invest in similar opportunities. The majority of Americans work for a company that provides them a paycheck, which in turn covers their bills. A portion of their income is invested passively into other investments, such as mutual funds, REITs and various retirement plans, including 401(k)s.

Passive investing has built, and will continue to build, great wealth for many Americans.

Ideally, your desired returns are in line with your projected needs from your financial game plan. For example, if you need to have $4 million of income-producing assets in 25 years, and you currently have $300,000 invested, thereby adding $30,000 per year, you need to earn a little less than 8 percent per year on average. The more you're able to save, the lower your required return to still reach $4 million—and vice versa.

My long-term estimates for an aggressive rate of return usually fall between 8 and 10 percent. If your calculations show you needing a return closer to 15 or 20 percent in order to reach your goals, then to stay realistic you may need to adjust the length of time to your goal, your future spending habits or the amount you save toward your goal. You also may need to take a much more active role in increasing your income for investing. As previously stated, the higher the anticipated annual rate of return, the greater the risks. As a rule of thumb, if you need access to your money in one to five years, then you might expect to earn a return up to 5 percent. If you have five to 10 years before needing to liquidate your money, then you might be looking for an investment that could produce gains of 5 to 10 percent. Of course, there could well be periods when your returns are much higher than that. Counting on a high return, however, can lead to overly optimistic expectations—and can cause you to take inappropriate and unwise actions.

> *Counting on a high return, however, can lead to overly optimistic expectations—and can cause you to take inappropriate and unwise actions.*

You might have periods when your long-term investments satisfy your short-term needs. I met with a middle-aged man, Jaime, who had stock he intended on investing for five or more years and other money invested in bond funds he intended on spending within that year. Almost overnight, the stock got some great press and became very popular, quadrupling in value. Jaime had only owned it for a few months, but he believed it was now over-valued and decided to sell it all. Although not his intended use, the gain was more than enough to satisfy his short-term needs.

Sometimes when this happens, people feel they can't go wrong in the market and invest aggressively for the short term when it isn't wise to do so. The problem is that the market could have turned the other way. Soon after Jaime sold his stock, it dropped below his original purchase price. Even three years later the stock wasn't worth more than what he had paid for it and would still be at a loss if he hadn't sold it when he did. It's tempting to invest for the short term with high-potential-return investments, but you had better have a back-up plan if you lose your shirt.

I met with someone in Michigan's Upper Peninsula who did quite well with his money in the late 1990s—so well, in fact, that he decided to no longer keep cash reserves in the bank. His logic was that if the market even did a fraction of what it did for him during the past five years it would still earn more interest than he was receiving at the bank. The only problem was his calculations assumed an indefinite *positive* rate of return, not factoring in what a negative (bear) market would look like. Indeed, the market took a serious turn for the worse from March 2000 through October 2002. Instead of earning more than the "measly" yield at the bank, he lost many thousands of dollars. He got too greedy and gambled his short-term money on long-term positions and lost.

Evaluating the projected return over a specified period of time is a great first test to evaluating the source's legitimacy. While working as a financial advisor in a small Northern Michigan town, I met someone, Wade, who made an investment with a friend who was buying property. Wade explained how he had been lending Sam money to buy rental properties. Sam would then use the money as the down payment on the property, do some fixing up and later refinance the money back out, with a guaranteed 15 percent return to the investor in just three months. If Wade allowed Sam to roll the money back in after three months and keep it invested for a year, Sam would guarantee twice the return on his money and a full liquidation anytime my client wanted. Wade also could roll the investment over again and continue earning double-digit rates of return.

Getting the details of the investment out of my client took much prodding because Sam told everyone to keep the opportunity under wraps. It turns out Wade wasn't my only client who had invested money with Sam. They were all very excited about how much money they were making on paper. I told Wade and my other clients to take their money out right away. Of course, most thought this advice was foolish. Why take money out when Sam was promising such a great rate of return? Conventional investments produced so much less.

I soon realized that this investment scheme was a hoax—for two reasons. First, Sam was promising way too high a rate of return over such a short period of time in an investment that couldn't sustain it. He borrowed money from multiple people throughout the year and was supposedly paying 15 percent in just a three-month time frame. If he had to pay people 15 percent every quarter, that meant his cost of borrowing was at least 60 percent a year. There were no residential real estate investments in that small Northern Michigan town that consistently provided in excess of 60 percent cash return to pay back his investors and earn a profit for Sam—let alone double that if they kept the money invested for a year. It was clear he needed money from "Peter" to pay "Paul."

The 1 to 5 percent theory for short-term investments would tell you right away that you needed to look into the specifics of the investment to determine why the stated return was so high.

> *I soon realized that this investment scheme was a hoax ... Sam was promising way too high a rate of return over such a short period of time in an investment that couldn't sustain it.*

In that real estate market, if Sam had been borrowing money from a bank, officials there would've charged him a rate of around 12 percent for the year ... 15 percent tops. Wade would've been better off had he checked with the local banks to see what their rates were, then immediately asked Sam why he was paying four times the amount he'd be charged at the bank. It's easy to assume the banks had already denied Sam the loan, so the next logical follow-up question would be: Why?

Second, Sam told his investors to keep the arrangement a secret. Unless you're privy to a very confidential business arrangement and signing confidentiality paperwork, being told to keep things a secret is generally not a good sign. Soon afterward Sam slithered out of town with $1.2 million in outstanding IOUs to many people in the community. He was eventually arrested. Once again, if something sounds too good to be true, it usually is.

When someone tells you an investment can produce a certain rate of return, find out why and how. Look at what it has done in the past—*everything* it has done in the past. The homework might be easy if the investment is a stock, mutual fund or other regulated investment with a public track record. But if the investment is more of an idea someone is telling you about or being offered by someone like Sam, then your research may be much more difficult. Nonetheless, do some digging!

Mutual funds are one of the most popular methods of investing money. They range from very conservative to very aggressive. Once you spend time asking probing questions and discovering the material differences in asset class from one mutual fund to another, you'll quickly find yourself in a comfort zone with building up portfolios of funds you can manage. Mutual funds have helped bring equity ownership to many an average household. For this reason, they are a great pioneer of individual wealth. They have helped people, who weren't comfortable buying individual stocks or going into other active business opportunities, to be worth more money and reach more financial independence. They also allow an investor to begin participating with small dollar amounts—some as low as $50 a month.

## WHAT IS MY *RISK*?

Once you've discovered all the upside potential in an investment and settled on a realistic rate of return, investigate the reasons you might not *obtain* that return.

Risk can be tough to determine in the case of some obscure private investments. I was once given a market analysis of a small-chain business that was looking to raise capital for further expansions. The chain owner came across as being a little arrogant, boasting frequently about his success. From what I was able to see, it did look initially like things were going his way. He claimed a 300 percent return on investment for himself on each store. Even if that were true, though, the return would be much less for the investor.

There are various levels of risk. With some investments, you risk losing all your money. With others, you risk losing more money than you put into it through extended liability or obligations to make future payments.

For most passive investments, you risk—for extended periods of time—the value of your portfolio being worth less than your initial deposit.

I asked him what the risk was. He snapped that there was no risk. According to him, all his stores were successful, and no competitor or condition could interfere with his growth. I noticed that the date on the market analysis he handed me was a year old. Apparently, he had been having difficulty finding someone to loan him the money for expansions. As soon as I was back in my office, the out-of-date market analysis found its way into the circular file. Anyone who isn't capable of understanding his or her investment risk is not a person I'm willing to give money to.

Your risk tolerance is generally determined by how much time you have to invest your money without needing to liquidate it or produce income from it. The longer you can ride through bad investment performance, the more risk you may decide to expose your money to in hopes of ultimately receiving a higher return. The shorter the time period, the less you may be able to let your investment go in the red. If somebody tells me, "Your investment should produce a return of over 50 percent in just one year," I'm going to assume there's a good chance of never getting any of my money back. It might actually be a great investment, but I'll be very skeptical at first. If it were that easy, everybody would be doing it.

Risk also helps you evaluate the actual return on an investment. For example, when you look at an investment's historical returns on a graph and see some highs and lows but, ultimately, a fantastic finish, the investment might look outstanding. The average annual return is determined by adding the total return and dividing by the number of years. This particular investment may have produced an average annual return of 14 percent. Be wary of how graphs can distort truths, which is a near cousin to "Figures don't lie, but liars figure." If you had purchased during one of the previous peaks rather than at the bottom, or if you had to sell prematurely, your investment may actually show a loss.

There is a very common investment strategy called "dollar cost averaging." If you invest into a 401(k), you're already dollar cost averaging. While you're in the accumulation phase of investing, having an investment fluctuate in value each month may actually be a good thing. During the market cycles, you buy shares at cheaper prices when they're worth less, allowing you to buy a greater amount of shares.

Investment fluctuation can have the opposite effect when you're spending your money. If you have to take out a consistent dollar amount each month (such as $5,000) when the share price goes down, you have to liquidate more shares to get the $5,000 than when the share price is up. If you experience a series of negative returns for months in a row, you may end up depleting your portfolio of shares quite quickly. Someone else saving into the same fund, however, will be purchasing your shares at a discount and may actually benefit from the same event that's causing your demise.

Once I met with a woman, Brandy, who back in the 1990s was investing her money rather heavily into mutual funds. Her returns were substantial and, even at a relatively young age she ended up with around $400,000. At that point Brandy wanted to stop working and spend some of that money over the next few years as she contemplated, then began moving into, job and life changes. She set aside money in conservative accounts to draw down from but ended up needing around three times the amount she anticipated. Soon she began selling funds that she thought she would be holding for a long time, right in the middle of the market decline in 2001, and continued spending through 2002. Her investments were down so much by then that she was selling three times the amount of shares in order to generate the same amount of money she took out two years earlier. Finally, Brandy started working again and stopped the withdrawals. She ended up benefiting during the market run in the late '90s, only to sell her gains at massive discounts a few years later.

Identifying the risk in anything helps you come back down to earth and establish realistic goals and expectations. Such risk identification also will be one of your key components in protecting your assets by naming various potential roadblocks, then building a strategy to help protect against them, as with crutch management (mentioned earlier in PRINCIPLE 3).

## WHAT WILL THIS *COST* ME (INCLUDING LIQUIDITY)?

"There is no such thing as a free lunch" was the favorite saying of Chuck Milliken, my college Economics professor. And he was absolutely right. Everything in life "costs" something, by hook or by crook, and when it comes to investing, the cost is real dollars and cents. In theory at least, costs need to be clearly labeled and easily identified.

In reality, however, this usually isn't the case. Many investments have a prospectus to help outline costs, but they're often much thicker and more confusing than most people care to read. Your advisor should be able to help you understand the costs of investing, but if those costs are wrapped up in his or her compensation, this may be a discussion he or she would like to avoid. To further complicate matters, even with ethical advisors, sometimes the costs are so layered that even they don't fully understand them all.

At the beginning of this principle I referred to a couple, Don and Alicia, who lost $100,000 in a life insurance policy. This is one of the examples where I'll bet the advisor didn't even understand all the costs. That said, I still think he knew it wasn't the right move for Don and Alicia. Insurance has multiple layers of costs, and many people don't take the time to figure them out.

First of all, the investment vehicle is going to have a different internal operating expense, generally expressed as a percentage, which commonly ranges from 0.3 percent to more than 2 percent. The insurance company may then charge a percentage fee. The policy is going to have certain costs that include insurance costs, operating expenses, contract fees and other miscellaneous expenses. Many of these fees are based on the investor's age; they increase as the investor gets older. Usually there are surrender charges for taking the money out within 10 or 15 years.

The advisor wanted to sell Don and Alicia a new policy for commission but was showing them only one side of the equation: gross potential return. He quoted a return of 12 percent (which, to be kind, I would classify as "optimistic") and compared that to the fixed-rate return of the old policy, which was around 6 percent. He did *not* show a net-return comparison after taking into consideration the multiple layers of costs, including the fact that the new insurance policy's costs were nearly three times the existing costs. It's quite a challenge to understand all the costs, then compare accurately with another insurance policy. However, if the clients had taken the time to probe and ask questions—even without discovering all the layers of costs—they would have learned that the proposed policy was considerably more expensive than their current one.

Many people also ignore future taxes as a cost when making comparisons. Most personal retirement investments today are in 401(k) plans, as well as other pre-tax retirement plans. While these plans provide a wonderful platform for systematic savings, under current tax law every dime spent in the future will be taxed as ordinary income. Most people are fine with this, as they believe they'll be in a lower tax bracket in the future. Sometimes, though, they discover it's actually higher. Itemized deductions are often at their lowest during retirement. The kids are out of the house (ideally), the mortgage is paid off (ideally), and there may not be business or other deductible expenses. Many retirees cringe at the thought of spending money from their 401(k)s because they have to give Uncle Sam as much as a third of it. Their money will last longer if they don't have to give such a large portion of it to the government each time they want to spend it. So don't just save blindly into every pre-tax account you can; take a minute to project what your income might look like in retirement and make sure you're balancing out the cost of taxes by using Roth IRAs and other tax-free or tax-advantaged investments.

> *Life insurance does play an important role in many people's planning; however, it isn't the cure-all investment some advisors would like you to think it is.*

That said, don't just assume that because an investment may help reduce future taxes it's a great investment. Life insurance is a common example where some advisors try to make it look more appealing than it may actually be. Life insurance does play an important role in many people's planning; however, it isn't the cure-all investment some advisors would like you to think it is.

I see this scenario all the time. A couple came in to meet with me and discuss their goals. One of the main investments they were using was a life insurance policy with high expenses attached. They put a modest amount of money into it each year and were expecting it to provide for their future. They thought it would pay for their kids' education and also a big part of their retirement "tax free." I told them it wouldn't and ran some numbers to show them why. They replied, "It's going to work because the advisor said it would, and he's our friend." If you invest a modest amount of money, and more than half of it is used up for various costs (such as insurance expenses), I don't care if it's tax-free or not (and it certainly doesn't matter if the advisor is your "friend"), it is unlikely to cover all the goals you have in life. *Numbers don't lie* (though people sometimes do).

Costs also come in the form of liquidity and surrender charges. The most mind-boggling example is with a 403(b), a retirement plan similar in tax nature to a 401(k). For some reason, the insurance industry has dominated the market, offering annuities to the 403(b) crowd. There might be 10 different 403(b) options, with nine of them being high-cost variable annuities. The one other choice might be a higher-cost, no-load, mutual-fund company, such as Vanguard or Fidelity. Often the gross investment performance of the variable-annuity sub-accounts and the mutual funds of Vanguard or Fidelity are quite similar. When you compare the net return after internal costs, however, it isn't uncommon for the variable-annuity charges to be two or three times the cost of the mutual funds—not to mention that variable annuities may carry a surrender charge as long as 12 years! Some variable annuities have additional riders that can protect your money,[15] but these riders come at an additional cost, and most people don't sign up for them.

Logically, if you have multiple choices for investing your money, and they're all similar with investment performance and risk, you'd choose the investment vehicle that provides the greatest flexibility and the lowest cost. Why so few choose that option, I simply don't understand. I'm convinced it will be a sign that people are starting to catch on and learn how to make investment decisions when more 403(b) investors begin using the lower-cost plans instead of the variable annuities—or they at least use the variable annuities for their unique functions, such as their living- or death-benefit riders.

A word of caution: If an investment has surrender charges, it often (though not always) is a more expensive and complicated investment, and you would be advised to approach it cautiously. This certainly doesn't mean the investment is bad; it might be exactly the right option for your situation. But it also can mean there's a higher commission, and that may distract the advisor. I also have seen some shorter-term, surrender-charge annuities have higher internal operating costs than longer ones. So the length of a charge calls for caution as well about the investment's internal expenses. Surrender charges also could appropriately exist within

---

15 Guarantees are subject to the claims-paying ability of the issuing insurance company.

illiquid investments to discourage investors from prematurely selling out. Liquidations in an illiquid market, such as real estate, make it very difficult for management to effectively invest the money.

We don't work for years, make sacrifices, educate ourselves and invest money just to have large portfolios; we do these things in order to some-day *spend* the money. Pay as much attention to how your money will be taxed or expensed when you spend it as you pay attention to investing and accumulating money.

I placed the discussion of cost third on the list of questions because sometimes too much focus is brought to bear on cost and not enough on what also matters—the return and the risk. As indicated earlier, just because one investment costs more than another doesn't mean it's bad. Also as stated previously, what you're ultimately looking for is a desired return. If a higher-cost investment has the ability to produce this ideal rate of return, all things being equal, pursue the desired return. If, however, the investments are similar in potential return and risk, costs can end up playing a significant role and might reduce overall performance.

## THE THREE QUESTIONS IN ACTION

I once took over a group of clients from an advisor who decided she wanted to get out of the investment business. As a result, the clients had nobody local to contact, so I made myself available to them. The previous advisor was fond of investing retirement accounts into variable annuities, similar to the example I gave earlier with 403(b)s. In my opinion, most of the clients were not well-served. They also had significant surrender charges, making it difficult to do something different with the money to lower their costs.

A few days after sending out a letter explaining that the original advisor was no longer in business, I received a phone call from one of the clients, Tom, and his friend Vinny, a financial advisor. Vinny was calling me, with Tom on speakerphone, inquiring about the investment in his IRA, specifically about the liquidity. I explained that it was a variable annuity and not originally purchased at my office—and had a surrender charge if it were cashed in. Tom said his original advisor hadn't made him aware of this, which didn't surprise me from what I saw of her business ethics.

The surrender charge amounted to around $2,400. Vinny explained that the new investment he was proposing offered a bonus of about 4 percent, which would offset the existing charge. There are very few investments that offer a bonus that aren't variable annuities. So I asked Vinny, "Are you rolling the investment into another variable annuity?" He replied that he was. I'm familiar with most of the variable annuities in the marketplace, so I asked which one he was using.

Shortly after the conversation ended, I called Tom back and made sure he understood what he was doing. Even though I had never met him, I wanted to make sure he was properly informed. I quickly realized that Tom had failed to ask his friend Vinny the three telling questions. Let's look at each question in the context of this example.

*What is the **return**?*

In this particular situation, both variable-annuity investments were similar. Theoretically, it's difficult to justify that one investment might produce a higher return than another one. Rather, it would be a function of the actual investment choices used inside the annuity that would determine investment success. Since the investments were so similar, Vinny didn't have to move the money out of the existing investment to increase return; he simply had to recommend a proper allocation inside the current annuity. Return, therefore, was identical.

*What is the **risk**?*

Since the investment choices in the two variable annuities were similar, so was the risk. Again, rather than one annuity being distinctly better than the other one, the actual allocation Tom or Vinny chose would prove to be the most crucial decision. They would be able to design a portfolio in either annuity that suited Tom's risk tolerance. This means that the risk in either investment was basically the same.

*What is the **cost**?*

Tom knew the obvious cost of getting out of the original investment—3½ percent, or $2,400. He also understood that he was receiving a 4 percent bonus for getting into a new investment. It thus seemed logical to Tom that his cost was being reduced. However, he never asked Vinny the question about what the investments' total costs were.

The internal operating expenses in the new investment exceeded the existing annuity by about 55 basis points, or 0.55 percent. That means that on every $10,000 of investment he would now be paying an additional $55 per year. This increased his internal cost by hundreds of dollars per year, thereby nullifying the new investment bonus and creating an instant loss.

In addition to the increased expense, Tom also had a new, heavier surrender charge. This is the liquidity portion of the cost. Tom had been in his existing variable annuity for almost four years. He had three years left on the surrender charge, and it was going down by 1 percent a year. The new variable annuity had a nine-year surrender charge, starting out at 9 percent. Tom was in his late 50s and planning to spend some of his money in the next few years. His surrender charge in the original investment would've expired by the time he needed the money. While any annuity contract would allow Tom to withdraw up to 10 percent of his account without a surrender charge, if he opted to withdraw more than that amount in any given year, he would in fact face a surrender charge. By getting into this new product, he tacked on an additional six years to the surrender period.

> *Tom simply needed to ask the value question ... And he would soon realize that Vinny wasn't being much of a friend.*

So the bottom line is this: If the client were to move his investment out of his existing variable annuity into the new one that Vinny was recommending, his potential return would remain the same and his risk control would also remain the same. His internal expenses and surrender charges, however, would increase. Tom simply needed to ask the value question, "Does this decision take me closer to or farther from my goal?" and he would soon realize that Vinny wasn't being much of a friend.

Ethical dealing with clients usually pays off—first figuratively, then literally—in the long run.

## KNOWLEDGE IS POWER

You can look at stories like this and quickly get fed up with the financial planning industry and some of the people who work in it. Whenever I see these types of things, I'm as appalled as you are. That's one of the reasons I'm writing this book. I believe that the best way to police the industry is to increase the level of consumer awareness. Since you can't always immediately tell if the person you're working with has the highest ethics, "arm" yourself and always ask the three telling questions:

- *What is the **return**?*
- *What is the **risk**?*
- *What is the **cost**?*

By asking these three questions before you invest your money, you save yourself from making many of the most common financial mistakes. Each time you cover these questions, you'll gain experience and become more proficient at evaluating opportunities.

Don't feel intimidated by asking what might even seem to be *simple* questions. I always like it when I hear someone say, "Explain it to me like I'm a 12-year-old." Some of my wealthiest clients ask me the most basic clarifying questions.

## TO SUMMARIZE

*1. Return*

- Active investing can provide you with more control and potentially a high return. It can also become a part-time or even full-time job.

- I define passive investing as hiring others to make the detailed investment choices for you, but you still need to be vigilant. It's your money!

- Don't gamble short-term needs on long-term investments. You also want to be wary of projecting great short-term experiences forward indefinitely. Try to maintain a healthy balance of optimism and realism.

*2. Risk*

- Evaluate the risk by asking why something might not produce a positive return. It may be easier to evaluate past risk and performance on publicly traded investments than on private opportunities. Difficulty, however, doesn't excuse you from doing your homework on a private investment opportunity.

- The more time you have before you need to spend your money, the more risk you may be able to assume. Volatility becomes quite important when you're in the spending (usually retirement) phase of your life.

*3. Cost*

- Some investments have multiple layers of costs, and you'll need to ask for them a number of times before you have unearthed all the layers. Don't forget to include taxes and surrender charges.

- All things being equal, lower costs will increase your return. However, all things usually are not equal, so don't let cost deter you from excellent opportunities.

- Practice asking the three questions ("What is the return? What is the risk? What is the cost?"), then ask another great clarifying value question: "Does this decision take me closer to, or farther from, my goals?"

*No question is a bad question, especially when it pertains to your money!*

## Principle 11
## Three Telling Questions

### Principles in Action

**Sample: Last three financial investment purchases**
**What did you do to determine their effectiveness?**

### Return, risk and cost

1. Bought a rental house

Return: The return looked minimal as far as positive cash flow goes. But it does like I'll have all my overhead covered and tweak out some positive money by the end of the year. I was able to buy the property without much of my own money, so through appreciation and debt service, I should enjoy a good return on investment in about five years having equity of around $60,000. We already have equity of $45,000.

Risk: The bulk of the risk is in not renting it out, which would put me in the red at $1,000 per month. This risk was reduced as I had a ready tenant before I bought the property. We currently have a two-year lease in place. I've reduced my liability risk by owning the property in an LLC and purchasing the appropriate insurances.

Cost: I only had to use $5,000 of my own money to purchase the property. But I put plenty of sweat into it. The house needed some good manual labor to get it into good shape. Thankfully there were no real big surprises. The cost could be significant if the tenant leaves and I can't get a new tenant or can't sell it.

2. Allocated out of company stock in my 401(k)

Return: I had 50% of my 401(k) in company stock. My wealth manager ran some numbers showing me that my returns would have been better (20/20 hindsight) if I'd had a more diversified portfolio of mutual funds. It's tough to predict the future, but it doesn't look like I'm gaining anything by owning so much company stock. And as far as the past is concerned, I lost money compared with what I could have had.

Risk: My risk was reduced from the simple standpoint that I don't like so much riding on one company. When I thought about it, my income is dependent on my company, my pension is dependent on it, my health benefits are dependent on it, and I didn't also want my 401(k) dependent on it.

Cost: The cost of the advice was small. I pay my wealth manager an annual fee, so I try to get as many good ideas out of him as I can. Whether or not we discussed this allocation change, my cost to him would not have changed. The cost to make the change in my 401(k) was close to nothing.

3. Made change to David's 401(k) options

Return: David's work offered him an option of transferring the balance of his 401(k) into a brokerage account, with thousands of fund options rather than just the 10 that he has now. Technically, the return is at least as good and quite possibly better than now. The new plan has all the same options that are available today, plus thousands more.

Risk: Depending on the quality of decisions we make, the risk is reduced as we now have a much greater selection of funds to choose from in his 401(k).

Cost: This depends on what kind of funds we buy. Some of the funds have high loads and some have none. The cost per transaction is pretty low at $25 per trade. So as long as we pick funds that have reasonable expenses, the cost is not that much different from what we have today.

## Principle 11
## Three Telling Questions

### Principles in Action

**Now list *your* last three financial investment purchases. What did *you* do to determine their effectiveness?**

**Return, risk and cost**

1. _____

Return:

Risk:

Cost:

2. _____

Return: _____

Risk: _____

Cost: _____

3. _____

Return: _____

Risk: _____

Cost: _____

## Principle 12

### Don't Forget That Your Story's Ending Is Predictable

The choices you make today will take you down a fairly predictable path. Depending on the quality of your decisions, the road may be paved in riches, or it may be filled with potholes and boulders. The good news is that where you end up is almost entirely within your control.

I asked a teacher nearing retirement what advice she had for younger teachers. She answered confidently and quickly: "I would have bought years for my pension immediately and would have started to save into my 403(b) the very first day." For those unfamiliar with some school pensions, "buying years" is a way to increase your future pension income. The cost of buying is usually based on your current income. Earlier in your career your income is lower, so the cost to buy is less. A 403(b) is very similar to the more popular 401(k). Contributions are made by the employee, pre-tax, into retirement-plan investments, which are managed by the employee and taken out for income upon retirement.

As noted previously, "If only I had started saving sooner" is the single most common statement I hear when asking people what they would have done differently. That gave me the idea to look for patterns of previous behavior while interviewing clients who were already retired. I also was curious if they had regrets about how they managed their money in years past. What I found is that people tend to end up in one of four possible scenarios—or "doors" (with apologies to "Let's Make a Deal," the old TV game show). There are many reasons why people wind up where they do in relation to money. In light of a number of client interviews, I've organized common behaviors as examples. They don't begin to touch on every reason why people end up in a particular financial position in life. But they do help to point out that there are patterns that lead each of us to those financial positions. Read each scenario and decide which door you'd like to open as you enter into your retirement years. Identify your own patterns and ask yourself which door you're now heading toward.

## **FOUR DOORS AWAIT YOU: WHICH ONE WILL YOU OPEN?**

### Door #1

Door #1 opens to financial freedom and flexibility. Most of the people in this scenario didn't get there by a windfall or through inheritance. Married or single, they worked hard and saved their pennies. A few of them did get a large influx of money at one time in their life, but that was the exception. Generally, they reached success because of their careful planning and hard work. It was the consistency of their efforts that put them into Door #1.

Their story was usually the same. They didn't depend on bonuses or overtime wages. Whenever they had a dual income, they mostly saved one and lived off the other. They avoided consumer debt and lived largely within their means through every stage of life. They invested early and often. They usually had a strong "offense" *and* "defense." The offense was the money coming in, and the defense was the budget and investment strategies. If they were married, they tended to split those duties as a team.

These people enjoyed the simple things in life. They had no need to keep up with the Joneses. They drove used cars and put a lot of miles on them. They didn't have much "junk" (bad assets) around the house, and they didn't move often. They had fixed-rate mortgages and worked on getting the balance down. If they had children, their kids didn't have all the "latest" things, but because many of these people started with next to nothing, they honestly felt they couldn't afford such luxuries at the time.

When their wealth started to grow, they were pleasantly surprised. Compound interest took small accounts and turned them into large accounts. They didn't intend to use the money before retirement, so their money continued to stockpile. Balances doubled, then tripled, and their net worth advanced sharply. The ball started rolling—like a snowball picking up speed and snow as it headed downhill—which, for some, led to early retirement and, for all, to very comfortable living.

They admit that saving was difficult at times, but they have no regrets. They're doing just fine now and enjoying the fruits of their labors. They had a good understanding of various investments and became more comfortable in some strategies than others. Not all these people are financial experts. Some of them just had a little more discipline than most people, along with an understanding of where they were headed in life.

## Door #2

Door #2 is also quite nice. These people have a decent understanding of money, and they're able to support themselves for the rest of their lives. They didn't necessarily live on a budget, but they knew how much they had available to spend. They also shared many of the same traits of those people who ended up in Door #1. Only they made a few more mistakes, didn't start as early or were not as concerned about building excess capital.

They also had an offense and defense, but the defense wasn't quite as committed to making the best decisions. They didn't talk as often about money or have as detailed a game plan. They knew it was important to stay out of debt, and some put as much money as they could toward paying off the mortgage. They also knew it was important to save, but sometimes they were more traditional, investing in things that produced a modest return with less risk.

They can now generally do most of the important things they want to in life. They travel frequently, visit friends and family, and enjoy life's amenities—all within reason. They protected most of their downside risk. They carried adequate life insurance polices in the event of early death. Many of them have long-term care policies to protect their current lifestyle or that of their spouse in the event of poor health.

As with those in DOOR #1, they made an effort to teach their children how to support themselves financially.

Some of the people interviewed had enough income and interest to make it to DOOR #1. Because of some periods of poor management, however, they slid over toward DOOR #2. This was their door as long as they finally learned to curb their spending once they reached retirement. If not, they could find themselves opening yet a third door—DOOR #3.

## DOOR #3

DOOR #3 begins to look less appealing. If nothing goes wrong, these people might have enough money to make it to the end of their respective lives. However, they'll have difficulty handling *"what if"* scenarios, such as poor health, nursing home expenses or an unexpected family burden.

They may have a small nest egg for the future and might be living on a fixed income. For most of these people, there will be a time (because of inflation) when their fixed income will be less than their fixed expenses. When that happens, depending on how long they live, their nest egg may be used up or their lifestyle adjusted. If they're hit with bad events, poor investment performance or large expenses, they'll be out of money quickly. If they're lucky, they own their house. It's not a fancy house, but it's a place to live.

The behaviors that got them to this more fragile financial position are quite common. They didn't save enough. Maybe they didn't fully understand how investing worked, and they didn't think they needed to have that much money. Many of them liked to buy things. They didn't know if they were going to be alive tomorrow, so they lived more for today. Being debt-free wasn't as important to some of them. They were more concerned with keeping up with the payments.

They made a lot of financial mistakes in their life. They were less organized and couldn't tell you what their strategy was. They lacked both a focused offense and a defense. In fact, the concept seemed foreign to them. They didn't live on a budget, knowing that was a mistake, but they continued spending anyway.

> *Many didn't see themselves as people who would be poor someday and thought they would hit it big in the future. Unfortunately, that didn't happen.*

Many didn't see themselves as people who would be poor someday and often thought they would hit it big in the future. Unfortunately, that didn't happen. In some cases they lost a job because of downsizing. In such instances their pension wasn't nearly as great as they thought it would be. They may have been surrounded by others with more money and tried to live the same lifestyle, but they couldn't really afford it. They sometimes were too eager to live well and spend freely. Their homes were too lavish, and they spent too much money on large items like luxury cars. They saw debt as a necessity and assumed they would be in debt forever.

## Door #4

For Door #4, take everything from Door #3 and compound it. Some of these people support their kids, even though they don't have enough money to support themselves, and their adult children have kids of their own. They have debt, low savings and low financial self-esteem. They never found time to talk about and understand money—or how to build it.

People end up in Door #3 or Door #4 for many reasons. One of the most common is making financial decisions due to pain. Some of these people make careless and selfish mistakes with money throughout their life.

They borrowed and spent with little or no regard for the effects, then hoped others would bail them out.

On the other hand, sometimes people in Door #3 and Door #4 have been quite supportive of others but seldom helped themselves. They may not have a lot of debt; they just don't have much income or good assets. They know they'll need financial support in the future. Some of these people may have the greatest hearts and the greatest intentions, but they never made the effort to understand and implement responsible fiscal behaviors. Sometimes they felt guilty whenever they had money because they realized somebody else had less. They got lost in the shuffle between a pension/Social Security society and one of individual wealth.

I feel for the people who got here by helping others more than themselves. If you're one of them, remember that to continue helping others you must also be helping yourself. If not, those who may have become dependent on you will discover you're suddenly unable to give anymore. Even more important than giving money is to teach people how to be independent and do the right thing with their own money rather than "enable" them to ignore their own fiscal responsibility.

## WHICH DOOR ARE YOUR CURRENT ACTIONS LEADING YOU TOWARD?

If you're like most people, Door #1 and Door #2 are the most appealing. But based on your current behaviors, you may honestly feel that Door #3 or even Door #4 is where you're headed. No matter which door your current actions or behaviors are pointing toward, you can take steps today to change your path. I believe that it's never too late or too early. The following are examples of balance sheets of people who are in Door #1 or Door #2. You'll notice they're displayed with "good" assets on the left and "bad" assets (and liabilities) on the right. This helps emphasize the importance that wealthy people place on building their good assets. I've shown a wide range of ages and incomes. See if any of them are similar to your current situation.

# Married, Mid-30s
## Income of $150,000

| APPRECIATING (GOOD) ASSETS | | DEPRECIATING (BAD) ASSETS | |
|---|---|---|---|
| Description | Value | Description | Value |
| Cash reserve | $50,000 | Home value | $350,000 |
| Brokerage account | 350,000 | Home mortgage | -200,000 |
| Husband's SEP | 140,000 | Wife's car | 20,000 |
| Husband's Roth IRA | 30,000 | Husband's car | 12,000 |
| Wife's Roth IRA | 105,000 | Car loans | -20,000 |
| Cash value, life insurance | 14,000 | Household items | 70,000 |
| Business interest | 350,000 | | |
| 529 plans | 55,000 | | |
| TOTAL | $1,094,000 | | $232,000 |

**APPRECIATING ASSET GOAL AT AGE 60:** $7,000,000

This couple has done a great job of living well below their means, saving a decent amount of money each year and growing their appreciating assets. They live in an area where many young people are purchasing much larger homes and driving nicer cars. They saved money into 401(k)s while working for someone else; now they're self-employed and invest into SEPs and non-qualified investments. Their current income is a little over $150,000 and growing.

**WHAT THEY HAVE DONE WELL:** Lived within their means all steps of the way. Even though they have accumulated a decent portfolio and know they could tap into it for anything, they still find ways of handling their annual expenses and home repairs with current earned income.

**WHAT THEY COULD HAVE DONE BETTER:** They carried some poor investments too long during the 2001 bear market decline.

**WHERE THEY ARE HEADED:** They're poised to have plenty of money for their retirement and college expenses. With those areas mostly covered, more attention will be spent building cash, real estate investments, and other methods beyond traditional stocks and funds. They'll never receive a pension. If their appreciating assets continue to grow at 9% for the next 25 years, they'll have accumulated in excess of their desired $7 million.

They are headed toward DOOR #1.

# Single, Late 30s
## Income of $80,000

| APPRECIATING (GOOD) ASSETS | | DEPRECIATING (BAD) ASSETS | |
|---|---:|---|---:|
| *Description* | *Value* | *Description* | *Value* |
| Cash reserve | $40,000 | Home value | $120,000 |
| Mutual funds | 120,000 | Home mortgage | -40,000 |
| Cash value, life insurance | 12,000 | Car | 20,000 |
| Roth IRA | 4,000 | Household items | 25,000 |
| Note receivable | 30,000 | | |
| Small business | 182,000 | | |
| Raw Land | 55,000 | | |
| Partnership property | 235,000 | | |
| Vacation rentals | 140,000 | | |
| TOTAL | $818,000 | | $125,000 |

**APPRECIATING ASSET GOAL AT AGE 60:** $5,000,000

She borrowed $200,000 in her 20s to start a business in a small town. Early on she had a drive to own good assets and had a knack for making profitable investments. She runs her business well and lean. She doesn't spend very much of her income on assets, which don't have the ability to earn her future income.

**WHAT SHE HAS DONE WELL:** Lived within her means from Day 1. She keeps her business and personal expenses low so that she'll never find herself in a position of lower business income and higher expenses, eroding her hard-earned appreciating assets.

**WHAT SHE COULD HAVE DONE BETTER:** While she's made some very good real estate purchases, she missed out on many traditional stock market returns during the declines early this century.

**WHERE SHE IS HEADED:** She's definitely on track to accumulate the desired amount of appreciating assets. She continues to make prudent investment decisions, funnels more money into the left column, and is increasing the market assets to help build liquidity and potential returns. She'll never receive a pension. If her assets continue to grow at 9% for the next 22 years, she will have accumulated her desired $5 million.

She is headed toward DOOR #1.

# Married, Mid-40s
## Income of $255,000

| APPRECIATING (GOOD) ASSETS | | DEPRECIATING (BAD) ASSETS | |
|---|---|---|---|
| *Description* | *Value* | *Description* | *Value* |
| Brokerage account | $200,000 | Home value | $750,000 |
| Stocks | 50,000 | Home mortgage | -600,000 |
| IRA | 70,000 | Wife's car | 30,000 |
| Husband's Roth IRA | 3,000 | Husband's car | 50,000 |
| Wife's Roth IRA | 3,000 | Car loans | -60,000 |
| Cash value, life insurance | 15,000 | Household items | 45,000 |
| Commercial real estate | 2,000,000 | Home appliances | 25,000 |
| | | Time share | 20,000 |
| | | Equity loans | -100,000 |
| **Total** | **$2,341,000** | | **$160,000** |

APPRECIATING ASSET GOAL AT AGE 60: $5,000,000

This couple has done an excellent job accumulating wealth with commercial real estate. They began less than 10 years ago with multiple partners buying a large commercial building. Since then, they've purchased a number of other properties with many of the same partners and continue to grow a portfolio of real estate positioned nicely for their future retirement.

WHAT THEY HAVE DONE WELL: Buying the right real estate. They're methodical in their efforts and are fortunate to have made prudent decisions when determining which properties to buy and with whom to partner up. They were responsible with their money, providing home equity to borrow against as investment seed money, thereby affording them the opportunity to get started in commercial real estate.

WHAT THEY COULD HAVE DONE BETTER: They're heavily invested in real estate, with less attention on financial market assets. This may create periods of liquidity issues or cash-flow concerns as interest rates and tenants will change throughout the years.

WHERE THEY ARE HEADED: They're poised to have the assets they desire and live a very comfortable life—if they just keep doing the things that got them where they are today. They learn more with each deal, and their reputation continues to improve, helping them find great future partnerships. They'll never receive a pension. If their appreciating assets continue to grow at 5% for the next 15 years, they will have accumulated in excess of their desired $5 million.

They are headed toward DOOR #1.

# Single, Late 40s
## Income of $80,000

| APPRECIATING (GOOD) ASSETS | | DEPRECIATING (BAD) ASSETS | |
|---|---|---|---|
| *Description* | *Value* | *Description* | *Value* |
| Cash reserve | $20,000 | Home value | $300,000 |
| Personal brokerage | 11,000 | Home mortgage | -195,000 |
| Variable annuity | 20,000 | Car | 6,000 |
| REIT | 20,000 | Household items | 70,000 |
| IRA | 11,000 | | |
| 401(k) | 250,000 | | |
| 403(b) | 25,000 | | |
| Roth IRA | 8,000 | | |
| Deferred compensation | 220,000 | | |
| Rental home net value | 36,000 | | |
| TOTAL | **$621,000** | | **$181,000** |

**APPRECIATING ASSET GOAL AT AGE 60:** $2,500,000

He has done an excellent job in capturing and investing earned income. Divorce and a declining market set him back significantly. Rather than give up, he took ownership in his future and found ways of investing massive amounts of income in just a short period of time. He stretched his comfort zones outside of the conventional methods and even entered the real estate market, purchasing some rental properties.

**WHAT HE HAS DONE WELL:** Realizing he was behind in his retirement savings, he capitalized on a few years of excellent income and, rather than splurging with a lavish lifestyle, he focused on securing his financial position. By doing so, in just a few years he was able to more than recover from recent losses and move into a position well above his previous income levels.

**WHAT HE COULD HAVE DONE BETTER:** It was a long and dedicated effort, rewarding yet exhausting. A couple of additional initiatives, such as fixing the interest rate on his rentals, would've helped secure his future even more.

**WHERE HE IS HEADED:** Things are on cruise control. He now has a consistent job and enough earned income to live comfortably. He continues to invest pre-tax earnings into 401(k)s and after-tax earnings into Roth IRAs. Other than that, he's enjoying his success today. He will never receive a pension. If his appreciating assets continue to grow at 7%, he will have accumulated the $2.5 million he desires. If he continues his 401(k) and Roth investing, the figure will be closer to $3.5 million.

He is headed toward DOOR #2.

# Married, Mid-50s
## Income of $70,000

| APPRECIATING (GOOD) ASSETS | | DEPRECIATING (BAD) ASSETS | |
|---|---|---|---|
| Description | Value | Description | Value |
| Cash reserve | $8,000 | Home value | $250,000 |
| Stock portfolio | 55,000 | Home mortgage | -120,000 |
| 403(b) | 200,000 | Retirement home | 280,000 |
| Speculative investments | 85,000 | Husband's car | 45,000 |
| Investment real estate | 620,000 | Wife's car | 40,000 |
| | | Car loans | -35,000 |
| | | Other vehicles | 35,000 |
| | | Household furnishings | 50,000 |
| TOTAL | **$968,000** | | **$545,000** |

**APPRECIATING ASSET GOAL AT AGE 58:** $800,000

They've had a good job throughout their married life and made responsible financial decisions. They avoided getting into debt and saved a percentage of their income. They didn't study money and made some mistakes through the years and had many missed opportunities. Fortunately, though, they made more right financial decisions than wrong ones.

**WHAT THEY HAVE DONE WELL:** More than 10 years ago they purchased a condo as an investment property in a popular vacation spot. Over the years this has proved to be their best financial decision. Not only did it provide them with a place to go to relax, it also produced working cash flow, which helped to pay down debt service and now presents a large amount of equity.

**WHAT THEY COULD HAVE DONE BETTER:** They were often swayed by people who could sell rather than provide proper advice. The investments they made were more expensive than necessary. If they had taken the time to learn about money a little sooner, they would've accumulated much more in financial assets than they have today, with basically the same effort.

**WHERE THEY ARE HEADED:** They're making the transition into retirement. For a few more years they'll work part time as they situate their house sales and remodels. Things should work out quite well. They're at a critical decision-making period, however, and must be sure to keep their belts tight these coming years to ensure a future of worry-free living. They will receive pensions. They already reached their accumulation goal; now they just have to keep the money they have.

They are headed toward DOOR #2.

# Married, Mid-50s
## Income of $125,000

| APPRECIATING (GOOD) ASSETS | | DEPRECIATING (BAD) ASSETS | |
|---|---|---|---|
| *Description* | *Value* | *Description* | *Value* |
| Cash reserve | $9,000 | Home value | $190,000 |
| Mutual funds | 25,000 | Home mortgage | -38,000 |
| Cash value, life insurance | 15,000 | Retirement cottage | 180,000 |
| Roth IRA | 23,000 | Household items | 45,000 |
| 401(k) | 385,000 | Collectables | 30,000 |
| 403(b) | 76,000 | | |
| Deferred compensation | 90,000 | | |
| TOTAL | **$623,000** | | **$407,000** |

**APPRECIATING ASSET GOAL AT AGE 60:** $650,000

Throughout most of their married life this couple lived within their means and relied sparingly on debt. They planned for things well in advance. For example, their retirement cottage is a wonderful place on a lake that they purchased as a cabin years ago. Their primary home is on a 15-year mortgage, with not much left to pay. They've been fixing the cabin over the years and, by the time they're retired, they'll have a very nice home built in place of the current structure. The eventual sale of their current residence will more than pay for their new home on the lake.

**WHAT THEY HAVE DONE WELL:** They knew accumulating wealth was important and took advantage of all work retirement programs early and often. They are good judges of people and were given decent advice over the years with regard to investing. They also take things into their own hands and do the necessary research on the recommended investments.

**WHAT THEY COULD HAVE DONE BETTER:** They are not natural savers. This is evidenced by the proportion of assets they have in retirement plans versus elsewhere, such as Roth IRAs and other funds. If it weren't for the forced out-of-sight, out-of-mind benefit of company retirement plans, they wouldn't be in as strong a position as they're in today. Participating in other outside investments would've further advanced their position.

**WHERE THEY ARE HEADED:** Retirement is just a few years away. They're young, healthy, definitely enjoying themselves and looking forward to the near future. They've done enough to ensure very comfortable living on their terms and can feel proud of that. They will receive a pension. If they maintain a reasonable rate of return, around 4%, they'll have more than enough money with which to retire.

They are headed toward DOOR #2.

## Married, Early 60s
### Income of $350,000

| APPRECIATING (GOOD) ASSETS | | DEPRECIATING (BAD) ASSETS | |
|---|---|---|---|
| *Description* | *Value* | *Description* | *Value* |
| Cash reserve | $50,000 | Home value | $400,000 |
| Company stock plan | 75,000 | Home mortgage | -180,000 |
| Brokerage account | 90,000 | Retirement home | 150,000 |
| Husband's 401(k) | 500,000 | Husband's car | 20,000 |
| Wife's 401(k) | 170,000 | Wife's car | 25,000 |
| Husband's IRA | 150,000 | Household items | 50,000 |
| Wife's IRA | 240,000 | Collectables | 25,000 |
| Annuity | 130,000 | | |
| TOTAL | **$1,405,000** | | **$490,000** |

**APPRECIATING ASSET GOAL AT AGE 62:** $1,300,000

This has been a family with strong offense but not the best defense. Fortunately, around five years ago they got organized and put their retirement needs in their sights. At the time they had more credit card debt than cash in the bank and, aside from saving money into their work retirement plans, they lived somewhat above their means.

**WHAT THEY HAVE DONE WELL:** Throughout their disorganization, they still managed to invest money into their retirement plans at work. Once they got things on track, they did some restructuring to gain control over the finance charges and started saving money into other areas, including a cash reserve. They took ownership of their investments and began making much better investment decisions.

**WHAT THEY COULD HAVE DONE BETTER:** With organization and a game plan, they would be "sitting pretty" with more than twice the amount they now have. They valued a strong offense and were able to redirect income toward buying good investment assets. They lost a lot of money during the recent recession when they had money invested in expensive accounts.

**WHERE THEY ARE HEADED:** They'll be retiring soon. Helping make this possible were compound interest on early retirement savings, experiencing great pre-retirement returns and some late career advancements. Now that they have enough money, they'll have to make sure to remain under control with their newly learned defense and invest their money wisely. They'll receive a small pension. They already reached their accumulation goal; now they just have to keep the money they have.

They are headed toward DOOR #2.

# Retired, Single, Mid-60s
## Income of $65,000

| APPRECIATING (GOOD) ASSETS | | DEPRECIATING (BAD) ASSETS | |
|---|---|---|---|
| *Description* | *Value* | *Description* | *Value* |
| Cash reserve | $40,000 | Home value | $130,000 |
| Mutual funds | 160,000 | Home mortgage | 0 |
| Variable annuity | 300,000 | Car | 20,000 |
| Roth IRA | 20,000 | Household items | 30,000 |
| IRA | 400,000 | | |
| Bonds | 90,000 | | |
| TOTAL | **$1,010,000** | | **$180,000** |

APPRECIATING ASSET GOAL AT CURRENT AGE: $900,000

He has never made more than $75,000 earned income in his best year. However, he managed to accumulate $1 million in appreciating assets. He's a great example of living within one's means and systematically saving from an early age. He is living proof that it doesn't take a tremendous income in order to afford a comfortable lifestyle.

**WHAT HE HAS DONE WELL:** Systematic savings, organization, lived within his means, aimed for a target, found good advice, didn't rely unduly on anything/anyone and learned how money worked. He stayed out of unnecessary debt and lived modestly, but he still enjoyed his life.

**WHAT HE COULD HAVE DONE BETTER:** Not a whole lot. There were a few investments made that didn't produce a return that hindsight proved weren't the best things to be in. All in all, he did quite well with his decisions.

**WHERE HE IS HEADED:** He's retired and doing well. He is actively enjoying the things he wants to do and is financially able to keep his options open to other opportunities. He doesn't live a lavish lifestyle and is realistic about how much money there is for him to spend. He will never receive a pension. He has reached his accumulation goal and now needs to make sure his money outpaces inflation in order to maintain his current living standards.

He is in DOOR #2.

# Married, Early 70s
## Income of $80,000

| APPRECIATING (GOOD) ASSETS | | DEPRECIATING (BAD) ASSETS | |
|---|---|---|---|
| *Description* | *Value* | *Description* | *Value* |
| Cash reserve | $30,000 | Home value | $350,000 |
| Brokerage account | 160,000 | Home mortgage | 0 |
| Husband's IRA | 320,000 | Wife's car | 16,000 |
| Wife's IRA | 62,000 | Husband's car | 10,000 |
| Deferred compensation | 150,000 | Household items | 75,000 |
| | | Jewelry and collectables | 25,000 |
| TOTAL | **$722,000** | | **$476,000** |

**APPRECIATING ASSET GOAL AT CURRENT AGE:** $675,000

They are modest people and live comfortably, not sacrificing very much. Throughout their married life they had a strong offense *and* defense. The husband made most of the income, and the wife saved it. Not only did they invest into retirement plans, she also worked very hard at buying stocks and making other investments. They always tried to live within their means, including paying off the mortgage.

**WHAT THEY HAVE DONE WELL:** Most of their success can be attributed to good, wholesome common sense. They worked, bought what they could afford and always saved a portion of their income for the future. Much of their flexibility today comes from the investments in stocks the wife made over the years. These turned out to be enough to put them over the top.

**WHAT THEY COULD HAVE DONE BETTER:** They are good people who hoped for the best—and, thankfully, many things worked out for them. If they had done a little more research or had better advisors, they would've ended up with even more money. Many of the investments they made were on the expensive side, and rarely did they implement tax or asset-allocation strategies while investing (no Roth IRAs).

**WHERE THEY ARE HEADED:** They're enjoying retirement and doing great. They travel throughout the year, live well and have much to look forward to. They receive his pension. They've reached their accumulation goal; now they just have to hang onto the money they have.

They are in DOOR #2.

# Single, Early 70s
## Income of $70,000

| **APPRECIATING (GOOD) ASSETS** | | **DEPRECIATING (BAD) ASSETS** | |
|---|---|---|---|
| *Description* | *Value* | *Description* | *Value* |
| Cash reserve | $15,000 | Home value | $350,000 |
| Brokerage account | 230,000 | Home mortgage | -190,000 |
| IRA | 400,000 | Car | 20,000 |
| Annuities | 310,000 | Household items | 50,000 |
| Mutual funds | 55,000 | | |
| TOTAL | **$1,010,000** | | **$230,000** |

**APPRECIATING ASSET GOAL AT CURRENT AGE:** $900,000

She is widowed and doing OK. She and her late husband were pretty decent savers, but they didn't always save as much as they should have. He passed away suddenly in his mid-60s. At the time of his death, both of them were still working and trying to get over the hump of accumulating enough wealth. When he died, the life insurance policies were sufficient to care for his wife's needs.

**WHAT THEY DID WELL:** As a couple they discussed money and made decent decisions throughout most of their married life. They saved into company retirement plans and tried to keep their debt at acceptable levels. Into their late 50s they began to really get things in shape. They started working with advisors who helped them make better investment decisions. One decision that proved to be helpful for the surviving spouse was to purchase adequate life insurance policies. Without both of them being able to work, however, money likely would have been lacking in her retirement.

**WHAT THEY COULD HAVE DONE BETTER:** Some of the individual stock purchases turned out to be a bust. They were sometimes caught up in the hype of a new company idea without really understanding the numbers behind it. They saved money, but when he died they were still struggling financially as they approached retirement. He had no pension, and hers was small.

**WHERE SHE IS HEADED:** She is retired and living comfortably. It would be nice if she didn't have to pay a mortgage, though the low interest rate is more advantageous than liquidating investments. All her bases seem to be covered now, including long-term care insurance, and it looks as if the money will last. She receives her small pension and has reached her accumulation goal.

She is in DOOR #2.

## TO SUMMARIZE

1. The choices you make today will take you down a fairly predictable path. Here's the great news: That means where you end up is almost entirely within your power to control.

2. When asking retirees what they would have done differently, almost everyone answers, "I would have started saving sooner." If this is so obvious, why isn't everyone doing it? No matter how behind you feel you might be, *today is sooner than tomorrow.*

3. DOOR #1: Total control of their lifestyle.

4. DOOR #2: Decent control with a rather comfortable lifestyle.

5. DOOR #3: If anything bad happens, they could be in trouble; otherwise, they live a satisfactory lifestyle but without the extra pleasures.

6. DOOR #4: Low financial self-esteem—in poverty or headed toward it; they're a financial burden on themselves and society.

7. Which door do you choose to open to your own retirement? Learn from the behaviors and actions of those who have gone before you.

# Principle 12
## Don't Forget That Your Story's Ending Is Predictable

### Principles in Action

**Sample: Which door do you believe you are headed toward based on your current actions? Why?**

DOOR #3: But we're making the changes toward head to DOOR #2. I'm headed toward DOOR #3 today because we're not on pace to meet our goals. It felt like we were saving a decent amount of money, but we haven't taken sufficient control of our cash flow and wouldn't be able to realistically live within the retirement we're projected to have unless we make some changes. Fortunately, we are making those changes now.

**Which door do *you* believe you are headed toward based on your current actions? Why?**

## Principle 13

## Stay Financially Healthy

Exercise gyms are filled with people working hard to get into great physical shape. Some gyms are so packed with sweating bodies you can't find an open machine. Yoga, kickboxing and Pilates classes fill the rooms. The weight room has guys with big muscles lifting hundreds of pounds. People are working hard and exerting great effort.

Why the dedication? It's the old pleasure-versus-pain theory we discussed earlier. When you're at the gym, you see beautiful people all around you. That's the pleasure. You want to look as good as they do; after all, it feels good to look good. Then there's the pain: at least two scales in every locker room—and mirrors everywhere! Reality sinks in that you don't look as good as you wish you did or, if you do look good, you want to keep that look going.

If I opened a financial fitness gym, do you think anyone would come? The budget machines, asset-allocation computers and financial planning stations might just sit empty. Yet having enough money can be as desirable as being in great physical shape. In fact, people often romanticize having money more than having a great physical appearance. Think about it ... While daydreaming about being a millionaire sailing in your yacht, living in the grand mansion or just longing for the day when financial stress is behind you, don't you look the same as you look today?

Why is a workout gym packed with people on diets willingly enduring physical pain in order to get in better shape—all the while our financial fitness is crumbling?

Here is one likely answer: Too many people focus on short-term satisfaction rather than long-term results. If I need to lose a few pounds and work out hard, I want to see the weight come off quickly. Even if I don't see the improvement on the scale the next day, working out still makes me feel better right away, so there's immediate satisfaction to compensate for my efforts. If I don't feel it or see it, it's all too easy to stop.

People also look for immediate satisfaction with their money instead of the long-term benefits that truly represent growth. It's easy to feel wealthier because of one's purchasing power. It's easy to go buy an expensive car, compare it to your last car and say, "I'm really moving up in the world." *It doesn't mean you're actually any wealthier, it just means you're spending more money.* Compounding the problem, most people don't have a constant measurement or understanding of their level of financial shape (though they do know about their ideal body weight). This makes it even easier to buy the expensive car instead of improving their long-term financial position. Eating cheesecake for dinner might be nice temporarily, but I know if I keep it up, eventually I won't like what I see on the scale (or in the mirror).

## TRACK YOUR PROGRESS

An exercise gym has an obvious advantage over a financial-fitness gym. It's easy to tell if you're in great physical shape. Just look in the mirror, step on the scale or notice that the jeans don't fit anymore. Then the annual physical at the doctor's office gives you the real facts. When it comes to financial shape, though, most people have no concrete way of measuring where they are or evaluating the real facts.

I try to stay in fairly good physical shape. There have been periods of my life when I've been in superb physical condition, and other times when I've gotten a little lazy. I know what it feels like to be in great shape, and I know what it feels like to be in not-so-good shape. I know what I look like in great shape, and I know what I look like in bad shape. I also know that the more I let my physical health slide, the harder it is to get back in tip-top shape.

A couple of years ago I reached a tipping point and was pushing an all-time high—and very little of the weight was muscle. I didn't feel good. I decided I could continue down the wrong path, or I could buckle down and do something about it.

I didn't totally dedicate myself like Rocky Balboa—but I did visit the legendary Kronk Gym in Detroit where a world-famous boxer, Thomas "Hit Man" Hearns, was training for an upcoming bout. What an awakening! Not only Hearns, but other guys there looked like they were getting ready to fight the fight of their life. I think there was more fat on my body than on all the other athletes combined. I don't think any of them wanted me to get into the ring with them—not because they were afraid, but because they didn't want the liability of injuring me!

I teamed up with a trainer who took me through a rigorous exercise regimen. Forty minutes into it and struggling to make my last five sit-ups, I had the look of defeat as my trainer yelled vulgarities in my face, challenging me in no uncertain terms to finish the set. It worked. By that time it appeared that the entire gym was placing side bets on whether or not I'd give up. I mustered the pride I had left and slowly, agonizingly pulled my head to my knees for the very last sit-up. After that I shadowboxed in the ring with a few other boxers. Let's just say I'm glad they boxed the air instead of me.

I soon "retired" from boxing, yet continued my physical exercise by playing hockey, doing more push-ups and sit-ups, and riding a mountain bike. Soon afterward I started to see and feel a difference, and within a few months I was right back on track. I should go back to the Kronk and redeem myself.

My maximum tolerance for getting out of shape physically is around 10 pounds—or 5 percent of my desired weight. I know if I work hard I can make gains physically in just a few short months. I have less tolerance regarding my financial shape, as it might take years to get back on track. Due to the long-term effects money can have on your life, I believe that you actually have to measure your financial shape with more intensity than your physical shape.

One simple measurement, when it comes to your money, would be great—if such a measurement or instrument existed. The closest thing I can find is measuring net worth and, most importantly, the good-asset side of the equation. In order for that number to mean anything, you'll need to understand, from your earlier exercises, what you need to be worth today in order to get you where you want to be tomorrow.

If you need $5 million in good assets to retire (based on your expected rate of return and how much money you continue to allocate in good assets every year), you can determine how much you'll need each year along the way. Then—and especially if your assets are such market assets as stocks and mutual funds—you may need to adopt a tolerance zone, depending on whether you're in a bear (down) or bull (up) market at the time.

Another more comprehensive measure of financial health that I have developed is to evaluate a person's finances as if he or she were a small business, then give a stock price. Just as officials with a publicly traded company know if they're doing well based on what their stock is trading for in the market, individuals also can track the progress of their overall financial position. The stock-price formula is a collection of equations that measure (1) what percentage of your desired good-asset portfolio you already have, (2) what you're doing to fill the gap, (3) what major financial events you have besides retirement and (4) how well-prepared you are should the unexpected happen. When I plug real numbers into the formula, it gives a price relative to each individual situation.

As I'm admittedly fond of saying, numbers don't lie. I compared two families, both worth around a half-million dollars. Members of one family were saving aggressively for their future, while members of another family had more material assets than appreciating assets. The savers had a higher stock price at $75, compared with the other couple's at $44/share. Clearly, the savers were doing most things right and were on target to have their desired level of wealth. On the other hand, each purchase the spenders made further deteriorated their chances of financial success. As the years go by, the spread between the two prices will most likely continue to widen.

> *Whatever method you use to organize the data, be sure to track your net worth of good assets against your goal for where you want to be at this stage of your life—and measure this number often.*

Today I also use a much more sophisticated method with technology. The numbers are fed daily into the system automatically and compared against income needs projected throughout your lifetime. Via visual graphs, it's easy to see if your assets are projected to outlive you.

Whatever method you use to organize the data, be sure to track your net worth of good assets against your goal for where you want to be at this stage of your life—and measure this number often. For fun, you can compare your own growth against common indexes, such as the S&P 500. Discuss your progress with your spouse and/or advisors every quarter; this discussion is mandatory every December/January. Paying attention to this number consistently will help you make better decisions throughout the year, providing the angel on your shoulder with good "ammunition" (that angel is the one who wants the right to "bare" arms!). Most people don't like going backward after exerting effort to get ahead. If you crunch your numbers, you're more likely to identify which actions will create more wealth. You'll also see more clearly when you're doing something that defeats your hard work, like wasting money buying unnecessary things. It's not unlike the cold "splash" of reality we sometimes get when stepping on a scale.

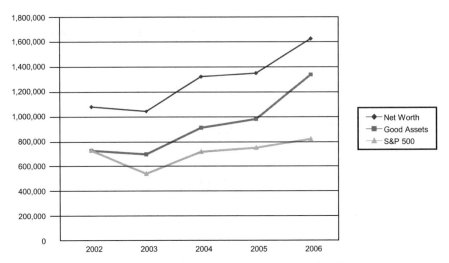

Here's a chart showing the hypothetical growth of a person's net worth and good assets, compared with the growth of the S&P 500 during the same time period. Compare your own progress with that of an index.

## WHY DON'T PEOPLE MEASURE THEIR FINANCES?

There's a general lack of accountability that keeps most people from improving themselves financially—and otherwise. For example, I'm noticing that clothing sizes are getting larger. I used to wear an extra large, then a large, and now sometimes I am buying mediums, all while the scale at the gym says I keep getting bigger. The same thing is happening with women's clothing. Size 8 is now a Size 6. The clothing industry is making it easier for people to stay out of shape, trying to fool their subconscious, and it's working.

Financially, I see many people with the same mindset. They believe that charge cards are meant to carry a balance, and if things get out of control you can always claim bankruptcy. It's as if people think they get a golfer's "mulligan," a second chance in life, without calculating how much it's costing them or society. Even though laws were recently passed that made declaring bankruptcy more difficult, some people will still see bankruptcy (or foreclosure) as a convenient crutch when times get bad. The people who measure financial success through material achievements rather than wealth accumulation tend to abuse the bankruptcy option. These people over-bought in an effort to front a life they couldn't yet afford.

I have always believed that if you understand where you are, you can figure out where you need to go. However, it's almost as if avoiding reality is a natural human behavior. I can't tell you how many people have told me they didn't want to meet with me because they didn't want me to hear how poorly they were doing. Once we met, though, they were relieved to know they were doing something positive to get in better financial shape. We focused on what they were doing well, capitalizing on their strengths but also addressing their weaknesses. Once they understood their position in life, a tremendous weight suddenly was lifted from their shoulders, and they were able to focus on productive actions. It's reassuring for most people to learn that they're doing many things well and are in fact on track toward a wonderful financial future if they just make some adjustments. Personalizing it (regardless of your success or lack thereof) and facing reality, then acting on it, will go a long way toward ensuring that you lead a much more productive and fulfilled life. While it's true that money can't buy happiness, it certainly doesn't hurt when it comes to having options.

You also have to answer to your own reality of good financial shape. Just as people aspire to varying levels of physical health, we also desire different levels of financial health. In the physical category you have Olympians, Ironmen and Ironwomen, and outstanding athletes from a variety of sports. Then you have regular people like me who just want to weigh 175 pounds and not "run out of gas" playing ice hockey. In the financial category, you have billionaires, mega-millionaires and millionaires. Then you have the folks who simply want to stay out of debt and have a sufficient nest egg (to supplement their future income) so they can retire comfortably.

## ACKNOWLEDGE THE SHAPE YOU'RE IN, RELATIVE TO YOUR PERSONAL GOALS

Regardless of the level of wealth you desire, you can measure and track your progress along the way. You can be in great shape, meaning you've already saved an adequate amount to reach your future goals (heading toward Door #1, as noted in the previous principle); good shape, meaning you're on pace to have enough so long as you keep doing what you're doing (heading toward Door #2); bad shape, meaning you have to change some behaviors because you're either off track or getting off track (heading toward Door #3); and terminal, meaning you'd better wake up and get it together because you're rapidly running out of options (heading toward DOOR #4).

Not long ago I was privileged to have an exciting meeting with some young clients of mine. They're a couple in their late 30s and have saved well for most of their lives. Over the past few years their savings are really starting to pay off. Their goal is to be worth $6 million in their 60s. *They already have more than $500,000 saved. Based on a 10 percent return, they have saved enough money to reach their goal.* They're in great shape. So for the next 20 working years, it's refreshing for them to know that all they really have to do is make good decisions with the money they already have and further insulate their goal (crutch management) by investing their money in other diverse opportunities. In addition, they also can spend money a little more freely if they'd like to!

Most of the people with whom I meet aren't in great shape, but they're in good shape. Based on the amount of money they have and the amount they're currently saving, they should be able to reach their retirement goals. I recently met with a couple in their 50s who have more than $400,000. If they keep saving 10 percent of their income from now until retirement, it looks as if they'll accumulate the $2.3 million desired. They generally have kept ahead of bills and stayed out of bad debt, but they didn't save money as aggressively as the couple in their late 30s who are in great shape. Thanks to their consistency and dedication, though, most of their important financial goals are within reach.

If you're in bad or terminal shape, you need to consider a serious financial diet and exercise program. You might need to save twice as much as someone in good financial shape, which probably means saving three or four times more than what you're saving right now. It may be time to start auctioning things on eBay, paying down larger chunks of debt, getting a second job or starting a business, cutting out cable TV, taking sack lunches to work or even downgrading from a Caribbean cruise to a family camping trip. You no longer have much "wiggle" room for bad investments, poor decisions, procrastination or lack of communication.

It's time to get serious because you're probably not too far from being in critical condition.

On that note, don't worry; measuring your progress can be a liberating experience! There will be highs and lows, just like stepping on the scale after working out. Sometimes the scale rewards me for the hard work, and sometimes it feels like I did a whole lot of work for nothing. Remember, you won't get where you want to be overnight, so try not to stress too much about being below your expectations. In the end, good physical exercise makes me a happier and more productive person. Measuring your financial shape and constantly improving on it also will keep your spirits high. Stay in reality with your numbers and reward yourself when you start hitting your desired targets or milestones. Even if you aren't in good financial shape, if you start doing the right things with your money today, your future outlook could change dramatically for the better!

When you achieve your goals—even intermediate steps along the way—remember to celebrate your gains.

The following charts could help you track your progress toward financial independence. The first four are in terms of $100,000 of expenses in retirement (adjusted for inflation), while the last chart is for $50,000 of expenses. The numbers are accurate based on the stated assumptions. You should, however, use the age on the left column that you were closest to in 2008. For example, if you look at the first chart and it's now 2013 when you are 45 years old, you wouldn't look at the age 45 columns in the GREAT SHAPE chart and see that you need to have $653,917 to be in great shape. Instead you would look at the age 45 column at the bottom of the chart and go up to the age 40 column from the left (because you were age 40 when these charts were designed) and see that you would need $762,126 to be in great shape. Because inflation is a moving target, it is very difficult to create a chart that will accurately illustrate needs in any given year. These charts, more than anything, are intended to illustrate the point that it's possible to run the numbers and recognize the type of financial shape a person is in relative to reaching his/her financial goals.

## GREAT SHAPE

| | |
|---|---|
| Inflation | 3.11% |
| Desired income | $100,000 |
| Retirement age | 65 |
| Savings rate | 9%* |
| Live till age | 105 |

> Under this hypothetical scenario, if a 40-year-old person has $495,330 saved in 2008, then he/she may have accumulated money sufficient to grow to the $4,271,267 required to fund his/her retirement goals, without saving another dime.

| | ANNUAL INCOME | FUTURE LUMP NEED | TOTAL COST |
|---|---|---|---|
| 20 | ($396,767) | $7,880,850 | $163,072 |
| 25 | (340,433) | 6,761,887 | 215,282 |
| 30 | (292,097) | 5,801,825 | 284,209 |
| 35 | (250,625) | 4,978,080 | 375,204 |
| 40 | (215,040) | 4,271,267 | 495,330 |
| 45 | (184,508) | 3,664,820 | 653,917 |
| 50 | (158,311) | 3,144,478 | 863,279 |
| 55 | (135,834) | 2,698,004 | 1,139,666 |
| 60 | (116,548) | 2,314,934 | 1,504,548 |
| 65 | (100,000) | 1,986,266 | 1,986,266 |

| | 20 | 25 | 30 | 35 | 40 | 45 | 50 | 55 | 60 | 65 |
|---|---|---|---|---|---|---|---|---|---|---|
| 20 | $163,072 | $250,907 | $386,052 | $593,989 | $913,925 | $1,406,187 | $2,163,593 | $3,328,956 | $5,122,012 | $7,880,850 |
| 25 | | 215,282 | 331,238 | 509,651 | 784,161 | 1,206,530 | 1,856,395 | 2,856,294 | 4,394,763 | 6,761,887 |
| 30 | | | 284,209 | 437,290 | 672,825 | 1,035,225 | 1,592,822 | 2,450,754 | 3,770,788 | 5,801,825 |
| 35 | | | | 375,204 | 577,297 | 888,243 | 1,366,672 | 2,102,795 | 3,235,410 | 4,978,080 |
| 40 | | | | | 495,330 | 762,126 | 1,172,625 | 1,804,229 | 2,776,030 | 4,271,267 |
| 45 | | | | | | 653,917 | 1,006,133 | 1,548,060 | 2,381,882 | 3,664,820 |
| 50 | | | | | | | 863,279 | 1,328,261 | 2,043,695 | 3,144,478 |
| 55 | | | | | | | | 1,139,666 | 1,753,517 | 2,698,004 |
| 60 | | | | | | | | | 1,504,548 | 2,314,934 |
| 65 | | | | | | | | | | 1,986,266 |

## GOOD SHAPE

| | |
|---|---|
| Retirement age | 65 |
| Savings rate | 9% |
| Live till age | 105 |

> If the 40-year-old person has $281,197 saved in 2008 and invests an additional $20,000 per year, then he/she should reach the desired retirement goal.

| | FUTURE LUMP NEED | PAYMENT | TOTAL COST |
|---|---|---|---|
| 20 | $7,880,850 | $13,749 | $618,714 |
| 25 | 6,761,887 | 18,360 | 734,405 |
| 30 | 5,801,825 | 20,000 | 753,852 |
| 35 | 4,978,080 | 20,000 | 751,238 |
| 40 | 4,271,267 | 20,000 | 781,197 |
| 45 | 3,664,820 | 20,000 | 854,915 |
| 50 | 3,144,478 | 20,000 | 987,556 |
| 55 | 2,698,004 | 20,000 | 1,199,761 |
| 60 | 2,314,934 | 20,000 | 1,519,754 |
| 65 | 1,986,266 | 20,000 | 1,986,266 |

| | 20 | 25 | 30 | 35 | 40 | 45 | 50 | 55 | 60 | 65 |
|---|---|---|---|---|---|---|---|---|---|---|
| 20 | $0 | $89,691 | $227,691 | $440,021 | $766,718 | $1,269,381 | $2,042,791 | $3,232,777 | $5,063,719 | $7,880,850 |
| 25 | | 0 | 119,769 | 304,049 | 587,587 | 1,023,844 | 1,695,080 | 2,727,860 | 4,316,921 | 6,761,887 |
| 30 | | | 53,852 | 213,324 | 458,693 | 836,223 | 1,417,099 | 2,310,849 | 3,685,994 | 5,801,825 |
| 35 | | | | 151,238 | 363,165 | 689,241 | 1,190,949 | 1,962,890 | 3,150,616 | 4,978,080 |
| 40 | | | | | 281,197 | 563,124 | 996,902 | 1,664,324 | 2,691,236 | 4,271,267 |
| 45 | | | | | | 454,915 | 830,409 | 1,408,155 | 2,297,087 | 3,664,820 |
| 50 | | | | | | | 687,556 | 1,188,357 | 1,958,901 | 3,144,478 |
| 55 | | | | | | | | 999,761 | 1,668,723 | 2,698,004 |
| 60 | | | | | | | | | 1,419,754 | 2,314,934 |
| 65 | | | | | | | | | | 1,986,266 |

* All numbers are based on a consistent pre-retirement rate of 9% annual return, in today's dollars, and all future lump needs are based on a consistent post-retirement rate of return of 7%.

## BAD SHAPE

| | |
|---|---|
| Retirement age | 65 |
| Savings rate | 9% |
| Live till age | 105 |

| | Future Lump Need | Payment | Total Cost |
|---|---|---|---|
| 20 | $7,880,850 | $13,749 | $618,714 |
| 25 | 6,761,887 | 18,360 | 734,405 |
| 30 | 5,801,825 | 24,676 | 863,643 |
| 35 | 4,978,080 | 33,505 | 1,005,164 |
| 40 | 4,271,267 | 35,000 | 995,598 |
| 45 | 3,664,820 | 35,000 | 1,005,663 |
| 50 | 3,144,478 | 35,000 | 1,080,764 |
| 55 | 2,698,004 | 35,000 | 1,244,832 |
| 60 | 2,314,934 | 35,000 | 1,531,158 |
| 65 | 1,986,266 | | 0 |

*If a 40-year-old person has $120,598 saved and invests an additional $35,000 annually, then he/she should reach the retirement goal.*

| Age | 20 | 25 | 30 | 35 | 40 | 45 | 50 | 55 | 60 | 65 |
|---|---|---|---|---|---|---|---|---|---|---|
| 20 | $0 | $89,691 | $227,691 | $440,021 | $766,718 | $1,269,381 | $2,042,791 | $3,232,777 | $5,063,719 | $7,880,850 |
| 25 | | 0 | 119,769 | 304,049 | 587,587 | 1,023,844 | 1,695,080 | 2,727,860 | 4,316,921 | 6,761,887 |
| 30 | | | 0 | 160,967 | 408,634 | 789,701 | 1,376,019 | 2,278,142 | 3,666,171 | 5,801,825 |
| 35 | | | | 0 | 218,567 | 554,860 | 1,072,288 | 1,868,416 | 3,093,357 | 4,978,080 |
| 40 | | | | | 120,598 | 413,872 | 865,110 | 1,559,396 | 2,627,640 | 4,271,267 |
| 45 | | | | | | 305,663 | 698,617 | 1,303,226 | 2,233,491 | 3,664,820 |
| 50 | | | | | | | 555,764 | 1,083,428 | 1,895,305 | 3,144,478 |
| 55 | | | | | | | | 894,832 | 1,605,127 | 2,698,004 |
| 60 | | | | | | | | | 1,356,158 | 2,314,934 |
| 65 | | | | | | | | | | 1,986,266 |

## FLAT LINE

| | |
|---|---|
| Retirement age | 65 |
| Savings rate | 9% |
| Live till age | 105 |

| | Future Lump Need | Payment | Total Cost |
|---|---|---|---|
| 20 | $7,880,850 | $13,749 | $ 618,714 |
| 25 | 6,761,887 | 18,360 | 734,405 |
| 30 | 5,801,825 | 24,676 | 863,643 |
| 35 | 4,978,080 | 33,505 | 1,005,164 |
| 40 | 4,271,267 | 46,264 | 1,156,597 |
| 45 | 3,664,820 | 65,720 | 1,314,391 |
| 50 | 3,144,478 | 70,000 | 1, 248 |
| 55 | 2,698,004 | 70,000 | 1,349,999 |
| 60 | 2,314,934 | 70,000 | 1,557,768 |
| 65 | 1,986,266 | 0 | 1,986,266 |

*If the 40-year-old person has nothing invested for retirement, then he/she would need to save $46,264 per year in order to reach this retirement goal.*

| Age | 20 | 25 | 30 | 35 | 40 | 45 | 50 | 55 | 60 | 65 |
|---|---|---|---|---|---|---|---|---|---|---|
| 20 | $0 | $89,691 | $227,691 | $440,021 | $766,718 | $1,269,381 | $2,042,791 | $3,232,777 | $5,063,719 | $7,880,850 |
| 25 | | 0 | 119,769 | 304,049 | 587,587 | 1,023,844 | 1,695,080 | 2,727,860 | 4,316,921 | 6,761,887 |
| 30 | | | 0 | 160,967 | 408,634 | 789,701 | 1,376,019 | 2,278,142 | 3,666,171 | 5,801,825 |
| 35 | | | | 0 | 218,567 | 554,860 | 1,072,288 | 1,868,416 | 3,093,357 | 4,978,080 |
| 40 | | | | | 0 | 301,795 | 766,144 | 1,480,602 | 2,579,885 | 4,271,267 |
| 45 | | | | | | 0 | 428,711 | 1,088,335 | 2,103,249 | 3,664,820 |
| 50 | | | | | | | 248,248 | 838,594 | 1,746,915 | 3,144,478 |
| 55 | | | | | | | | 649,999 | 1,456,737 | 2,698,004 |
| 60 | | | | | | | | | 1,207,768 | 2,314,934 |
| 65 | | | | | | | | | | 1,986,266 |

## COST TO RETIRE

|    | GREAT SHAPE | GOOD SHAPE | BAD SHAPE | FLAT LINE |
|----|-------------|------------|-----------|-----------|
| 20 | $163,072    | $618,714   | $618,714  | $618,714  |
| 25 | 215,282     | 734,405    | 734,405   | 734,405   |
| 30 | 284,209     | 753,852    | 863,643   | 863,643   |
| 35 | 375,204     | 751,238    | 1,005,164 | 1,005,164 |
| 40 | 495,330     | 781,197    | 995,598   | 1,156,597 |
| 45 | 653,917     | 854,915    | 1,005,663 | 1,314,391 |
| 50 | 863,279     | 987,556    | 1,080,764 | 1,298,248 |
| 55 | 1,139,666   | 1,199,761  | 1,244,832 | 1,349,999 |
| 60 | 1,504,548   | 1,519,754  | 1,531,158 | 1,557,768 |
| 65 | 1,986,266   |            |           |           |

This helps illustrate that the earlier you save, the less "out of your pocket" retirement will cost you.

## $50,000: GOOD SHAPE

| Retirement age | 65 |
|---|---|
| Savings rate | 9% |
| Live till age | 105 |

|    | FUTURE LUMP NEED | PAYMENT | TOTAL COST | FUTURE INCOME |
|----|------------------|---------|------------|---------------|
| 20 | $3,940,415       | $6,875  | $309,356   | ($198,383)    |
| 25 | 3,380,943        | 9,180   | 367,203    | (170,216)     |
| 30 | 2,900,922        | 10,000  | 376,926    | (146,049)     |
| 35 | 2,489,030        | 10,000  | 375,618    | (125,312)     |
| 40 | 2,135,634        | 10,000  | 390,599    | (107,520)     |
| 45 | 1,832,410        | 10,000  | 427,457    | (92,254)      |
| 50 | 1,572,249        | 10,000  | 493,781    | (79,156)      |
| 55 | 1,349,013        | 10,000  | 599,885    | (67,917)      |
| 60 | 1,157,477        | 10,000  | 759,883    | (58,274)      |
| 65 | 993,133          | 0       | 993,133    | (50,000)      |

Here, if the 40-year-old person wanted to live on $50,000 instead of $100,000* per year, then he/she would need to have $140,599 invested today and continue saving an additional $10,000 per year for retirement.

|    | 20  | 25       | 30        | 35        | 40        | 45        | 50          | 55          | 60          | 65          |
|----|-----|----------|-----------|-----------|-----------|-----------|-------------|-------------|-------------|-------------|
| 20 | $0  | $44,845  | $113,845  | $220,010  | $383,358  | $634,689  | $1,021,393  | $1,616,384  | $2,531,853  | $3,940,415  |
| 25 |     | 0        | 59,885    | 152,025   | 293,793   | 511,922   | 847,540     | 1,363,930   | 2,158,460   | 3,380,943   |
| 30 |     |          | 26,926    | 106,663   | 229,348   | 418,113   | 708,552     | 1,155,428   | 1,843,003   | 2,900,922   |
| 35 |     |          |           | 75,618    | 181,581   | 344,619   | 595,472     | 981,441     | 1,575,302   | 2,489,030   |
| 40 |     |          |           |           | 140,599   | 281,562   | 498,451     | 832,162     | 1,345,618   | 2,135,634   |
| 45 |     |          |           |           |           | 227,457   | 415,205     | 704,077     | 1,148,544   | 1,832,410   |
| 50 |     |          |           |           |           |           | 343,781     | 594,182     | 979,457     | 1,572,249   |
| 55 |     |          |           |           |           |           |             | 499,885     | 834,369     | 1,349,013   |
| 60 |     |          |           |           |           |           |             |             | 709,883     | 1,157,477   |
| 65 |     |          |           |           |           |           |             |             |             | 993,133     |

\* In today's dollars and then inflated out at 3.11%

## TO SUMMARIZE

1. Financial fitness doesn't happen overnight. Focus on long-term results.

2. Measure your net worth and good assets as a constant reference for tracking the progress of your wealth accumulation. Based on your end-goal retirement number, you should be able to calculate what your net worth needs to be at any given moment. Chart your progress and, for fun, compare your growth to a popular index, such as the S&P 500.

3. Beware of "lack of accountability" prevalent in society, and don't act as if you will get a second chance. Never confuse being approved for credit (to purchase expensive toys) with financial stability.

4. Don't fear reality. Instead, let it set you free. Live life in reality so that you have a basis for great decisions. Besides, it's generally easier to get into good financial shape than most people think it's going to be.

5. Answer to your own numbers—and don't worry about "the Joneses." Some people want to be filthy rich, while most merely desire a comfortable level of security in retirement. Do what's right for you.

6. Great shape means you have done the heavy lifting. Now your assets can take care of the rest (see previous principle regarding DOOR #1).

7. Good shape means that based on your current activities you can expect to end up with the money you want to have (DOOR #2).

8. Bad shape means you need significant lifestyle adjustments to get where you want to go (DOOR #3).

9. Terminal means you're in seriously poor financial shape and need drastic adjustments in order to have any hope of reaching financial independence (DOOR #4).

10. Reward yourself when you reach milestones. Celebrate!

# Principle 13
# Stay Financially Healthy

## Principles in Action

**Sample: What is your number?**

*I got this number with the help of my wealth manager; 2.5 million dollars is the amount of good assets we need in order to retire comfortably.*

**What amount of that number do you have completed in today's dollars and as a percentage?**

*We have $250,000 of good assets today, which is 10% of the ultimate goal.*

**What should your good-asset number be by year end?**

*Based on having another 18 years before we retire, we want to have $300,000 by the end of the year.*

# Principle 13
# Stay Financially Healthy

### Principles in Action

**What is *your* number?**

**What amount of that number do *you* have completed in today's dollars and as a percentage?**

**What should *your* good-asset number be by year end?**

## Principle 14

## Get Organized and Stay Organized

Why are some people in tune with their finances and consistently make great financial decisions, while others only fret about money and claim they have no time to deal with it? In a word: *organization*. Assuming you now know your "number" of good assets that you need to retire, have established your financial goals, have taken ownership of the accomplishment of those goals and have set the path … organization now plays a vital role in helping you reach your summit.

People often tell me they feel a little overwhelmed with money, and life gets in the way of managing it well. Many business owners say they're too busy at the office to manage their personal affairs. One wealthy executive told me he gets to the office every day at 5 o'clock in the morning and works two hours until 7 o'clock on his personal finances, then begins his work for the company.

It's easy to become overwhelmed by the challenge of saving money while simultaneously sorting out work, kids and a personal life. People face unlimited distractions and have a boatload of reasons why they can't allocate time for organizing their finances. The sad truth for them is that the less organized they are, the harder they have to work. On the flip side, the more organized you are with your money, the less you have to work to obtain even better results. Therefore, poor organization ensnares you in the frustrating game of chasing your tail, while good organization will allow you to live the balanced life you dream of having someday. You need to have a well-thought-out financial plan. Lift your head above the rat race and take the bird's-eye view, then find a system that works for you. Most of us work to make an income; you owe it to yourself and your family to get the most out of that income.

## THE TRUTH BEHIND ORGANIZATION

Here's an example of how organization helps you to be prepared. I have been working with a couple, Sung and Nicki, for almost six years now. When we first met, they brought in a binder full of statements, spreadsheets and forecasts. This is what I quickly learned about them:

- They looked up the value of each of their investments on a daily basis and tracked their progress diligently.
- They monitored their expenses on a software program and did their own taxes.
- They invested money at every opportunity and paid for their cars with cash.
- They were aware of ways to cut expenses while still enjoying life.
- They had one household income that never exceeded $80,000 per year.
- They used our relationship to help find ways to gain intellectual leverage.
- They maximized my knowledge of tax strategies, investment opportunities and other money-related efficiencies.

Now Sung and Nicki use my online program to monitor their numbers, which frees up hours of work per month to do other things. Even though I haven't seen that binder in a couple of years, I'll bet it's still somewhere in a filing cabinet in their house.

Recently Sung's company informed him that he was going to be laid off, so they called me with the details. At 58, his planned retirement was scheduled to be a few years away. We ran the numbers and had to make a few minor adjustments, but because of "lack of waste" during the majority of their working years and their (especially Nicki's) incredible organizational skills, they were able to retire early with more than $1 million of good assets. They're now fully enjoying the fruits of their labor, while many other workers fear layoffs.

Examples like this remind me of the reason we work so hard—and why everyone must take control of one's own life. Your income-earning potential can change in an instant, and you're advised to be ready for it. I cannot emphasize enough that it's the little things done well, time after time, that make the big difference in the end. Very few people in life get the "big break" that sets them free. And even if that "big break" does occur, it usually happens for the person who was ready for it. Get something in return for the years of your life you'll spend on the job. Lay other distractions aside for a day, take control of your life and get organized with your money. Every day you're unorganized is another day you worked longer than you had to—to get the same net financial results for your family. In today's world, technology replaces the big file folder. Getting organized is as easy as using a software program on your computer or using a Website organizer.

## DEVELOP AN ORGANIZED STATE OF MIND

It's all right to spend a little money for organization. The cost of being disorganized is a far greater expense—usually measured in years of your life. In fact, if you could add up all the money you waste throughout the year because of being disorganized, the number would stun you (let alone the value of time lost spent worrying about your future). Just think about the money you fritter away each year on fast food, impulse buys, late fees, interest charges, poor investments, unnecessary taxes, premium-priced goods, convenience charges and procrastination. Multiply that by the number of years you have been working. You would probably have enough to retire two times over already. I'd also wager the waste didn't add to your current standard of living one bit. In fact, you're probably more stressed and in worse physical and mental shape because of it.

I met with a couple who made a great income, yet somehow managed to have tens of thousands of dollars in credit card debt. They didn't appear to live any better than others who made similar incomes, and they couldn't tell me where all the money went. Thankfully, they finally got organized and in just a few short years had freed up more cash flow and experienced more growth in their net worth than they had in the previous 10. They were now in control, clear-headed and happy.

HERE WE SEE A SET OF IDENTICAL TWINS. THEY BOTH HAVE THE SAME JOB AND THE SAME INCOME. HOWEVER, ONLY ONE IS FINANCIALLY ORGANIZED. CAN YOU GUESS WHICH ONE?

Just as bad as wasting money because of disorganization are the families I meet who are so worried about having enough money that they aren't enjoying life today. They have sleepless nights, frequent arguments and insecurity. Often they're already doing more than enough to become wealthy, they just don't know it. After getting organized and gaining control of their finances, their life literally turned around. They didn't suddenly become rich. Their increased satisfaction didn't even come from the prospect of having money in the future. Their happiness was more a result of knowing that they were in control. As I've said before, the anxiety in my life has come during periods when I wasn't sure where I was going. Organization is like having a compass in the woods. As long as I have my compass, I know I'll be able to find my way out.

I knew another couple who also was in fantastic financial shape but didn't know it. They were nearly out of the woods but, without a compass, they had no way of knowing which direction they were headed. They were already doing all the hard work; they just needed to make a few adjustments in their strategies. Only a few years later, they went from a net worth of $600,000 to more than $1,000,000. They didn't work any harder; they just made better decisions with less stress, thanks to a little organization.

When you're organized, you accomplish the tasks that are in your best interests. By being able to easily evaluate your numbers, you also know when things are working well. Accumulating wealth need not be a stressful venture. When done right, living within the principles of a wealth will put you in control of both your present and future. Stress with money usually comes from the unknown. Organization puts you in the know. It gives you accurate information, which in turn identifies where you can focus resources for the maximum return on your efforts.

## THE 'KISS' METHOD OF ORGANIZATION

KISS stands for "Keep it simple, Stupid." People, including me, like things simple. Here's one example: My wife and I buy everything on credit cards. Even if I'm going to spend $3 for a few apples, I'll charge it. Why? It's our budget. Every month we get a breakdown of where we spent our money. At the end of the year, the credit card company sends us a nice book that categorizes our spending. Granted, the potential downside to using credit cards as a budget tracker is that psychologically it's easier to buy with plastic than with cash. So if you don't have much self-control when it comes to spending, I wouldn't recommend using credit cards to track your spending.

If the organization system you choose isn't easy and simple, however, you won't stay with it very long. Consider this: "Getting better with money" is usually one of the top five New Year's resolutions. If so many people are concerned and have the desire to "get better," why is just a very small percentage of Americans independently wealthy? Why are so many people trapped in consumer debt? People start out in January trying to "get better with money" and quickly give up. Part of the problem is that "getting better" provides no measurable or real starting point—and no defined goal. Proper organization, on the other hand, gives you all those things, meaning your New Year's resolution might actually make a difference in your life, enabling you to make it to the following New Year, let alone to February!

So how can you get organized in a simple way that you'll actually use? Here's a hint: Use technology to do the grunt work. You want to be looking *at* information, not putting paperwork together every week. I have found that good financial planning software is a key to good organization.

Financial planning software is essential because it will allow you to not only track your existing assets and liabilities, it also will tie them in to your financial goals. I tie software in to my advice, setting up a Website for clients that organizes and encompasses most of their financial and estate strategies. Doing so allows us to spend our time together on intellectual-strategy meetings and making improvements in their future, rather than spending all our time gathering documents. It also puts the clients in charge, as they're able to access all the information about their money no matter where they are in the world, so long as they can get on the Internet. You want to be able to macro- or even micro-manage your financial world quickly. Think about how ineffective people would be at work if they didn't have a good system for evaluating their business. It's just as important for people to set up a strong system that allows them to organize their personal finances.

Make sure you use your organization software consistently. You want something that is going to provide you with accurate real values of all your accounts—together in one place—regardless of the time of month or quarter. You can't wait for statements to come in the mail and then put the information together. That takes too long, and, if you're like most people, you won't keep doing it long term. Just looking at the balances of your accounts won't be revealing unless they're somehow tied in to your goals. The financial planning software is what ties them in. You could use an online system, such as the one we use at our financial services firm, or buy one specifically for your home computer.

You would be making a big mistake if you think organization is just about organizing your statements. What's needed is looking at finances "holistically," taking into account all the other aspects of your life. Do you have a trust, will or patient advocate? Are you efficient with your tax strategies? Are you anticipating financial opportunities and obligations? This isn't just about balancing your asset allocation. This is your life and what you're working 40 to 80 hours a week for! So take the time to get the most out of all your hard work.

If you're using a Web-based system, make sure it's secure. The last thing you want is to make a concerted effort to get organized, only to have your information stolen and used negatively. Use good, safe technology when you're organizing your money—and know what risks you may be exposed to. Hackers are a problem and won't be going away anytime soon. If you have all your numbers organized into one central data center, it's a good idea to use a "read only" program that doesn't allow access to any of your accounts; it just shows values, keeping information current. Under this arrangement, trades can't be made directly from your consolidated site.

## BALANCE SHEET AND OWNERSHIP

Once all your numbers are organized, go through your balance sheet with a fine-tooth comb. Structure the information by account name, with the ability to see the details of each account. Pay close attention to which assets are appreciating versus which ones go down in value every year—or will never be turned into income. The appreciating assets are your money-making partners that will someday give you financial independence, so be well-connected with those numbers. I can't tell you how many times I hear people say they have an account here and there, but they're small so they don't pay that much attention to them. "Here and there" often add up to tens of thousands of dollars if not more. Besides, no matter how small they are, it took hard work for you to get the money in there, so don't ignore them after you've already done the heavy lifting!

Look at your liabilities. Know the interest rates, payment terms, why you have the liability and where it came from. You can use one or a combination of many different debt-reduction techniques to help eliminate liabilities.

Generally, debt-reduction strategies follow two main paths, depending on how high the interest rates are:

- Maximize the amount of money going to principal in order to focus on and accelerate the repayment of debts.
- Minimize the amount of money that goes toward principal and funnel all freed-up cash flow into appreciating assets, which will eventually pay off the remaining debt.

Research the methods available and choose the ones that work best for your life. Even though debt isn't always uplifting to review, don't ignore it. The behaviors necessary to elevate you out of debt also will carry you into permanent wealth.

I don't spend a great deal of time in this book on debt, even though I know many people struggle with it. There are a couple of reasons why I don't. One is because there's a tremendous amount of good information already out there on how to reduce debt. The other is because I don't want to focus on getting out of debt. *I see having no bad debt as a given, not a goal.* I want people to focus on building wealth and migrating back to the belief that debt is *not* something used to make material purchases. Rather, it's to be used solely for the purpose of advancement: furthering education, buying real estate, and starting a business or other productive method of leverage for future gain.

> *I want people to focus on building wealth and migrating back to the belief that debt is **not** something used to make material purchases.*

## ESTATE STRUCTURE

Pay close attention to how things are owned. If you have a trust, and it owns property, title it as such. If things are owned jointly or individually, report it accurately. This will be important in projecting the probate and possible estate-tax scenarios and can be a real eye-opener to estate taxes. What happens to your estate after you die can be a complicated process. In today's environment, a trust can help minimize the confusion and expenses beyond a simple will.

The trust generally keeps most of your assets out of probate court and can make for a much smoother transition of your assets to your heirs than a will. A trust also can provide you with control over your estate, even after you're gone. For example, you might stipulate that your assets are not to be distributed to your heirs until they reach a certain age, such as 30 or 40. This may help ensure that someone too young or inexperienced doesn't spend the money unwisely.

Trusts have been around for years and will continue to be a useful tool in the future. The laws change constantly, and knowing which trust makes the most sense for you usually depends on the current law. So meeting with a qualified professional or reviewing your estate plan on a regular basis is very important.

A trust generally doesn't provide the benefit desired unless your assets are owned in the name of the trust. This process is called "funding" and is critical to helping make sure you will receive the desired benefit from the document. This is usually a simple process but one that is seldom done. If a trust is drafted and not properly funded, you may find that it's as functional as a simple will, and much of your estate planning will have gone to waste.

When is the right time to pursue estate advice? Many people wait until they're advanced seniors to begin, but that can be a complicated time for such matters. Drafting estate documents at an older age is sometimes difficult for people, as it forces them to confront their mortality. Thinking processes also may not be as clear. Estate planning isn't something you have to wait for. It's just as important to have a good plan in your 30s or 40s as it is in your 70s or 80s, especially if you're married and have children. Estate planning is also very important after a divorce, if remarrying and in same-sex partnerships. Your organization software also should be able to identify if your estate planning has done its job, or if you are subject to estate taxes.

In addition, you need to pay close attention to any business or real estate you own and properly evaluate the legal structure. I often see people own investment real estate in their own name rather than through a limited liability company (LLC) or other business structure. Owning it outside of your personal estate, such as with an LLC, can help lessen your potential liability. While you're reviewing your estate plan with your attorney, be sure to also discuss any other assets you own from which you may need liability protection. You never want to have a good thing going financially just to have someone sue you and take it all away. Structuring proper ownership is a simple process that won't take you long to figure out but could cost you plenty if something goes wrong.

Review all your insurance policies and how they're owned. Life insurance proceeds are usually brought back into the value of an estate for estate-tax purposes. So if you have a couple of million-dollar policies for your children (in case you and your spouse die in a plane crash), don't be surprised if one of those policies goes directly to pay the estate tax it helped create, unless you've already addressed that with a proper estate plan.

## ASSET ALLOCATION

Detroit is a huge hockey town. Most everyone in this area is a Red Wings fan. We recently had a string of unbelievable seasons and even some Stanley Cups. What made it possible? Having great talent, a deep bench and outstanding coaching. Detroit is able to attract some of the best players in the league, but great players can get hurt just like anyone else. Having a couple of star players isn't as important as having a great team. Each "string" the Red Wings put on the ice is strong, hence the term "deep bench"—a long line of very good players. We also were blessed with having a coach who has won more Stanley Cups than anyone in history, Scotty Bowman. He knew how to rotate his team in order to capitalize on the game situation. If someone was hurt and missing some games, the team was strong enough to compensate. The new coach, Mike Babcock, appears to be doing just as well. In fact, the Red Wings won the Stanley Cup again in 2008. Most great sports teams, businesses and investment strategies have a similar formula. You can use asset allocation to build a deep investment bench. You're continuously working to improve each individual player, while simultaneously improving your mix of investment to reduce risk and advance in value through many different types of markets.

Once you're comfortable that everything is reporting properly, review your current asset allocation. Asset allocation is a logical strategy: Don't put all your eggs in one basket. Your organization system will be a key component of maintaining a desired asset allocation. If you really don't know how your money is invested, it's pretty difficult to evaluate when you need to make adjustments. The more traditional asset classes include:

- Large-cap growth stocks
- Large-cap value stocks
- Mid-cap stocks
- Small-cap stocks

- International stocks
- Emerging-market stocks
- Real estate
- High-yield bonds
- Intermediate bonds
- Government bonds
- Short-term bonds
- Cash

Asset-allocation diversification strategies can reach much more broadly than this. For example, a person may have money in all these categories and directly own various commercial properties. He or she also may be investing in small businesses, debt instruments, raw land, rentals and many other appreciating assets.

I often find that people are improperly diversified. For example, they'll have two 401(k)s allocated across all the major asset classes in equal proportions. In theory, this looks good. If you look farther, though, you may find that one 401(k) offers a great small-cap fund but doesn't have a very good mid-cap fund. Why use an inferior fund in one account when you can satisfy the better small-cap allocation in one 401(k) and the preferred mid cap in another? Many times people don't know how their spouse's investments are allocated, and they rarely have a side-by-side comparison of fund choices. Having the data organized in front of you enables you to identify these scenarios and leverage the information.

One couple I met years ago, Jason and Claudia, showed me statements with a $350,000 variable-annuity IRA, $500,000 in 401(k)s, and a joint brokerage account with stocks and mutual funds for $100,000. In total, they had approximately 25 different stocks and mutual funds. They felt diversified. Unfortunately, the statements they showed me were six months old. Now they had only $210,000 in the IRA and $70,000 in the joint account. They continued to put money into their 401(k) so it had maintained a steady balance.

When we sat down together, the first thing we did was evaluate what asset classes they were in as an entire portfolio. To their surprise, even though they had 25 different investments, they were invested in only three different asset classes, and their IRA was actually invested in only one asset class, which is one reason why it lost so much money. Then

I asked, "Why didn't you reallocate your investment, as it was losing so much money?" Jason answered, "We thought our *advisor* was doing something." Claudia said, "We didn't get one of the statements, and by then it had already declined. So we wanted to leave the money in there and wait for it to come back." Their first problem was not having a good allocation. Their second problem was ignoring things and relying on someone else to do the work.

> *... $3,875 an hour. How does that compare with what the current hourly rate for employment is?*

## BEING ORGANIZED IS 'PLENTY WORTH IT'

Again, organization allows you to spend less time on the grunt work and more time on the learning and decision-making side of your money. The simple strategy of evaluating what you have and making appropriate changes could earn you thousands of dollars—much more money than the hour you think you lost to get organized! If someone has $100,000 currently and saves $10,000 annually into that account, at 8 percent in 20 years it will grow to $983,530. If the same person earns 10 percent, it will grow to $1,365,614. If it grows at 12 percent it will reach $1,913,634! That's almost twice as much ($930,104) as what one would get with 8 percent. I cannot emphasize enough how important it is to pay attention to assets and getting the most out of them. Saving the money is the hard part; don't ignore the returns after the labor is already done! What if someone had to spend an hour a month reviewing his or her allocation and making some adjustment in order to get a higher return? That would be a grand total of 240 hours over a 20-year period. Let's see, 930,104 divided by 240 is $3,875 an hour. How does that compare with what the current hourly rate for employment is? Is anyone really too busy to get organized?[16]

If you're getting overwhelmed with the thought of all this work, don't. Remember, you can hire out much of this work to your team of advisors. You don't have to do everything, but that doesn't excuse you from not knowing which tasks are important.

Without undue effort or knowledge, you can structure a pie chart that will sort by taxable versus tax-deferred assets. It's likely you'll structure

---

16 Using diversification/asset allocation as part of your investment strategy neither assures nor guarantees better performance and cannot protect against loss in declining markets.

a different model for both categories. For example, you might have good-asset allocation as a whole, though most of your income-producing assets are held outside of retirement plans and add to your taxable income every year—even though you don't plan to spend them until you retire. It can make more sense to defer that investment in your retirement plan and use more growth-related investments outside the plan. Being organized with the tax structure of your investments can provide significant efficiencies in your financial plan.

Organizing your investments on one page will help you to identify the costs of each. All investments carry operating costs. Even if an investment has an up-front charge, it probably still has an internal operating cost. Some costs are appropriate, but some investments are just plain expensive. *Know what you're paying for, as well as how much it costs, and be able to evaluate the investment's effectiveness.* To help understand cost structure, ask your trusted advisor. Some people in the industry would just assume you don't know about the expenses. But it's your money; you have a right to know everything that's important. The best way to understand what level of cost is appropriate is to pay attention, to dig around like a gardener who isn't afraid to get his or her hands dirty. Before long, you'll begin to recognize when something may be priced higher than necessary. As I said before, make sure your investments are performing well. In the final analysis, performance is more important than costs. All things being equal, though, costs directly affect your performance.

## AUTOMATIC

Systematic savings is a great way to build wealth consistently. Most family wealth is in home-equity and retirement plans. I've met with many people who have hundreds of thousands of dollars in 401(k) plans and in home equity—and no other wealth. Why is it so much easier to accumulate wealth in a 401(k) or through home equity? Simply put, they both rely on consistent strategies that become habit.

Most people buy their homes with a mortgage. Back in the day (and, one would hope, again soon) when most mortgages were on either a 15- or 30-year fixed rate, the seemingly endless monthly mortgage payments eventually increased your equity. I'm not very far into a fixed-rate mortgage, and hundreds of dollars get paid off the balance of the loan with each monthly payment. The mortgage payment becomes part of life, and you may forget that you're also making headway toward increasing your net worth. As this book was being completed, we in the United States were experiencing a housing slump, and some home prices have been declining in value. During most periods, however, home values consistently rise, automatically increasing your net worth.

A 401(k) builds equity in much the same way. People get into the habit of saving a percentage of their paycheck and, before long, it becomes a regular part of life. The balance starts out very small, but through systematic investing, your portfolio begins to grow. A key element to systematic investing is that your money is put into the market through many market cycles, without your trying to time the market. If, on the other hand, your savings weren't automatic, and you simply invested monthly into investments when you thought the timing was right, you could see an entirely different outcome—and not usually for the better.

I was talking to a new client who was sitting on cash until the market "did better." This woman felt more comfortable investing after the market showed signs of growth. The problem with that strategy is she was waiting to invest money *after* a large rebound while watching from the sidelines. Investing at the peaks of the market and withdrawing in the valleys is the exact opposite of what you want to do. But when you're trying to time the market, that's often exactly what happens. Some of the people who chose to put their investment life on hold and stopped investing during the recession in 2000–02 still haven't gained back the money they lost. The smart ones kept investing when others were afraid and profited while the "market timers" finally started getting back in—after the market had already experienced significant growth. The "robotic" method of payroll going directly into the 401(k) helps take emotion out of the equation and improves your wealth accumulation by buying right through the cycles.

Emotion tends to play too large a role when people invest. Many people lost significant amounts of money during the recession of 2000–02, especially in the technology sector, as many of those stocks went belly-up. But look at your 401(k). If you had good-asset allocation, chose decent funds and kept investing 15 percent of your income every pay period in the late '90s—through the recession and up to today—you would most likely be looking at a large portfolio. Even though (during those years) the market experienced severe ups and downs, dollar-cost averaging your investment allowed you to purchase through the cycles. You bought more shares while the prices were lower and gained value as the prices rose.

Having money isn't something you want to have had once and then lost. Money is something you build up for a lifetime, which will in turn produce a lifetime of income for you and quite possibly income for your family and charity as well. Systematic investing and asset allocation are a strategy that creates discipline and structure around your wealth accumulation. It also helps you to capture income that otherwise would have slipped through your fingers. As your wealth grows, you'll continuously look for ways of improving return and, just as important, insulating against loss.

> *Go to* **www.jpstudinger.com** *for a free cash-flow report worksheet.*

## CASH FLOWS

Next, tally up your cash inflows and your expenses. Whether you have a strict cash-only budget or use credit cards, get the information in the program. Project your desired income in retirement. Don't forget the "what if" scenarios, such as an early death or disability. When calculating expenses, don't leave out taxes. You want your tax information so organized that you can quickly identify whether an expense is an itemized expense to automatically be crunched by the software for a projected tax return. In addition, your income projections should be an accurate reflection of what you expect to earn that year and through what sources. While projecting income in retirement, the application also can calculate the source of income and compute the taxable distribution based on current tax law. Since tax laws change periodically, make sure your program has a mechanism for changing with them. Go to *www.jpstudinger.com* for a free cash-flow report worksheet.

## DON'T GET OVERWHELMED

Once you have all the facts in place, you're ready to start learning, strategizing and growing. The initial inputs may take some time, but you can hire out much of that job to a professional. If you do it on your own, remember to use a system that keeps things updated automatically, making life relatively simple after things have been loaded up. If you have to redo the work every time you try to get your hands around money, consistent financial self-evaluation won't happen. Also, do your utmost to keep the *big* picture in focus; no financial decision is made in isolation. Recall Newton's "third law of motion," as quoted in Principle 1: "To every action there is an equal and opposite reaction."

## ORGANIZATION SUCCESS

I have countless stories of how organization can lead to wealth. I met with a single woman, Bridget, who was looking to retire the following year. She wasn't currently putting money away into a retirement plan and had few itemized deductions. Although her debt level was low, her payments were large. Bridget also was technically a little behind the eightball in having enough investments to retire.

If all we did was look at her existing investments and make improvements in allocation and investment quality, certainly she could have improved financially and would have been worth a little more because of it. I started, however, by looking at the big picture. I knew that Bridget not only needed to improve her returns and take out volatility (she had lost well over $100,000 during the previous couple of years), she also needed to physically add more money to her investments. So I looked for ways to reduce her expenses, including taxes and debt-service costs.

We got organized with my system and made sure we were reviewing accurate information and seeing the entire picture. Then we needed to find a way to max out her retirement plan before the year was over. We accomplished this by tax-harvesting her existing taxable investment accounts, refinancing her debt and significantly lowering her monthly payment, then putting almost all of her income for the rest of the year into the retirement plan. It may sound impossible, but we did this without decreasing her current standard of living. We implemented similar strategies a few months later in the beginning of the next year, including funding Roth IRAs for both years. In one and a half years she was worth $170,000 more and had no debt, all on a $90,000 salary. Bridget is now retired and living quite well.

By ignoring organization, people make it much more difficult to accomplish financial goals. Yes, you may need assistance putting this information together and developing the strategies. And yes, it takes a little time up front to get organized. But if Bridget had kept doing what she was doing, she wouldn't have retired with enough money, or she would've had to work years longer to get the same results.

If your organizing is really state-of-the-art, you'll be able to implement alerts and triggering events that notify you or your advisor when things need attention. Money can move fast, and if you're looking at it only once a month, you may be *over*looking important strategies. Take as much human error as possible out of the equation by utilizing technology to provide at least a degree of "automaticity" with your money.

## BOTTOM LINE: NET WORTH

Once you have all this figured out, pay attention to the bottom line. What is your net worth? What does it need to be in order to retire? Where is your primary 12-month focus? What do you predict your net worth to be at that time? Then build your strategy to address these questions.

Most investment returns, especially in the short run, are notoriously unpredictable. Some years you may greatly exceed the goal because of investment performance. Some years you may go backward. The key is to focus on what is in your control, mainly maximizing cash flow (driving down expenses and/or increasing income) and astutely allocating investments. Look at the strategies you implement regarding spending, debt, taxes and insurance. Then work with the investments to the best of your ability and the ability of your advisors. By taking the same disciplined approach year after year, you'll find yourself amassing money and having fun doing it. You'll find that being "in the know" simply feels better than when things were disorganized. The best part is you'll know how well you're doing with your money and be proud of your accomplishment.

Look at your net worth each time you pull up the system on your computer. Is it up or down? If it's down, ask *why*. Do you need to change something, or is it normal (and acceptable) market movement? If things are up, also discover *why*. Did you generate substantial profits in something that you can now capitalize on? Have you paid a debt down? Is your cash reserve building?

Now that you have information at your fingertips, you can see, think and react to improve your financial life. If you're married or have joint finances with someone, do these exercises together. Communication and working as a team are of vital importance to eventually reaching your dreams. And the key to all this? *Get organized and stay organized.*

## TO SUMMARIZE

1. Being organized with your money puts you in control. The less organized you are, the harder you have to work to get the same results.

2. KISS: Keep it simple, Stupid. Use a simple method of organization, or you likely won't stay with it. Financial planning software will touch on much of your life beyond just evaluating your portfolio. Especially if you're using an online system, make sure the software is secure.

3. Even though it may be depressing to review, get organized with your liabilities. You'll probably save thousands of dollars and, as a bonus, develop some healthy habits that will help you create permanent wealth.

4. Organize your estate with a will or trust. At the same time, pay close attention to the structure of your business or real estate properties and make sure they aren't endangering the stability of your personal wealth by exposing you to excessive financial risk.

5. Develop a "deep bench" of investments through asset allocation. Asset allocation diversifies your good assets in an attempt to have your overall portfolio function well in many different types of markets.

6. When comparing the asset-allocation grouping of your portfolio, be sure to use the strengths each investment account has to offer in order to develop a cost-efficient and strategically sound overall investment portfolio.

7. Automatic investments are a great way to consistently build wealth. A 401(k) is one of the best automatic investments available.

8. Develop an overall plan to increase your portfolio by investing straight through market cycles rather than trying to time them. You

don't want to be left watching on the sidelines while the market goes up, then finally invest and watch the market go down.

9. Review your cash-flow expenses and search to cut inefficient overhead.

10. Make sure itemized deductions are identified in your cash-flow report so that the financial planning software can automatically make tax projections.

11. Get to know your net-worth numbers and review them often. In order to help you make better decisions with your money, look for reasons why your net worth is advancing or declining. Money isn't something you want to have had and lost. Stay focused, disciplined *and organized* for the long haul.

## Principle 14

## Get Organized and Stay Organized

### Principles in Action

**Sample: How quickly can you put your numbers together?**

*Cash-flow numbers are a little difficult to get organized. It may take an hour or more for us to know they're accurate. We know our balance-sheet numbers (good and bad assets) within minutes.*

**What is your primary method of financial organization?**

*I have to look at my checkbook and credit card statements to get the budget organized. I use a software system through my wealth manager to keep track of our net worth and goals.*

**When was the last time you reviewed your entire financial position and strategies?**

*We used to review it once a year, if that. Now we're are reviewing our numbers at least monthly. It has made a big difference in our communication and has increased our level of success.*

# Principle 14
## Get Organized and Stay Organized

### Principles in Action

**How quickly can *you* put your numbers together?**

**What is *your* primary method of financial organization?**

**When was the last time *you* reviewed your entire financial position and strategies?**

# Principle 15

## Put Your Money on a Mission

The dictionary defines "legacy" as "money or property bequeathed to another by will" or "something handed down from an ancestor or a predecessor or from the past." A financial legacy is a way of ensuring that your lifetime of hard-earned wealth can be used for people or institutions that share the same ideals and discipline as you, which will in turn secure your efforts for a long time.

In 1785 a Frenchman wrote a story making fun of Benjamin Franklin's American optimism. He tells a tale of a man leaving a small sum of money in his will, which grows to a fortune in 500 years. Rather than be offended by the story, Ben Franklin embraced the idea and changed his own will to leave around $4,500 each to Boston and Philadelphia to be invested for 100 years before some of it could be paid out. Then the remainder was to be reinvested for another 100 years before it could again be put to good use. According to the *Stanford Social Innovation Review,* in 1990, after the second century of investing and the money having been spent as instructed, Boston's fund had grown to $5 million. Philadelphia's had grown to $2.25 million.

In a world with fewer and fewer pensions, as well as reduced Social Security, we're now faced with the task of accumulating enough money to last us our entire life, which may very well be to age 100 or longer. Even if people in their 90s aren't as active and don't spend as much leisure money, their healthcare costs generally are significant. If you didn't think you would live that long and find yourself in your 90s and still spending, your last years in this world may be very difficult financially. Just look at the examples of some elderly people who have to choose between buying food and prescription drugs. On the other hand, if you think you just might live to be 100 and accumulate a nice nest egg worth millions of dollars, then you pass away at 65, your large amount of money will go to people you care about, to charity, to the government or to any combination of the three (and attorneys). So rather than just accumulate wealth for your retirement or for your family's future, think in terms of the bigger picture: the legacy you can leave to the world. Although the aphorism "You can't take it with you" is certainly true, you worked hard and made sacrifices to accumulate wealth. With your passing, make sure the people or institutions that receive your wealth share the same values and will put your funds to good use.

Today much of the wealth that passes to family isn't taxed unless it's in an IRA or an annuity. Unless people are in the top tier of wealth, estate taxes don't usually factor in very heavily. Once an estate (often including life insurance death benefits) does cross a wealth threshold, however, estate taxes can erode that wealth rather quickly.

Estate taxes have been around much longer than the United States has. They were a method of redistributing wealth rather than having individual families amass fortunes, which tends to further separate the economic classes. People argue whether estate taxes are necessary—and the pros and cons of eliminating them. The tax creates a significant source of income for the government, so it will likely always remain or be replaced with another form of taxation, such as income tax or capital-gains tax. Even if this book is in circulation 200 years from now, estates will almost certainly be taxed in some form or another.

By today's standards, an estate worth a few million dollars could very likely have taxes in the hundreds of thousands or even millions of dollars, depending on how the estate is positioned. Or, with proper planning, the taxes could be minimized to mere thousands or less, with much of the difference going to your family and/or charities. If your estate is large enough to trigger estate taxes, by all means evaluate your options immediately. Ignoring this can result in a tremendous waste of your money.

Let's look at a few of the more common ways you can leave a financial legacy:

## CHARITABLE CONTRIBUTIONS

The U.S. government collects taxes from individuals with the intention of running programs that benefit society as a whole. However, the U.S. Congress recognized many years ago that this process was inefficient. Therefore, Congress passed tax laws to encourage Americans to directly help those in need, rather than relying on the government bureaucracy to do so. By passing these laws, Congress empowered American citizens (with incentives) to self-direct our contributions to charities and causes we believe in.

Rather than blindly giving to any charity that calls you on the phone or sends a request in the mail, evaluate the effectiveness of each dollar you give. Some charities put much more of your money to support the cause than others do. Custom-design a planned giving strategy and help maximize your money and your goodwill. Working directly with your charity of choice can be a great way to also maximize the benefits the U.S. government provides and ensure that your planned giving is benefiting the cause(s) you wish to support. Tremendous personal and financial benefits can be the result of this partnership.

Why would you want to give charitable contributions? Some of the benefits to you include providing an annual income for life, passing assets to family members tax-free, increasing income-tax deductions, minimizing capital-gains taxes, reducing or eliminating estate taxes, and giving you the satisfaction of helping causes you believe in—for years to come.

I'm of the mindset that estate and charitable planning is best structured, first and foremost, to provide the desired benefit to the donor and charity. Ideally, the act of giving is driven by a desire to help others—and tax savings are not the primary motivation. Far too detailed for the scope of this book are specific tax, charitable-giving and estate strategies. That's why I recommend that you talk with your trusted advisor about your options. I've seen a number of families engaged in complicated strategies with the best of intentions, but because of a misunderstanding or bad advice, they discovered that their efforts were worthless or even costly. Good charitable planning can be well worth the effort. Bad planning can be devastating.

Many people think "leaving a legacy" is something only the ultra-rich do. If you discuss planned giving with your spouse, family and advisors, you may actually find current or future tax and income benefits, as well as provide a means to help a greater cause. You may not have been able to give as much of your time and energy to your favorite charities throughout much of your working career, but perhaps in the sunset of your life you can help by making significant financial contributions.

As you pursue philanthropy, one mental hurdle you'll have to overcome is the understanding that giving goes way beyond the standard tax deduction for writing a check to a charity. While some of your money will always be subject to taxation, you can use a number of strategies beyond just giving cash or tangible property to a charity to help reduce your tax liability.[17]

---

17 This overview has been created to provide accurate and reliable information on the subjects covered. It is not intended to provide specific legal, tax or other professional advice. The services of an appropriate professional should be sought regarding your individual situation.

## REBALANCE YOUR GAINS

Even during your accumulation phase of wealth, planned-giving strategies for charities can support your efforts. For example, many people give a few thousand dollars each year to various charities. At the same time they also may have stocks and other assets with an appreciated value that they'll have to pay a capital-gains tax on what they sell. So rather than give with cash, they can transfer an appreciated asset instead. Here's how it works: You intend to write a check for $3,000 to a charity. Let's say you also purchased a stock for $1,000, and it's now worth $3,000. Instead of writing a check for $3,000, you gift the stock, and you receive a deduction for the entire amount of the gift ($3,000). Because you're transferring the stock rather than selling it and giving cash, you don't have to pay taxes on the $2,000 gain. Now, rather than giving cash, put the $3,000 in your 401(k) by deferring more income from your paycheck. You can buy a similar asset-class investment and thereby not reduce the amount of money you had allocated toward your future.

By using this strategy, you'll receive a tax deduction of $3,000 for the gift to the charity. You also will have reduced your taxable income by the $3,000 deferred into the 401(k).

> *This is a great example of how having knowledge regarding taxes and investments can help you receive the maximum return financially on a good deed. It's a win-win.*

Assuming you're in the 25 percent tax bracket, you've reduced your overall income by $6,000 (rather than just $3,000 by giving cash), thus lowering your federal tax liability by $1,500. Now if you really want to be efficient, invest the $1,500 you just saved into a Roth IRA. The tax-free status of the Roth will help to offset the future taxable income generated by the $3,000 you put into the 401(k).

So the bottom line to this strategy is that you avoid a capital-gains tax while rebalancing your portfolio. You benefited a charity, just as you had planned, by $3,000. Then you increased your tax-deferred portfolio by $4,500—$3,000 into the 401(k) and $1,500 into the Roth—with $1,500 of it as a future tax-free withdrawal!

This is a great example of how having knowledge regarding taxes and investments can help you receive the maximum return financially on a good deed. It's a win-win.

## GIFT ANNUITY PROGRAMS

Some charities are involved in gift annuity programs. When you take part in such a program, you receive lifetime payments with reduced taxes. Here's how it works: In exchange for irrevocably transferring your cash or securities to the charity, the charity promises to pay you and/or another beneficiary a specified dollar amount on an annual or quarterly basis for as long as you or the other beneficiary live. A large portion of the initial gift you give to the charity is tax-deductible, and a portion of the payments you receive also may have tax advantages.

This program is basically an immediate annuity with a charitable twist. Generally speaking, the interest rate may be lower than what you could get if you went directly to an insurance company. The immediate charitable deduction, however, can be quite significant and may in some circumstances more than offset the lower return. It also may be possible for you to use an appreciated asset to fund the gift annuity, thereby also helping to reduce capital-gains taxes on an investment.

With this program, the older you are the higher the payout is going to be. Therefore, this strategy often works best for people who are already retired and are looking for ways of increasing their fixed income and helping a charity. It doesn't work well for someone who has limited assets or who needs access to cash, since you're giving your money in exchange for a fixed-income stream.

A charity may either self-insure the payments to you or transfer the risk to an insurance company. Generally, I prefer that the charity sell it to a highly rated insurance company. This will insure the payments even if the financial status of the charity isn't all that great. It also provides the charity with immediate revenue from your gift annuity. If instead, the charity is making payments to you directly from your donated money, it technically has a vested interest in you dying soon. The longer you live, the less money the charity will have from your gift and the longer before it benefits from your strategy.

## CHARITABLE REMAINDER TRUSTS

A charitable remainder trust (CRT) can have significant advantages to income and tax deductions. Although with today's lower long-term capital-gains rates, this strategy is less appealing than in years past. Again, make sure you're working with good advisors, as I've seen this strategy botched due to bad implementation. It has some similarities with a gift annuity in the sense that it's often a strategy used to generate lifetime income.

Here's a common situation for a CRT: Suppose you as a couple have $500,000 of highly appreciated assets, such as an investment portfolio. If you were to sell the investments outright and put them into something to generate an income stream, you would be facing a significant capital-gains tax, thereby generating income on a smaller portfolio. You may consider transferring the portfolio to a special charitable remainder trust, then selling the asset in the trust. In the trust you'll have identified an income stream, usually a percentage of assets in the trust, for a couple's lifetime. The lower the percentage payout, the higher the tax deduction. It's common for people to take out 5 to 7 percent.

Most trusts are set up so you can change the charity at any time, or you can identify multiple charities. Whatever money is left in the trust at the time of your death will be distributed to the charity.

This strategy removes assets from your estate and therefore can be a significant method of reducing or eliminating estate taxes. It also means your heirs won't be inheriting the money. If you want your heirs to receive some of your money, you also can establish a separate irrevocable life insurance trust (ILIT), which can pass to your heirs at your death, generally income- and estate-tax-free. Because the tax deduction is so great with a CRT, some people justify the insurance premium of the ILIT and figure it into the overall cost/benefit analysis while evaluating the CRT.

## GIVE YOUR GRANDCHILDREN THE GIFT OF EDUCATION

College is expensive and appears to be getting even more so as the cost of school has been exceeding the rate of normal inflation. There appears to be less government money available, and student loans are beginning to look more beneficial to the lender than they are to the student. In the midst of all this, families are struggling to make up lost ground on retirement savings and are realizing how much more money they need to have saved than was previously thought. This leaves families with less money available to pay for the cost of college. At the same time the world economy is reminding everyone that good education is paramount to the success of our country and our future.

Some grandparents may be in the "perfect position" to calm education's "perfect storm."

One of the more common education savings plans today is the 529 plan. There are quite a few 529 plan varieties out there, and many states may offer a plan that provides unique benefits to the residents of their state. The Website *www.savingforcollege.com* is one of the more popular sites out there, breaking down the specifics of each plan. The core functions of the plans, however, are similar. 529 plans allow you to invest money into bond- or equity-type investments designed to grow in value and help pay for "qualified higher education" expenses. The best news is, that when done right, the money taken from the plan can be used tax-free. Especially if the account began when the child was very young, and there are substantial gains in the account, the tax-free nature of the plan can have significant advantages.

I have quite a few clients who are funding their grandchildren's education by investing the maximum allowed into the plan each year, gift-tax-free, so as not to trigger other estate taxes down the road. This not only helps the grandparents remove assets from their estate that they've identified as in excess of their needs (and subject to taxes at their death), it also helps give their family members a much-needed education. Further, these plans currently allow the beneficiary to be changed, thereby allowing the assets to be passed on to other generations if not all the money was used up for the intended participant.

Years ago many people bought savings bonds for their grandchildren. Then Coverdell ESAs (education savings accounts) became popular. Now 529 plans appear to be one of the best options. Over time, the specific vehicle may change, but the story remains the same. How wonderful would it be to know that you have established the framework of a family scholarship fund that helps give loved ones a chance to excel in life!

## YOUR FUTURE AND BEYOND

Realize that many of the charitable strategies are irrevocable, meaning you cannot undo them once you set them up. I once met with a couple who were advised to construct a charitable remainder trust to reduce a capital-gains tax and create lifetime income. The strategy was poorly conceived and became a point of great frustration for them. They worked with advisors for years to try to undo the trust, but they were unsuccessful. It's likely their mistake cost them hundreds of thousands of dollars. So be very methodical in your planning before you decide on anything.

When charitable giving is properly constructed, however, the benefits of leaving a living legacy like this can be great, and the satisfaction of supporting your beliefs is immeasurable. Additionally, if your estate is positioned through direct wealth or life insurance proceeds to pay a large tax upon your death, utilizing charitable strategies can increase the amount of money that goes toward your family by benefiting charities at the same time.

## TO SUMMARIZE

1. Lack of pensions and uncertainty with regard to Social Security means we need to save more money. Those who die early may leave very large estates that will benefit others. Estates transfer to heirs, charities, or the government and attorneys. Take control of that distribution process.

2. Taxes redistribute wealth for social causes. You can direct which social cause(s) you wish to support by designing a planned-giving initiative.

3. Look beyond the obvious tax deduction of charitable giving. Meet with advisors to discuss if there are charitable strategies that could improve your situation or your family's financial position while also benefiting a charity.

4. Most charitable-giving strategies are irrevocable. Be sure to receive good advice and think through your options thoroughly before proceeding.

5. College is expensive—and getting more so. Some grandparents are building education funds for their grandchildren to help assure them a chance for a good education.

6. Enjoy the immeasurable satisfaction of knowing that you are doing something in both life *and* death that supports your deeply held values, convictions and beliefs.

# Principle 15

## Put Your Money on a Mission

### Principles in Action

**Sample: Which philanthropic causes are important for you to support and why?**

*Children: We want to do what we can to help kids get a good start in life. I can't imagine my own children not having a chance or living in fear.*

*The environment: We really enjoy the outdoors and want it to be around for generations to come. It takes a conscious effort to make sure that will happen.*

**Which philanthropic causes are important for *you* to support and why?**

## Principle 16

## Share the Wealth of Experiences

People routinely share golf tips, fishing techniques, cooking recipes, religious beliefs, political theories, parenting techniques, pick-up lines, business war stories, relationship secrets, home-repair tips and much more. It's fun to tell people about things we're good at. But rarely will we share financial success—and almost never our failure stories. If you hear someone telling a financial success story, it may come across as bragging, whereas nobody wants others to know about their financial blunders. People can be quite competitive with money, but if nobody talks about it, then no one really knows who's succeeding and who's struggling. That attitude, however, contributes to a society in which everyone keeps making the same mistakes, unable to learn from each other's experiences. We go about our lives making financial decisions inside a "bubble." *No wonder so many people struggle when it comes to money!*

Many of the things we learn in life we learn from those around us. Family traditions passed through the generations, success stories told by parents and mistakes made by older siblings all help mold us into who we are today. We generally believe that some people are *better with money* than we are. Since we never know the actual details, it's just a perception. Sometimes, however, those people aren't any more successful with money than anyone else is.

## PERCEPTIONS ARE NOT ALWAYS REALITY

A number of years ago I implemented a retirement plan for a company in a small Michigan town. In doing so, I met individually with many of the employees. Almost everyone I met apologized for the amount of money they had saved. Pretty soon conversation turned to others, and several people said I really needed to talk to Nick and Erin because they were the rich ones in town. I thought most of the people I had met with were doing rather well, so the 10$^{th}$ time I heard this I was eager to meet Nick and Erin. It sounded like they were the local millionaires.

When I finally met Nick and Erin, the meeting didn't go quite as I expected. I thought there would be numerous statements showing massive investment portfolios. Instead, I saw various statements showing massive ... debt. They were overspending their income by thousands of dollars every year. All told, they had less than $30,000 in savings. As Nick and Erin were in their early 50s, it was obvious they were running out of time and needed to change their behaviors fast. They didn't want to face reality—and they certainly didn't want others in town to know about their problems. So rather than take my advice and change their ways, they kept asking me how to find creative financing to postpone the inevitable, something I obviously couldn't support.

## GET TALKING

For some reason most people, it seems, would rather stand naked in the middle of Main Street at high noon than reveal how they look financially. Even people who are usually very forthright with sharing both positive and negative life experiences shy away from the topic of money. The fact is no one is without financial mistakes. We can limit our families' and others' future mistakes by sharing stories of what worked for us, as well as what didn't work. We also can limit our own errors by learning from the successes and failures of others. The dialogue about money, debt and financial strategies needs to begin if we want to *get better with money* and ensure that our children grow up to be financially responsible.

Indeed, start with your children. If you're cutting back in order to free up money for good assets, let your children know what you're doing and why. Tell them you established a savings goal for their college and your future—and you must save 15 percent of your income to accomplish those goals. Let them know when you had a great year and are on schedule to meet your goals. Explain to them early your strategies for accumulating wealth, and you'll be less likely to have problems with them undervaluing money and becoming a financial drain. Talking to them about this as they enter their teens is not too soon!

In Michigan we have a major interstate highway, I-75, which runs north and south. Every Friday afternoon many of us scramble north to escape the city. This routinely causes miles of backups. On occasion, to make matters worse, there's an accident, and your best bet is to get off the freeway and find your way on the country roads. Sometimes, though, the backups are the natural congestion from traffic merging onto the freeway and clear quickly. Everyone sitting idle (and idling!) in line has the same question: "How long will this last, and should I get off the road?" I watch southbound traffic driving 80 miles per hour in the other direction, and they know the answer to my question (because they have just passed our line of cars), but to this day I haven't figured out how to get it from them!

Regarding money, people all around you are struggling with (or have already researched) the same things you would like to know. But unlike traffic headed in the other direction, you can ask someone sitting right next to you. Being able to openly discuss strategies that you may have heard on the radio, seen on TV, read in a book or learned from an advisor will help you to better understand them and discover the practical truth for your situation. In order for the public to master wealth-accumulation skills (that today few really know) will require a more open dialogue with people you respect and trust. Likewise, as you're experiencing and understanding money and the financial services industry, don't keep what you learn a secret from others struggling around you. Here are three kinds of things to ask others about:

1. Ask your good friends or siblings if they try to max out their Roth IRAs.

2. Ask them about a strategy someone suggested to you and see if they have any experience with it or if they have considered it in the past.

3. Ask them what might be wrong with an idea you love, and let them be your devil's advocate. You don't have to ask or share specific dollar amounts. You can start by talking more conceptually about strategies and ideas.

Open up positive dialogue. Yes, money can be a sensitive subject, and some people may not hear your feedback well—and, in some cases, you may have difficulty receiving feedback yourself. Use active-listening skills and check your negative emotions to really hear what the other person is saying. Being aware of the defenses we tend to build around our insecurities about money will help us discuss ideas or strategies in ways that explain things we've done, rather than taking the tone of telling people what they *should* do. Use more "I" statements, fewer "you" statements. We can thereby share information without being judgmental or standing on a soapbox.

Chuck and Scott are brothers—and friends of mine. One day I heard Scott tell Chuck that he really liked his Corvette. Chuck said, "If you would save your money like I do, then someday you might be able to afford one too." That may have been a true statement, but Scott didn't take it very well. Scott is the younger brother, and I'm sure there are some psychological insecurities and competition in relation to the two of them. Scott isn't doing as well financially. He has a lot of credit card debt, doesn't own his own home and has a tough time finding consistent work. Chuck, on the other hand, has very little debt, saves his money and has been advancing well throughout his career. If Chuck were really trying to make a positive impact on his brother, he might have had more success by saying, "If you'd like, I'll be happy to tell you how I could finally afford to buy this car."

If you're having a conversation with someone, and the discussion starts getting into specifics, avoid phrases like "You *should* do this" or "You never *should* have done that." Remember, there is often great sensitivity regarding finances, so have empathy during the conversation. When you're discussing success stories, start by saying, "Here are some things that worked for me," or "When we experienced something similar, this is what we did." Be sure to also share something that didn't work so well. People will often open up and take your advice better if they realize you aren't perfect either.

> *Being taken for any kind of ride may prick our pride, but we have to move past that and learn from the experience—while at the same time helping others not experience the same misfortune.*

Earlier in my career I would sometimes bad-mouth an investment or strategy that new clients had used in the past. I soon realized that when I was discussing the negative components of a strategy or product they were using, what they heard was judgment on them and their decision-making ability. Even if they had been hurt with blatantly improper or unethical advice, if I approached it the wrong way, I would soon find myself at loggerheads with them while they vigorously defended the person who had given the bad advice. Outwardly they were defending the advice, but inwardly they were really defending their own intelligence—because they had made the decision to take the advice. Eventually I learned that fixating on a mistake is not the best way to begin an open and productive discussion. All of us have erred or have been taken advantage of in the past. Regarding the latter, I know I have been taken "down the garden path" more than once and likely will be again. Being taken for any kind of ride may prick our pride, but we have to move past that and learn from the experience—while at the same time helping others not experience the same misfortune.

A hot investment tip is something else you would do well to share sparingly. Suggesting a specific stock or other investment that, in reality, very few people (often you included) know much about, can lead not only to lost money but strained relationships. Even if you think the investment is sound, many factors beyond your control—such as when the other person bought, how long he or she held the investment and, the market's volatility—are important factors that have a bearing on the viability of the tip. In these kinds of situations I never forget Murphy's Law: "Whatever can go wrong will go wrong." By the time you share a hot tip that already made money for you, the market likely changes, and the big investors take their money out. Your friend invests at the absolute wrong time and experiences massive decline. You certainly don't have to be a licensed professional to have good ideas. But if you're sharing a tip, beware of the reality of the risk because your friend could lose all of his or her money.

The goal is to share strategies and methods that have influenced your life either positively or negatively. Families and friends who talk openly about other things may have the greatest potential to also share financial ideas in a comfortable atmosphere—and, as a result, grow financially with each other. Use their insight as information to help pinpoint your areas of further research, not to replace them. I recently was meeting with a woman named Ann to discuss her financial strategies. I asked her why she had been making monthly investments into one particularly risky strategy. It was illiquid and didn't seem to fit with the rest of her goals. She said her dad told her to buy the investment a long time ago, and so she did. She couldn't describe to me the nature of the investment or how she could redeem her money. The investment may have been a good one for her father, but he's in an entirely different financial position from Ann, and it doesn't make sense for her to own so much of it. Just because someone you respect says you *should* be doing something doesn't keep you from also understanding the investment. As noted before, ultimate financial responsibility rests in one place only: on your shoulders.

Above all else, allow yourself and others to prosper. Also as discussed earlier, getting rid of your financial crutches is a major step in advancing with wealth accumulation. If talking about money becomes more socially acceptable with you and those around you, information about who has more and less money also may be known. People with less money may wish to borrow yours, but *don't cripple their future by becoming their crutch.*

> *People with less money may wish to borrow yours, but* **don't cripple their future by becoming their crutch.**

If you really want to help them, discuss your experiences—especially the greatest strategy, which is "buying good assets to create wealth." Giving or even loaning people money because they have poor monetary practices is pouring your hard-earned wealth into the bad-asset column. You're really not helping them by becoming their crutch. Yes, it can be difficult to have money when others you care about have a lot less. But if you take it upon yourself to solve their short-term problems, soon you may not have money either. You must realize that having money doesn't automatically mean it's available for you to give or loan. Hundreds of thousands of dollars in an IRA is the same as having a pension in retirement. You're going to need that money in order to survive. If you do give or loan money to someone, be sure to identify what money you have that is necessary to keep for your own financial solvency—and what money you have that is surplus and can be parted with.

To make sure I'm clear: I'm not saying that it's bad to share your wealth. What I am saying is that you don't want to keep others from also achieving financial success by allowing them to depend on you for their necessities. It's the old "buy them a fish or teach them to fish" parable. If you buy them food, they'll eat for a day, but if you teach them how to get their own food, they'll never go hungry again.

## WE ALL CAN POSITIVELY INFLUENCE OUR OWN AND OTHERS' SUCCESS WITH MONEY

In order for our society to survive and prosper with money, each generation must make more intelligent financial decisions than the previous. Virtually everyone shares a common goal: to be financially secure. It's odd, then, that we don't share our stories more often. We go through many stages of life with our friends—childhood, puberty, relationships, partying, learning, developing philosophies—and then when we enter the earning stage of life, we stop talking (at least about money). If small groups of people who genuinely care about each other's outcome are able to share some of their experiences, then we can accelerate our learning curve about how to accumulate money and all reach our goals sooner. You might even schedule regular "money talk" meetings, much as some folks meet to discuss books.

Remember, talking about money is neither boastful nor inappropriate. Such conversations are necessary for our country and our future generations to move forward and build a legacy for the whole world to benefit from. I have one friend who is so humble about her wealth that she'll tell you anything. It's refreshing, and I love that honesty in her. It helps others who know her learn from those experiences and make better decisions themselves. One can hope her willingness to share will become the norm, not the exception.

So get out there and get talking! Compare notes. Share what you've learned from this book as a starter, then move into your own personal experiences. By so doing, you're making the world a better place in which to live—one friend at a time.

## TO SUMMARIZE

1. Most people make financial decisions in a "bubble." People need to talk more openly about money. We especially need to share our financial failures.

2. Let your children know what you're doing and why.

3. When you talk about strategies, you don't need to include specific dollar amounts if you don't want to.

4. Be empathetic when discussing money with other people. We often build defenses around our finances. Avoid saying "You *should*" or "You *should never*" and other judgmental phrases. Say things like "Here is what has worked for me" and "This is what we tried."

5. When you share your failures, as well as your successes, others will have an easier time opening up to you. We've all made mistakes and have been taken for a ride by someone—and probably will be again. Be humble about your experiences.

6. Beware of passing on "hot investment tips." Many things are out of your control, and your friend's actual experience may end up being the polar opposite of yours.

7. Don't let others' experiences replace your own due diligence. Always follow your own values when making investment decisions.

8. Don't become someone else's crutch, especially if you're farther along financially. Give people information first, not money.

9. Each generation needs to make better decisions than the one before. Share your experiences with others in order to advance their financial position as you also improve your own.

# PRINCIPLE 16
## SHARE THE WEALTH OF EXPERIENCES

### PRINCIPLES IN ACTION

**SAMPLE: WHOM DO YOU TALK FREELY WITH ABOUT MONEY?**

*My big brother.*

**WHOM COULD YOU BE MORE OPEN WITH WHEN TALKING ABOUT MONEY?**

*Some of my friends who are in similar situations in life. We all work two jobs, have kids, want to retire comfortably and could use each other's support and experiences to help us all make better decisions.*

**WHOM COULD YOU MENTOR?**

*My kids for sure. We also could help David's family like my brother has helped us.*

**WHOM DO *YOU* TALK FREELY WITH ABOUT MONEY?**

**WHOM COULD *YOU* BE MORE OPEN WITH WHEN TALKING ABOUT MONEY?**

**WHOM COULD *YOU* MENTOR?**

## Principle 17

---

### Always Remember the *Why*

---

I'm keeping this principle very short. I want the message to be totally clear: *You cannot quit!*

Your *will* must meet, even exceed, the challenge at hand. Never forget your personal *why*. It is the fuel—and determines the strength—of your will. If you forget *why* something is important, you lose the courage it takes to tackle the task.

You are the one who determines how much wealth to attain. Some desire to be extremely rich, while others would like to live a simpler, more secure life. Try to answer the age-old question: "When is enough enough?" I believe that enough becomes enough when you have reached a level of wealth that allows you to live the lifestyle you desire, without having dependencies on others or social (welfare) programs to take care of you. As people pursue wealth, many find that the material items they once longed for to distinguish themselves as "arrived" aren't as important as they once seemed to be. As more people continue to understand and practice the principles of living in a sustainable wealthy lifestyle, laying aside most of their material desires, they may find they have both the time and capacity to more fully understand complexities in health, food, and energy—and move away from the processed, detached world we too often inhabit today.

Success is your only option! You owe it to yourself and to those you love. No matter what age you are today, retirement is something you want to get right with the first "shot." Pull the string back, find your anchor point, aim at the target and let your arrow fly.

To shift the metaphor, which one wins? The angel or the devil—the good assets or the bad assets?

*The one you feed the most!*

Good luck. I know you can make it happen! Please share your thoughts and experiences with me. I'm pulling for you.

# Principle 17

## Always Remember the *Why*

### Principles in Action

**Sample: Why will you reach your goals?**

*Because we have no other choice. It's great to live in financial freedom rather than live in fear like we used to. Nobody is going to be there to bail us out. It's time for us to realize this and build a strong, financially secure family for generations to come.*

*Because I want to be able to say, "My word is good!" and my kids will believe it!*

**Why will *you* reach your goals?**

# Glossary

**401(k):** Type of employer-sponsored, defined-contribution retirement plan under section 401(k) of the Internal Revenue Code in the United States, as well as some other countries. This plan allows a worker to save for retirement while deferring income taxes on the saved money and earnings until withdrawal. Most commonly, the employee can select from a number of investment options, usually an assortment of mutual fund type accounts.

**403(b):** Tax-advantaged retirement savings plan available in the United States for public education organizations, for some non-profit employers (such as hospitals and school systems) and for self-employed ministers. It has tax treatment and investment structure similar to a 401(k) plan.

**457:** Type of tax-advantaged, defined-contribution retirement plan available for governmental and certain non-governmental employers in the United States. The employer provides the plan, and the employee defers compensation into it on a pre-tax basis. For the most part the plan operates similarly to a 401(k) or 403(b).

**529 plan:** Tax-advantaged investment vehicle designed to encourage saving for future higher-education expenses of a designated beneficiary, usually a son/daughter or grandchild.

**Accumulation:** Gathering or amassment of objects of value, the increase of wealth or the creation of wealth.

**Accumulation goal:** Process of contributing cash to invest in securities over a period of time in order to build a portfolio of desired value.

**Active investing:** Investment strategy involving ongoing buying and selling actions by an investor. Active investors purchase investments and continuously monitor their activity as they seek to exploit profitable conditions.

**Aggressive investing:** High-risk method of portfolio management and asset allocation that attempts to achieve maximum return.

**Amortization:** Paying off of debt in regular installments over a period of time—also known as the reduction of the value of an asset by prorating its cost over a period of years.

**Anchor point:** In *Wealth Is a Choice* this term is used synonymously with financial values to describe having a basis for making consistent financial decisions. Generally an anchor point is determined by the specific goal the decision affects. An anchor point can be as simple as *Does this decision take me closer to or farther from my goal?*

**Annuity:** Income from capital investment paid in a series of regular payments (for example, "His retirement fund was set up to be paid as an annuity").

**Appreciating asset:** One that has a higher market value than its book value or taxable value and which, upon its sale, will generate a capital gain.

**Appreciation:** Increase in value.

**Asset:** Useful or valuable quality.

**Asset allocation:** Investment strategy that aims to balance risk and reward by apportioning a portfolio's assets according to an individual's goals, risk tolerance and investment horizon.

**Asset classes:** Various investment vehicles, such as cash, money markets, bonds, stocks, real estate, foreign currency, natural resources, precious metals, REITs (real estate investment trusts), international investments and life settlements. A further breakdown of equity investments into additional asset classes can be done by size (large-cap, mid-cap and small-cap) or by style (growth, blend and value).

**Assisted living:** Usually refers to a non-institutionalized facility used by people who are not able to live on their own but who do not yet need the level of continuous care that a nursing home offers. Assisted-living arrangements are for people who are partly independent but need some help in various areas, such as bathing, cooking, medications, laundry and lawn care.

**Automatic investment:** See "Systematic saving."

**Bad asset:** In *Wealth Is a Choice* the phrase "bad asset" is not suggesting that all the assets listed are "bad" to own, especially in the case of a personal residence. Rather it is to make a distinction that there are assets where one has no intention of converting their value into income, especially assets that depreciate in value, such as retail-product purchases.

**Balance sheet:** Record of the financial situation of an institution, organization or even household on a particular date by listing its assets and the claims against those assets.

**Balanced budget:** Current expenditures equal current revenues.

**Bankruptcy:** Legally declared inability (or impairment of ability) of an individual or organization to pay its creditors, who may file a bankruptcy petition against a debtor in an effort to recoup a portion of what they are owed.

**Basis points:** Unit equal to 1/100th of a percentage point. It is frequently used to express percentage-point changes less than 1. It avoids ambiguity between relative and absolute discussions about rates. For example, a "1 percent increase" in a 10 percent interest rate could mean an increase from 10 percent to 10.1 percent or from 10 percent to 11 percent. A 100 basis-point increase would indicate it changed by a full 1 percent to 11 percent (following the previous example).

**Bear market:** Characterized by falling prices for securities on the stock exchanges.

**Bond fund:** Mutual fund (see mutual fund definition) invested in corporate, municipal or U.S. government debt obligations—or some combination thereof.

**Bonds:** Certificates of debt (usually interest-bearing or discounted) issued by a government or corporation in order to raise money. The issuer is required to pay a fixed sum annually until maturity, then a fixed sum to repay the principal.

**Bonus:** Additional payment (or other remuneration) to employees as a means of increasing work-related performance.

**Bottleneck:** Impediment that creates an obstruction.

**Broker:** Someone who acts as a buyer or seller in a transaction—or is responsible to mediate between a buyer and seller. A sales person working for a securities or commodity brokerage firm is commonly called a "broker."

**Brokerage account:** Account opened with a firm for the purpose of purchasing, selling and holding a portfolio of securities.

**Budget:** For planning purposes, a sum of money allocated for particular purposes.

**Bull market:** Characterized by rising prices for securities on the stock exchanges.

**Burn rate:** Timetable at which a new company uses up its venture capital to finance overhead before generating positive cash flow from operations (in other words, a measure of negative cash flow).

**Business cycle:** Refers to the fluctuations of economic activity regarding its long-term-growth trend. The cycle involves shifts over time between periods of relatively rapid growth of output (recovery and prosperity), and periods of relative stagnation or decline (contraction or recession). The five stages are growth, peak, contraction, trough and recovery. Despite being named cycles, these fluctuations in economic growth and decline do not follow a purely mechanical or predictable periodic pattern.

**Capital:** Assets available for use in the production of further assets.

**Capital appreciation:** Rise in the market price of an asset.

**Capital gains:** Profits realized on the sale of an asset that was purchased at a lower price. The most common capital gains are realized from the sale of stocks, bonds, precious metals and property.

**Capital-gains tax:** Levy charged on the capital gains of an asset. Generally when the asset is sold and not sheltered in a 401(k), IRA, Roth IRA or other tax-deferred vehicle, the gains realized by the sale are taxed at varying rates. When applicable, the tax is owed regardless if the asset is sold for liquidation and spending purposes—or if the asset is sold and reinvested into another asset.

**Cash flow:** Amount of money being received and spent by a business (or personal finances) during a defined period of time, sometimes tied to a specific project. Free and clear cash flow refers to leftover revenues after all expenses are paid.

**Cash-flow analysis:** Estimate of the timing and amounts of cash inflows and outflows over a specific period (usually one year). A cash-flow analysis shows if a firm needs to borrow, how much, when and how it will repay the loan. Also called cash-flow budget or cash-flow projection.

**Cash reserve:** Account set aside by an individual or business to meet unexpected costs that may arise in the future, as well as the future costs of upkeep. Also known as a rainy-day fund. In most cases, the fund is simply a savings account or another highly liquid asset, as it is impossible (by definition) to predict when an unexpected cost may arise. However, if the fund is set up to meet the costs of scheduled upgrades, less-liquid assets may be used.

**Certificate of deposit (CD):** Debt instrument issued by a bank. Usually pays interest.

**Charitable giving:** Gift made by an individual or an organization to a nonprofit organization, charity, religious entity or private foundation. Charitable donations are commonly in the form of cash but can also take the form of real estate, motor vehicles, appreciated securities, clothing, and other assets or services.

**Charitable remainder trust (CRT):** Tax-exempt irrevocable trust commonly used in an estate plan to generate income and also create significant tax advantages. Generally, appreciated assets are placed within a charitable trust, with a percentage of the income generated by the trust's investments paid out to the donor and at his or her death the remainder paid out to designated charities.

**Clarifying questions:** To make clear and (more) comprehensible.

**Commercial (real estate) property:** Property used solely for business purposes.

**Commission-based advisor:** Compensation for services rendered based on a percentage of an amount received or collected or agreed to be paid (as distinguished from a salary). The advisor is generally paid by the product company for selling the company's product rather than collecting a fee directly from the client.

**Commodity:** Anything for which there is a demand but which is supplied without qualitative differentiation across a market. In other words, copper is copper. Rice is rice. Stereos, on the other hand, come in many varieties of quality. And the better a stereo is, the more it will cost. The price of copper, however, is universal and fluctuates daily based on global supply and demand.

**Compound interest:** Accrued capital (interest) calculated on both the principal and the additional money (interest) that has accumulated over time. Compare with simple interest, which is an increase to the original investment, and not on its earnings.

**Conservative:** Investment strategy that seeks to minimize risk and preserve a portfolio's value, with a high return having less importance than preservation of the capital itself.

**Consolidate:** Bring together into a single whole or system.

**Consumer debt:** Borrowings (debt) which is used to fund consumption rather than investment. The most common type of consumer debt is held on credit cards.

**Contractual obligation:** Legal responsibility to meet the terms of a contract. If the requirements are not met, there is often recourse for the other party to the contract.

**Conventional:** Conforming to accepted standards.

**Cost basis:** Original price of property adjusted for various factors, including depreciation. When property is sold, the difference between the sale price and the basis is the income or loss reported on U.S. tax returns.

**Cost of investment:** See "Cost basis."

**Credit card:** Actual card (usually plastic) that assures a seller that the person using it has a satisfactory credit rating and that the card owner will see to it that the seller receives payment for the merchandise delivered.

**Credit card balance:** Unfortunately, many credit card purchases are not paid off immediately, which gives the account a carry-over amount. Carrying a balance is something credit card companies prefer most people do, as the companies make a tidy profit on the interest charged to the account.

**Credit limit:** Maximum amount of money that a financial institution or other lender will extend to a debtor for a particular purpose (for example, the maximum that a credit card company will allow a card holder to borrow at any given point on a specific card).

**Creditor:** Person to whom money is owed by a debtor—someone to whom an obligation exists.

**Credit score:** Numerical expression based on a statistical analysis of a person's credit files—in order to represent the creditworthiness of that person, which is the perceived likelihood that the person will pay debts in a timely manner. The higher the score the better, ideally reaching the high 700s and into the 800s.

**Crutch:** Something that one depends on for support. In *Wealth Is a Choice* it is discussed in terms of the reality of having something that we are dependent on for financial support. Sometimes the dependency is well-founded, forming an interdependent relationship, and sometimes it is not, thereby potentially contributing to financial failure. A 401(k) is an example of a healthy crutch where one is applying a strategic plan to help accomplish independence goals for retirement. Expecting to win the lottery and counting on Dad and Mom's inheritance would be examples of unhealthy crutches, especially if the expectations are so great that they cause one to neglect fiscal responsibility.

**Crutch management:** Described in *Wealth Is a Choice* as a process of identifying the strategies one is using to reach financial independence, then brainstorming ways of further insulating the possibility of reaching financial independence by finding alternatives other than the core strategies—giving credence to the phrase "Don't put all your eggs in one basket."

**Debt:** State of owing something (especially money) or having an obligation (legal and/or moral) to pay someone back.

**Debt consolidation:** Action of combining several loans or liabilities into one loan. Stated another way, the process of taking out a new loan to pay off a number of other debts. Most people who consolidate their debt are usually doing so in order to attain a lower interest rate—or for the simplicity of a single loan. Also known as a "consolidation loan."

**Debtor:** Person who owes a creditor. Someone who has the obligation of paying a debt.

**Debt service:** Amount of money required to be paid over a given period for the repayment of outstanding financial obligation (debt).

**Debt-service cost:** Cash required over a given period for the repayment of interest and principal on an outstanding financial obligation (debt). Monthly mortgage payments are a good example of debt service.

**Deductible:** Amount that can be subtracted or deducted (especially for the purpose of calculating income tax).

**Deduction:** Act of subtracting (removing a part from the whole). Such as with computing tax owed on a tax return, the more deductions one qualifies for, generally the less in total taxes one will be required to pay.

**Dependent:** Person who relies on another person for support.

**Depreciating asset:** Tending to decrease or cause a decrease in value to the asset, usually over a period of time.

**Derivatives:** Contract whose value is derived from that of other quantities.

**Disability:** Condition of being unable to perform as a consequence of a lack of physical or mental fitness or capability.

**Distribution:** Act of disbursing, spreading or apportioning—such as a company disbursing profits in the form of dividends to the shareholders of the company.

**Diversified:** Having varied forms or components—or having increased variety.

**Dividend:** Payment made by a corporation to its shareholder members. When a corporation earns a profit or surplus, that money can be put to two uses: It can either be reinvested in the business (called retained earnings), or it can be paid to the shareholders as a dividend.

**Dollar cost averaging:** Technique of buying a fixed dollar amount of a particular investment on a regular schedule, regardless of the share price. More shares are purchased when prices are low, and fewer shares are bought when prices are high.

**Dow Jones Industrial Average:** Also called the DJIA, Dow 30, or (informally) the Dow Jones or The Dow, it is one of several stock market indices created by 19th-century Wall Street Journal editor and Dow Jones & Company co-founder Charles Dow (along with Edward Jones and Charles Bergstresser). Dow compiled the index as a way to gauge the performance of the industrial component of U.S. stock markets. It is the oldest continuing U.S. market index, aside from the Dow Jones Transportation Average, which Dow also created. Today, the average consists of 30 of the largest and most widely held public companies in the United States. The "industrial" portion of the name is largely historical; many of the 30 modern companies have little to do with heavy industry.

**Earned income:** Income derived from active participation in a trade or business, including wages, salary, tips, commissions and bonuses.

**Emerging markets:** Term used to describe a nation's social or business activity in the process of industrialization. The term "rapidly growing economy" is now being used to denote emerging markets. The opposite end of the spectrum is "developed markets," such as most of North America, Europe, Australia and Japan.

**Entrepreneur/small-business startup:** Person who has possession over a new enterprise or venture and assumes full accountability for both inherent risks and outcome.

**Equity:** Difference between the market value of a property and the claims held against it. For example, a house worth $500,000 and a mortgage of $300,000 have equity of $200,000. Equity also is used as a term to indicate that ownership of an asset, such as owning stock in a company, connotes having equity in that company.

**Equity partner:** Individual or entity in a partnership that is a part owner of the business and is entitled to a proportionate share of the distributable profits of the partnership.

**Estate strategy:** Ideas generally discussed during an estate planning meeting. Common estate strategies are often devised to reduce taxes, to control the passing of an estate to desired heirs, and to avoid costs associated with disability or dying. Common vehicles used in estate strategies are wills, trusts, powers of attorney, patient advocates, guardianship documents and sometimes life insurance policies.

**Estate tax:** Levy issued on the total material worth/wealth of a deceased person.

**Federal tax:** Levies issued by the U.S. Internal Revenue Service (IRS) on the annual earnings of individuals, corporations, trusts and other legal entities.

**Fee-based:** Investment account in which a set percentage of a client's assets are paid to the advisor as compensation. It also can be used to describe an advisor who does not earn a commission on selling a product but charges a fee for time spent on consultation.

**Financial defense:** Used in *Wealth Is a Choice* to describe a method of increasing cash flow by reducing overhead and investing available income for wealth accumulation and/or to pay down debt—as opposed to financial offense, which is to improve cash flow by increasing income (although income also can be increased through defense when a good investment is made that creates additional income). A strong defense also would reinvest that new income into other investments.

**Financial independence:** Mathematically, financial independence is a state of wealth in which a financial entity (such as an individual, family or business) can self-finance, usually because it possesses assets that either (a) generate a stream of income that sufficiently satiates the entity's consumption needs and/or (b) are sufficiently large that they cannot be entirely depleted by future consumption. Because consumption needs are subjective and vary greatly between entities, the level of income-generating assets required for financial independence also will vary accordingly. Further, because satiation is another subjective metric, some entities may include only their basic survival needs in that definition, while others also may include less-important needs—and possibly some of their wants (or even all of their wants).

**Financial Industry Regulatory Authority (FINRA):** Self-regulatory organization under the Securities & Exchange Act of 1934, successor to the National Association of Securities Dealers, Inc. (NASD). FINRA is responsible for the regulatory oversight of all securities firms that do business with the public; for professional training, testing and licensing of registered persons; for arbitration and mediation; and for market regulation by contract for much of the financial services industry involved with the sale of stocks and other securities.

**Financial offense:** Method of increasing cash flow by increasing income—as opposed to financial defense, which focuses on increasing cash flow by reducing overhead and investing for the future and/or paying down debt. In *Wealth Is a Choice* it is generally recommended that people first become proficient at financial defense before they spend time specifically trying to increase income. It is believed that if you are good at defense, then you can accumulate wealth much faster as your income increases. However, if you have poor defense, then even when personal income increases, the underlying bad habits will still exist and block opportunities for wealth accumulation.

**Financial planning:** Comprehensive evaluation of an investor's current and future financial state by using currently known variables to predict future cash flows, asset values and withdrawal plans.

**Financial services:** Industry that encompasses a broad range of organizations that deal with the management of money. Among these organizations are banks, credit card companies, insurance companies, consumer finance companies, stock brokerages, investment funds and some government-sponsored enterprises.

**Financial values:** In *Wealth Is a Choice* values are used synonymously with anchor points and describe the importance of having a baseline, foundational approach for making consistent financial decisions. Also see "Values."

**Financing:** Act of providing funds for business activities, making purchases or investing. Banks are in the business of providing money, usually through loans, as a catalyst for businesses, consumers and investors to help them reach their goals.

**Fiscal responsibility:** Most commonly associated with having a balanced budget (spending within one's means) so that individuals are making financial decisions that are in the best interests (both short and long term) for themselves or those they represent.

**Fixed annuities:** Insurance contract in which the insurance company makes fixed dollar payments to an annuitant (receiver of an annuity). Usually guaranteed for at least as long as the annuitant is alive.

**Fixed expense:** Meant to describe in *Wealth Is a Choice* those costs that are mandatory, necessary or difficult to adjust easily.

**Fixed overhead:** Cost that remains constant, regardless of any change in a company's activity. In *Wealth Is a Choice* the term is used almost interchangeably with fixed expense; however, it generally describes a grouping of expenses rather than just a single item.

**Fixed-rate mortgage:** Mortgage that has a set interest rate for the entire term of the loan. The distinguishing factor of a fixed-rate mortgage is that the interest rate over every time period of the mortgage is known at the time the mortgage is originated. The benefit of a fixed-rate mortgage is that the homeowner will not have to contend with varying loan-payment amounts that fluctuate with interest-rate movements.

**Free cash flow (FCF):** Cash flow available for distribution among all the security holders of a company. Or, with personal finances, it is the cash flow from revenues (income) available after all expenses and savings have been accounted for.

**Funding:** Financial resources that make a project or projects feasible.

**Futures contract:** Standardized and legal agreement to buy or sell a certain underlying instrument at a certain date in the future—at a specified price.

**Gain:** Rise in rate or price.

**Game plan:** Carefully thought-out strategy for achieving an objective.

**Gift annuity:** Arrangement under which a qualified charitable organization pays a fixed-sum annuity over the life of one or two persons in exchange for an irrevocable transfer of cash or property.

**Good assets:** In *Wealth Is a Choice* the phrase "good asset" is not meant to imply that all the assets listed are good. It is a term being used to indicate that some assets are purchased with the intent of growing their value and creating income.

**Goods:** In economics, any objects (assets) or services that increase utility, directly or indirectly, such as inventory or promotional items.

**Government bond:** Financial instrument that is an IOU on the U.S. Treasury, considered the safest security in the investment world.

**Gross:** Entire amount of income before any deductions are made.

**Habit:** Pattern of behavior acquired through frequent repetition. In *Wealth Is a Choice* having good financial behaviors are exemplified as paramount to achieving financial independence.

**Hedge fund:** Flexible investment company for a small number of large investors (usually the minimum investment is $1 million). Can use high-risk techniques (not allowed for mutual funds), such as short-selling and heavy leveraging.

**High-yield bond (junk bond):** Debt security in which the authorized issuer owes the holder a debt and is obliged to repay the principal and interest at a later date. High-yield or junk indicates the quality of the debt is lower than normal—and there is a higher risk of default or other adverse results. Usually, because of the increased risk, these bonds pay a higher yield than safer bonds would.

**Home-equity loan:** Borrowings (debt) secured by equity value in the borrower's residence.

**Hot investment tip:** The word "hot" implies that you need to act fast in order to benefit from the tip—before everyone else knows about it and the investment loses its advantage. Many investors recommend steering clear of so-called hot tips, voicing the old adage, "If it sounds too good to be true, it probably is." One also must be careful that the tip is not of non-public information and therefore illegal if acted upon.

**Hot issue:** Stock or similar offering that sells in excess of the public price on the first day of trading.

**Immediate annuity:** Contract purchased that has a specified payment plan that starts right away.

**Income:** Financial gain (earned or unearned) that accrues over a given period of time.

**Income-tax deduction:** Fixed amount or percentage permitted by taxation authorities that a taxpayer can lawfully subtract from his or her adjusted gross income to arrive at the taxable income. Deductions typically include allowances for home-mortgage payment, home-repair expenses, and some job-related expenses.

**Index:** Single number calculated from a set of prices or quantities. Examples are the price index, a quantity index (such as real GDP), and a market performance index (such as a labor market index/job index or a stock market index). Values of the index in successive periods (days, years, etc.) summarize level of the activity over time or across economic units (regions, countries, etc.). Some investment funds (index funds) manage their portfolio so that their performance mirrors the performance of a stock market index or a segment of the stock market.

**Index annuities:** Special class of annuities (see annuity above) that yield returns on contributions based on a specified equity-based index. These annuities can be purchased from an insurance company and, similar to other types of annuities, the terms and conditions associated with payouts will depend on what is stated in the original annuity contract.

**Index fund:** Collective investment scheme that aims to replicate the movements of an index of a specific financial market—or a set of rules of ownership that are held constant, regardless of market conditions. Tracking can be achieved by trying to hold all of the securities in the index in the same proportions as the index. The lack of active management (stock picking and market timing) usually gives the advantage of lower fees and lower taxes in taxable accounts.

**Individual retirement account (IRA):** Investing tool used by individuals to earn and earmark funds for retirement savings. There are several types of IRAs: traditional IRA, Roth IRA, SIMPLE IRA and SEP IRA.

**Inflation:** General and progressive increase in prices. When forecasting for future income needs it is very important to include a rise of cost due to inflation. If this is not done properly, it is possible to have dramatic shortages of resources as the cost of goods exceeds the anticipated wealth necessary to retire. It is common for retirees who experience this to re-enter the work force in order to make up for the shortage of income.

**Inheritance:** That which is passed on to a family member or members. A title or property or estate that passes by law to the heir on the death of the owner.

**Initial public offering (IPO):** Corporation's first issue of stock being sold to the public.

**Interest:** Fixed charge for borrowing money. Usually a percentage of the amount borrowed.

**Interest charge:** Amount reported by a company or individual as an expense for borrowed money.

**Interest-only loan:** Borrowing arrangement in which periodic installments cover the interest (see interest above) amount and do not reduce the outstanding principal, which is paid in lump sum at the end of the loan period.

**Interest-only mortgage:** Type of mortgage (see mortgage below) in which the mortgagor is required only to pay off the interest that arises from the principal that is borrowed. Because just the interest is being paid off, the interest payments remain fairly constant throughout the term of the mortgage. However, interest-only mortgages do not last indefinitely, meaning that the mortgagor will need to pay off the principal of the loan eventually.

**Interest payment:** Contractual debt disbursement based on the coupon rate of interest and the principal amount.

**Interest rate:** Monthly effective rate paid (or received, if one is a creditor) on borrowed money. Expressed as a percentage of the sum borrowed.

**Internal rate of return (IRR):** Discount value (rate) often used in capital budgeting that makes the net present value of all cash flows from a particular project equal to zero. Generally speaking, the higher a project's internal rate of return, the more desirable it is to undertake the project. As such, IRR can be used to rank several prospective projects a firm is considering. Assuming all other factors are equal among the various projects, the project with the highest IRR would probably be considered the best and would be pursued first.

**Invest:** To create more money through the use of capital.

**Investment:** Laying out money or capital with the expectation of profit.

**Investment allocation:** Process of dividing portfolio of assets among different kinds of assets, such as stocks, bonds, real estate and cash, in order to optimize the risk/reward tradeoff based on an individual's or institution's specific situation and goals. A key concept in financial planning and money management.

**Investment asset:** Usually purchased or, equivalently, a deposit is made in a bank in hopes of getting a future return or interest from it.

**Investment real estate:** Investment asset specifically in property and/or structures, with the intent of realizing income and/or appreciation in value. The buyer of such real estate, however (at least for the time being), generally has no intention of living in the dwelling that is purchased.

**Investment strategies:** Investor's plan of attack to guide investing decisions based on individual goals, risk tolerance and future needs for capital.

**Irrevocable life insurance trust (ILIT):** Estate planning document set up for the purpose of owning a survivor's aid (life insurance) policy. If the insured is the owner of the policy, the proceeds of the policy will be subject to estate taxes when he or she dies. But if he or she transfers ownership to an ILIT, under current tax law the proceeds will be completely free of estate taxes.

**Joint finances:** In general, a legal term describing an arrangement in which two or more parties act together.

**KISS (Keep it simple, Stupid):** Philosophy in the world of finances that is easier to espouse than to actualize.

**Large cap:** Shortened version of "large market capitalization." Market capitalization is calculated by multiplying the number of a company's shares outstanding by its stock price per share. The expression "large cap" is used by the investment community as an indicator of a company's size. For example, a large-cap stock would be from a company with a market-capitalization dollar value of more than $10 billion.

**Large-cap growth:** When an investment is termed a "growth" investment, it is believed that it will appreciate in value and yield a high return on equity. Analysts determine whether or not an investment should be considered "growth" by evaluating the projected earnings and other historical growth measures.

**Large-cap value:** When an investment is termed a "value" investment, it is perceived to be an undervalued stock and has a smaller market capitalization than would otherwise be the case. Its price-to-book ratio is also lower, and thus it is closer to the value end of the growth/value spectrum. See also "Value fund."

**Legacy:** Gift of personal property by will.

**Lender:** Someone who loans money or provides credit in business matters.

**Leverage:** Investing with borrowed money as a way to amplify potential gains (at the risk of greater losses).

**Life expectancy:** Age to which a person is expected to live based on gender, nation where living, cultural factors, etc.

**Life insurance:** Financial settlement paid to named beneficiaries when the insured person dies. Also sometimes known as survivors' aid.

**Limited liability company (LLC):** Corporate structure whereby the shareholders of a company have a limited liability for the company's actions. An LLC is in essence a hybrid between a partnership and a corporation.

**Line 39:** Federal tax return Line 39 where total itemized (or standard) deductions are listed. Generally, the practice of increasing deductions lowers taxes owed.

**Line of credit:** Agreement that allows a borrower to take advances, during a defined period, up to a preset "line limit" and repay the advances at the borrower's discretion (with the exception that the entire principal balance plus accrued interest is due on the maturity date).

**Liquidate:** Convert into cash.

**Liquidation:** Process by which a company (or part of a company) is brought to an end, and the assets and property of the company are redistributed.

**Liquidity:** Asset's ability to be easily converted through an act of buying or selling without causing a significant movement in the price—and with minimum loss of value.

**Load:** Percentage charge levied on a purchase or sale of shares. A load is a type of commission. Depending on the type of a load a mutual fund exhibits, charges may be incurred at time of purchase, time of sale or a combination of both.

**Long-term-care (LTC) insurance:** Product that helps insure that the costs of an individual's nursing needs are met over a period of years beyond a predetermined period. Long-term care insurance handles care generally not covered by health insurance, Medicare or Medicaid.

**Long-term goals:** Projected state of affairs a person or system plans or intends to achieve or bring about. Unlike short-term goals, these objectives tend to have timelines measured in years (similar to LTC above).

**Margin account:** Collateral that the holder of a position in securities, options or futures contracts has to deposit in order to cover the credit risk of his or her counterpart (usually the brokerage firm).

**Market decline:** When a security's price falls in value over a given trading day and subsequently closes at a lower value than its opening price. A decline can happen for any number of reasons, including a reduction in the firm's intrinsic value or as a result of the security's price dropping below its support level.

**Maturity:** Final payment date of a loan or other financial instrument, at which point all remaining interest and principal are due to be paid.

**Mentor:** Wise and trusted counselor or teacher.

**Mid-cap:** Company with a market capitalization (total value of a company's shared outstanding multiplied by current market price of the stock) between $2 billion and $10 billion.

**Milestone:** Significant event in life (or in a project). In *Wealth Is a Choice* it is discussed of the importance in recognizing the accomplishment of achievements along the path to financial independence. For some people, being wealthy may appear to be a far distant mountain, too difficult to climb. Finding fulfillment in reaching milestones along the way is an excellent strategy to staying focused. It may even provide the motivation necessary to actually reaching the destination, rather than giving up early.

**Monetary value:** Worth of real goods, measured or measurable in terms of their efficacy relative to their monetary equivalent.

**Monthly obligations:** Total of all expenses that one needs to pay every 30 days. It is important to calculate this number, as it helps identify how much money to pay out each month just to survive. Once one knows this number, one can more easily find ways of reducing expenses or increasing income to lessen the financial burden. Such obligations do not normally represent discretionary or "fun" expenses.

**Mortgage:** Conditional conveyance of property as security for the repayment of a loan.

**Mortgage payment:** Amount of principal and interest owed monthly to the lender as determined by the loan structure.

**Municipal fund:** Debt security issued by a state, municipality or county in order to finance its capital expenditures. Municipal bonds are exempt from federal taxes and from most state and local taxes, especially if one lives in the state where the bond is issued.

**Mutual fund:** A professionally managed firm of collective investments that collects money from many investors and puts it into stocks, bonds, short-term money market instruments and/or other securities.

**Nasdaq or NASDAQ (National Association of Securities Dealers Automated Quotation system):** American stock exchange. It is the largest electronic screen-based equity securities trading market in the United States. With approximately 3,200 companies, it lists more companies and has more trading volume per day than any other stock exchange in the world. It tends to have a preponderance of Internet- and technology-related stocks.

**Net:** Excess of revenues over outlays in a given period of time (including depreciation and other non-cash expenses).

**Net worth:** Amount by which a company's or an individual's assets exceed liabilities.

**No load:** Mutual fund (unit trust) that does not charge a sales commission (called load) when an investor buys its shares (units). It sells directly to the actual investor without involving a broker or dealer. Its net asset value (NAV), market price and offer prices are identical because there is no sales charge. Some no-load funds, however, levy an annual fee for advertising and marketing. Listing of a no-load fund's share (unit) price in the print media is denoted by the designation "NL."

**Operating expenses:** Essential things a company must pay for in order to stay in business.

**Options:** Financial instruments that convey the right, but not the obligation, to engage in a future transaction on some underlying security or in a futures contract.

**Overhead:** Ongoing operating costs of running a business.

**Overtime:** Work done in addition to regular working hours, usually in excess of 40 hours per week.

**Passive investing:** Investment strategy involving limited ongoing buying and selling actions. Passive investors tend to purchase investments with the intention of long-term appreciation and limited maintenance.

**Patient advocate:** Person designated to speak on behalf a resident of a hospital or nursing home in order to protect his or her rights and help the individual obtain needed information and services. The role of patient advocate is frequently assumed by nurses, social workers and other healthcare providers.

**Pension:** Regular payment to a person that is intended to allow the individual to subsist without working for pay.

**Personal loan:** Temporary transfer of funds that establishes consumer credit that is granted for personal use. Usually unsecured and based on the borrower's integrity and ability to pay.

**Planned giving:** Substantial gift given as a bequest or charitable annuity, which is often planned by the donor to be disbursed after his or her death.

**Portfolio:** List of the financial assets held by an individual, bank or other financial institution.

**Precious metals:** Rare metallic chemical element of high economic value. The best-known precious metals are gold and silver. Other precious metals include the platinum group of metals: ruthenium, rhodium, palladium, osmium, iridium and platinum.

**Pre-tax savings retirement plans:** Generally, work-related retirement savings platforms, such as 403(b), 401(k) and 457 plans where the employer takes savings out of the employee's paycheck before taxes are calculated. This then reduces take-home pay, which in turn reduces taxable income.

**Principal:** Original amount of a debt or investment on which interest is calculated.

**Principal balance:** In regards to a mortgage or other debt instrument, it is the amount due and owing to satisfy the payoff of the underlying obligation.

**Principals:** Major parties to a financial transaction at a stock exchange; they buy and sell for their own accounts.

**Private equity funds:** Ownership (equity) capital that is made available to companies or investors but not quoted on a stock market. The funds raised through private equity can be used to develop new products and technologies, to expand working capital, to make acquisitions and/or to strengthen a company's balance sheet.

**Private investment:** Situation in which an investor (either individual or institutional) purchases all of the shares (or a fraction thereof) in a non-public firm. Private purchases do not involve the use of capital markets and will likely require the skills of a broker.

**Probate:** Venue where the act of proving that an instrument purporting to be a will was signed and executed in accord with legal requirements.

**Profit:** Excess of revenues over outlays in a given period of time (including depreciation and other non-cash expenses).

**Prospectus:** Formal written offer to sell securities, filed with the U.S. Securities & Exchange Commission (SEC), that sets forth a plan for a (proposed) business enterprise: "A prospectus should contain the facts that an investor needs to make an informed decision."

**Purchasing power:** Amount of value of a good/service compared with the amount paid. As legendary economist Adam Smith noted, having money gives one the ability to "command" others' labor, so purchasing power is, to a certain degree, power over other people—to the extent that they are willing to trade their labor or goods for money.

**Rate of return (ROR):** Ratio of money gained or lost on an investment relative to the amount of money invested. Sometimes it also is referred to as return on investment (ROI).

**Real estate:** Property consisting of structures (houses, commercial buildings, etc.) and land.

**Real estate investment trust (REIT):** Tax designation for a corporation investing in structures and land that reduces or eliminates corporate income taxes. In return, REITs are required to distribute 90 percent of their income, which may be taxable in the hands of the investors. The REIT structure was designed to provide a structure for investment in real estate in similar fashion to the way mutual funds provide for investment in stocks.

**Reallocate:** Distribute or apportion anew.

**Recession:** Decline in the overall health of an economy. A widespread drop in the gross domestic product (GDP), employment and trade lasting from six months to a year.

**Refinance:** Renew the financing of.

**Regulation T (Reg T):** Governs the extension of credit by securities brokers and dealers in the United States. Its best-known function is the control of margin requirements for stocks bought on margin.

**Rental property:** Combination of land/structure bought or developed to earn income through renting, leasing or price appreciation. Income property can be residential or commercial. Residential income property is commonly referred to as "non-owner-occupied." A mortgage for a "non-owner-occupied" property may carry a higher interest rate than an "owner-occupied" mortgage, as it is viewed by lenders as a higher risk. It can be residential (meant for personal use) or commercial (intended for business purposes).

**Residential (real estate) property:** Land/structure used solely for private dwelling purposes.

**Retirement:** Withdrawal or departure from one's position or occupation.

**Retirement pension:** Periodic or lump-sum income received as a benefit when one stops working for pay.

**Revenue:** Income received from activities, usually from the sale of goods or for services rendered.

**Revenue source:** Identification of each individual income stream, rather than just looking at total income as one number.

**Rider:** Provision in an insurance policy that allows for changes to its terms and/or coverage.

**Roth IRA:** Named for its chief legislative sponsor, U.S. Senator William Roth of Delaware, a Roth IRA differs in several significant ways from other IRAs—primarily that the contributions are not tax-deductible and withdrawals are tax-free.

**Rule of 72:** Investing rule of thumb that explains how long it takes to double your savings, approximately, for a given savings rate. To use the rule: Start with the number 72. Divide by the rate of return you expect to earn. This is your investment horizon—or number of years you need to double your savings. For example, if the interest rate you earn is 7.2 percent, you would double your money in about 10 years.

**Salary:** System of financial compensation that remunerates an individual for services rendered.

**Sales tax:** Levy imposed by the government at the point of sale on retail goods and services. It is collected by the retailer and passed on to the government.

**S&P (Standard & Poor's) 500:** Index consisting of 500 stocks chosen for market size, liquidity and industry grouping, among other factors. The S&P 500 is designed to be a leading indicator of U.S. equities and is meant to reflect the risk/return characteristics of the large-cap universe.

**Savings:** Fund of money set aside as a reserve.

**Security:** Fungible, negotiable instrument representing financial value. Securities are broadly categorized into debt securities, such as banknotes, bonds and debentures and equity securities (for example, common stocks).

**SEP (simplified employee pension) plan:** Retirement plan adopted by business owners to provide retirement benefits for the business owners and their employees. There are no significant administration costs for self-employed person with no employees. If the self-employed person does have employees, all employees must receive the same benefits under the plan.

**Severance pay:** Compensation that an employer gives to someone who is about to lose his or her job—at either the employee's or employer's initiative.

**Share:** Unit of ownership interest in a corporation or financial asset. While owning shares in a business does not mean that the shareholder has direct control over the business's day-to-day operations, being a shareholder does entitle the possessor to an equal distribution in any profits, if any are declared in the form of dividends. While shares are often used to refer to the stock of a corporation, shares also can represent ownership of other classes of financial assets, such as mutual funds. The owners (individual or company) are called shareholders.

**Share class (mutual fund):** Each fund company establishes its own formula for how it will calculate whether an investor is entitled to receive a discount. For that reason, it is important to seek out the breakpoint information from your advisor or the fund itself. Generally, Class A shares impose a front-end sales load. They also tend to have a lower 12b-1 (internal expenses of the fund). Class B shares typically do not have a front-end sales load; instead many impose a contingent-deferred sales load (back-end fee) and have a higher internal operating expense than an A share. There are also other share classes with various fee structures.

**Short sale (short-selling):** Seller does not own the security that he or she is selling.

**Short-term bonds:** Refers to the length of time before a bond matures. The duration is generally described as short-term or intermediate-term (one to 10 years) and long-term (usually longer than 10 years).

**Short-term goals:** Expected accomplishment in a brief period of time, such as trying to get a bill paid in the next few days. The definition of a short-term goal need not relate to any specific length of time. In other words, one may achieve a short-term goal in a day, week, month, six months, etc.

**SIMPLE (savings incentive match plan for employees) plan:** Type of employer-provided retirement plan. Specifically, it is a type of individual retirement account that is set up to be an employer-provided plan. It is much like a 401(k) or 403(b), but it offers simpler and less costly administration rules.

**Small cap:** Refers to stocks with a relatively small market capitalization. The definition of small cap can vary among brokerages, but generally it is a company with a market capitalization between $300 million and $2 billion.

**Social Security:** Federally sponsored welfare program in the U.S. that began with President Franklin Roosevelt in the 1930s. Includes survivors insurance, unemployment insurance and old-age assistance.

**Speculative investment:** Stock with extremely high risk relative to potential return.

**Stock investment:** Type of security that signifies ownership in a corporation and represents a claim on part of the corporation's assets and earnings.

**Stock market:** Private or public economic setting for the trading of a company stock, as well as derivatives of a company stock, at an agreed price; these are securities listed on a stock exchange, as well as those traded only privately.

**Stock market volatility:** Standard deviation of the change in value of a financial instrument with a specific time horizon. The volatility concept is often used to quantify the risk of the instrument over that time period.

**Stock option (employee):** Financial instrument awarded by a company to its employees as a form of incentive compensation. Such instruments convey the right, but not the obligation, to engage in a future transaction on some underlying security. Usually they provide the employee the opportunity to buy company stock in the future at a predetermined price. If this price is lower than the market price when the waiting time has expired, then the option is "in the money" and can be financially rewarding for the employee.

**Stocks:** Capital raised by a corporation through the issuance of shares entitling holders to an ownership interest (equity).

**Strategy:** Systematic plan of action.

**Sub-account:** Term generally depicting individual investment options within a contract. For example, variable annuities usually have many investment choices for the owners to invest their money within the annuity itself. Investors generally design a portfolio of these investments that would be in line with their investment objectives.

**Surrender charge:** Fee levied, usually on a life insurance policyholder, upon cancellation of his or her life insurance policy. Other investments besides insurance policies also can have surrender charges (common in a B-share mutual fund).

**Systematic saving:** Regular method or strategy of accumulating money on a regular basis, such as an automatic bank draft from one's checking account into one's Roth IRA (or other investment) for a set dollar amount on a particular day each month.

**Target:** Goal intended to be attained (and which is believed to be attainable).

**Taxable:** Of goods or funds subject to levies by governmental entities.

**Taxable event:** Any event or transaction that results in creating a taxable liability. Common examples are investors selling securities and realizing a gain, withdrawing money from a regular IRA, and exercising options.

**Tax bracket:** Category of taxpayers based on the amount of their income.

**Tax credit:** Direct reduction in levy liability (not dependent on the taxpayer's tax bracket).

**Tax-deductible:** Deduction representing an expense incurred by a taxpayer. It is subtracted from gross income when the taxpayer computes his or her income taxes. As a result, the tax deduction will lower overall taxable income and the amount of tax paid. The exact amount of tax savings is dependent on the tax rate and can be complicated to determine.

**Tax-deferred:** Refers to investment earnings—such as interest, dividends or capital gains—that accumulate free from taxation until the investor withdraws and takes possession of them. The most common types of tax-deferred investments include those in individual retirement accounts (IRAs) and in deferred annuities.

**Taxes:** Charges or levies against a citizen's person, property or activity for the support of government at any/all levels.

**Tax harvesting:** Process of selling securities at a loss to offset a capital-gains liability. It is typically used to limit the realization of short-term capital gains, which are normally taxed at higher federal income-tax rates than long-term capital gains (also known as "tax-loss selling").

**Tax liability:** Total amount of money owed for an occurrence. For example, in preparing a tax return the total tax liability will be calculated in order to determine if one will receive a refund or if more taxes are still owed.

**Tax withholding:** Amount of money held back from a paycheck, usually by the employer who sends the payment to the government. The amount withheld is generally within reason to fully fund what the total tax liability would be by the end of the year. Some people prefer to have extra money withheld and call it "forced savings," as they receive a large refund. Others like to have the minimum withheld and would rather use that money for their benefit throughout the year.

**Ticker symbol:** Unique two- or three letter symbol assigned to each listed company by a stock exchange where its securities are traded. These symbols may be different from the symbols used in the stock tables of newspapers. Also called trading symbol.

**Ticket charge:** Also called "trade fee" (see below). An actual cost generally associated with purchasing a stock or mutual fund in a brokerage account. It is common for the charge to range from $10 to $25 per trade placed.

**Tipping:** Practice in which an insider or related party has access to trade based on relevant, non-public information obtained during the performance of an insider's duties at a corporation—or otherwise in breach of a fiduciary duty or other relationship of trust and confidence (or where the non-public information was misappropriated from the company).

**Tolerance zone:** Permissible difference. Allowing some freedom to move within limits. For example, a person might be willing to have their portfolio increase or decrease by 10 percent before they would consider making a change to their investments.

**Total return:** Combines the share-price appreciation and dividends paid to show the entire investment performance to the shareholder or investor.

**Trade fee:** Also called "ticket charge" (see above). An actual cost generally associated with purchasing a stock or mutual fund in a brokerage account. It is common for the charge to range from $10 to $25 per trade placed.

**Traditional IRA:** Individual retirement account held at a custodian institution, such as a bank or brokerage, and may be invested in anything that the custodian allows. Unlike the Roth IRA, the only criterion for being eligible to contribute to a traditional IRA is sufficient income to make the contribution. The traditional IRA also has more restrictions on withdrawals than a Roth IRA.

**Trust:** Arrangement whereby property is managed by one person (or persons or organizations) for the benefit of another. A trust is created by a "settler," who entrusts some or all of his or her property to people of his or her choice (the trustees). The trust is usually used for estate planning purposes to help avoid probate and/or provide for a greater amount of control over an estate after death than would a will.

**Trusted advisor:** Person or company responsible for making investments on behalf of, and/or providing advice to, investors.

**Vacation rental by owner (VRBO):** Term used to describe a leisure-time home that the owner is managing directly, rather than using the services of a management company or real estate broker. The landowner often does this to create an income stream or to help offset the expense of owning the property. These properties can usually be found by consumers online or advertised in related publications.

**Value fund:** Mutual fund (see also mutual fund) that primarily holds value stocks, also defined as stocks deemed to be undervalued in price. See also "Large-cap value."

**Values:** Values are usually associated directly with moral or ethical standard, which is not the primary thrust of this book. In *Wealth Is a Choice* values are used to describe an "anchor point" as a method of establishing a strong basis from which one makes consistent financial decisions. Also see "Financial values."

**Variable annuity:** Investment that pays amounts that vary according to the performance of a specified set of investments, typically bond and equity investments.

**Variable expense/overhead:** Cost that changes in proportion to a change in a company's activity or business.

**Venture capitalist:** Speculator who makes money available for innovative projects (especially in high technology).

**Visionary goals:** Objectives that are not necessarily perfectly clear but that represent the types of things a person would like to have attained in the future—or have the ability to do in the future. They can become the framework for other more tangible short-term goals.

**Wealth accumulation:** Process of building one's personal material goods and finances. A common example would be saving money into a 401(k) in an effort to increase the account value, thereby also increasing personal net worth.

**Wealth management:** Professional service that is a combination of financial/investment advice, accounting/tax services and legal/estate planning—all for a fee.

**Wealthy:** Being rich or affluent. Having a plentiful supply of material goods and money.

**Will:** Legal document declaring a person's wishes regarding the disposal of his or her property upon that individual's death.

**Windfall:** Sudden occurrence that potentially brings good fortune (as a quickly revealed opportunity to receive and/or make money).

**Yield:** Quantity of something (as a commodity) that is created (usually within a given period of time).

# INDEX

## NUMBERS

**401(k):** 36, 37, 55, 57, 59, 61, 62, 65, 79, 99, 104, 135, 144, 148, 164, 167, 172, 175, 176, 182, 187, 193, 196, 198, 199, 231, 233, 234, 238, 247, 267, 270, 272, 282, 285, 289

**403(b):** 118, 136, 164, 176, 187, 196, 197, 198, 267, 282, 285

**457:** 164, 267

**529 plan:** 193, 250, 267

## A

**Accumulation:** 17, 20, 22, 30, 31, 72, 73, 95, 172, 197, 199, 200, 201, 202, 210, 217, 234, 235, 247, 256, 258, 274, 275, 289

**Accumulation goal:** 267

**Active investing:** 166, 180, 267

**Aggressive investing:** 166, 169, 268

**Amortization:** 268

**Anchor point:** 26, 27, 28, 264, 268, 288

**Annuity:** 199, 248, 268

**Appreciating asset:** 73, 87, 99, 193, 195, 196, 197, 198, 199, 200, 201, 202, 209, 227, 231, 268

**Appreciation:** 182, 268

**Asset:** 8, 17, 65, 87, 88, 89, 90, 91, 96, 98, 135, 171, 193, 194, 195, 196, 197, 198, 199, 200, 201, 202, 205, 208, 218, 219, 226, 230, 231, 232, 233, 234, 235, 238, 247, 248, 249, 259, 268, 270, 272, 273, 275, 276, 278, 281, 284

**Asset allocation:** 65, 226, 230, 232, 233, 234, 235, 238, 268

**Asset classes:** 230, 231, 268

**Assisted living:** 268

**Automatic investment:** 268

## B

**Bad asset:** 87, 88, 89, 90, 91, 94, 98, 99, 100, 146, 189, 240, 264, 268

**Balanced budget:** 269, 275

**Balance sheet:** 13, 86, 102, 227, 268, 282

**Bankruptcy:** 64, 71, 73, 210, 269

**Basis points:** 179, 269

**Bear market:** 135, 163, 193, 269

**Bond fund:** 168, 269

**Bonds:** 7, 8, 9, 31, 89, 164, 200, 231, 250, 268, 269, 270, 276, 278, 281, 284, 285

**Bonus:** 15, 31, 32, 44, 102, 178, 179, 238, 269

**Bottleneck:** 58, 269

Broker: 269, 281, 282, 283, 288

Brokerage account: 31, 183, 231, 287, 288

Budget: 72, 74, 87, 94, 101, 108, 118, 159, 189, 191, 205, 225, 235, 240, 269, 270, 275

Bull market: 269

Burn rate: 269

Business cycle: 7, 269

## C

Capital: 10, 60, 89, 171, 189, 244, 246, 247, 248, 249, 250, 268, 269, 270, 271, 278, 281, 282, 286, 287

Capital appreciation: 89, 270

Capital gains: 10, 268, 270, 286, 287

Cash flow: 9, 69, 70, 72, 73, 74, 77, 78, 79, 81, 89, 90, 103, 104, 110, 112, 113, 134, 146, 147, 182, 197, 204, 224, 227, 237, 269, 270, 274, 275

Cash-flow analysis: 72, 78, 270

Cash reserve: 102, 193, 194, 196, 197, 198, 199, 200, 201, 202, 237, 270

Certificate of deposit: 89, 164, 270

Charitable giving: 251, 270

Charitable remainder trust: 248, 249, 250

Clarifying questions: 29, 39, 137, 166, 180, 181, 270

Commercial real estate: 164, 167, 195, 270

Commission-based advisor: 126, 127, 270

Commodity: 269, 271, 289

Compound interest: 98, 104, 189, 199, 271

Conservative: 86, 171, 271

Consolidate: 103, 110, 272

Consumer debt: 118, 189, 225, 271

Contractual obligation: 102, 271

Conventional: 167, 170, 196, 271

Cost basis: 271

Cost of investment: 271

Credit card: 12, 16, 32, 43, 63, 72, 75, 102, 103, 105, 109, 134, 199, 223, 225, 235, 240, 257, 271, 275, 299

Credit card balance: 271

Credit limit: 102, 271

Creditor: 272, 278

Credit score: 44, 47, 271

Crutch: 53, 54, 56, 57, 58, 59, 60, 61, 62, 64, 67, 173, 210, 212, 259, 261, 272

Crutch management: 58, 67, 173, 212, 272

## D

Debt: 7, 12, 14, 16, 32, 43, 55, 70, 71, 72, 74, 75, 79, 81, 85, 89, 99, 100, 102, 103, 104, 109, 110, 112, 116, 118, 134, 135, 138, 146, 182, 189, 190, 191, 192, 197, 198, 199, 200, 202, 211, 212, 223, 225, 227, 228, 231, 236, 237, 254, 257, 268, 269, 271, 272, 274, 276, 278, 282, 284, 299

Debt consolidation: 272

Debtor: 7, 77, 269, 271, 272

Debt service: 14, 72, 182, 197, 272

Debt-service cost: 272

Deductible: 95, 108, 175, 248, 272, 284, 286

Deduction: 246, 247, 248, 249, 251, 272, 277, 286

Dependent: 14, 21, 53, 55, 58, 67, 183, 192, 272, 286

Depreciating asset: 96, 272

Derivatives: 272, 285

Disability: 79, 235, 273, 274

Distribution: 10, 235, 251, 275, 284

Diversified: 148, 183, 231, 273

Dividend: 273, 285, 288

Dollar cost averaging: 172, 273

Dow Jones Industrial Average: 273

## E

Earned income: 32, 34, 73, 78, 90, 94, 95, 104, 193, 196, 200, 273

Emerging markets: 273

Entrepreneur: 273

**Equity:** 47, 59, 77, 78, 88, 94, 99, 103, 134, 164, 171, 182, 195, 197, 233, 234, 250, 268, 273, 276, 277, 279, 281, 282, 284, 286

**Equity partner:** 77, 94, 273

**Estate strategy:** 274

**Estate tax:** 228, 229, 230, 244, 245, 246, 249, 250, 274, 279

# F

**Federal tax:** 7, 104, 247, 281, 289

**Fee-based:** 126, 127, 138

**Financial defense:** 17, 107, 274

**Financial independence:** 2, 31, 33, 34, 36, 46, 53, 56, 59, 66, 67, 89, 90, 91, 96, 171, 213, 217, 227, 272, 274, 276, 280

**Financial offense:** 17, 69, 78, 274

**Financial planning:** 123, 124, 134, 180, 205, 226, 238, 239, 275, 278, 299

**Financial services:** 5, 12, 29, 31, 35, 44, 118, 120, 128, 166, 226, 256, 274

**Financial values:** 28, 38, 123, 268, 275, 288

**Financing:** 31, 103, 105, 254, 275, 283

**FINRA:** 274

**Fiscal responsibility:** 36, 101, 192, 272, 275

**Fixed annuities:** 164, 275

**Fixed expense:** 275

**Fixed overhead:** 73, 79, 81, 275

**Fixed-rate mortgage:** 189, 233, 275

**Free cash flow:** 77, 275

**Funding:** 229, 236, 250, 276

**Futures contract:** 276, 281

# G

**Gain:** 20, 23, 31, 32, 67, 69, 76, 78, 85, 93, 94, 95, 118, 129, 138, 168, 181, 199, 208, 218, 222, 228, 247, 268, 277, 287

**Game plan:** 59, 151, 152, 153, 159, 168, 190, 199, 276

**Gift annuity:** 248, 249, 276

**Good assets:** 74, 87, 89, 90, 91, 93, 94, 97, 98, 99, 100, 103, 136, 157, 164, 192, 194, 208, 209, 210, 217, 218, 221, 223, 238, 254, 259, 264

**Goods:** 16, 223, 277, 280, 283, 284, 287, 289

**Government bond:** 276

**Gross:** 72, 106, 174, 176, 276, 277, 283, 286

# H

**Habit:** 101, 233, 234, 276

**Hedge fund:** 276

**High-yield bond:** 276

**Home-equity loan:** 134, 276

**Hot investment tip:** 258, 276

**Hot issue:** 276

# I

**ILIT:** 249, 278, 279

**Immediate annuity:** 248, 277

**Income:** 6, 7, 8, 10, 12, 14, 15, 16, 17, 23, 30, 31, 32, 34, 37, 38, 40, 46, 47, 54, 55, 60, 61, 62, 63, 64, 65, 66, 68, 69, 70, 71, 72, 73, 74, 75, 76, 77, 78, 80, 82, 84, 85, 86, 87, 88, 89, 90, 91, 94, 95, 96, 98, 99, 100, 101, 104, 106, 107, 108, 109, 110, 112, 113, 119, 129, 144, 146, 147, 148, 157, 161, 167, 168, 172, 175, 183, 187, 189, 190, 192, 193, 194, 196, 197, 199, 200, 201, 209, 211, 212, 214, 222, 223, 227, 233, 234, 235, 236, 237, 244, 246, 247, 248, 249, 250, 254, 255, 267, 268, 270, 271, 272, 273, 274, 275, 276, 277, 278, 281, 282, 283, 284, 286, 288

**Income-tax deduction:** 277

**Index:** 164, 277, 284, 291, 293, 295

**Index annuities:** 164, 277

**Index fund:** 277

**Inflation:** 8, 62, 64, 118, 190, 200, 213, 214, 249, 277

**Inheritance:** 15, 17, 54, 66, 67, 68, 188, 272, 277

**Interest:** 7, 8, 9, 18, 32, 48, 71, 74, 75, 76, 77, 95, 98, 102, 103, 104, 116, 126, 128, 129, 134, 135, 155, 169, 180, 189, 190, 193, 195, 196, 199, 202, 223, 227, 248, 269, 270, 271, 272, 275, 276, 277, 278, 279, 280, 281, 282, 283, 284, 286, 287

**Interest charge:** 278

**Interest-only loan:** 278

**Interest-only mortgage:** 278

**Interest payment:** 278

**Interest rate:** 7, 196, 202, 248, 269, 272, 275, 283, 284

**Internal rate of return:** 134, 278

**Invest:** 10, 13, 16, 29, 30, 31, 32, 33, 34, 39, 60, 93, 94, 97, 98, 126, 134, 135, 144, 166, 167, 169, 172, 176, 177, 181, 193, 196, 199, 201, 234, 239, 247, 250, 267, 278, 286

**Investment:** 5, 6, 7, 8, 9, 10, 13, 16, 19, 29, 30, 31, 34, 37, 39, 57, 62, 65, 66, 70, 74, 75, 85, 86, 87, 88, 89, 98, 118, 124, 125, 126, 127, 128, 129, 132, 133, 134, 135, 137, 139, 155, 157, 164, 165, 166, 167, 168, 169, 170, 171, 172, 174, 175, 176, 177, 178, 179, 180, 181, 182, 185, 189, 190, 194, 195, 197, 199, 202, 222, 229, 230, 232, 233, 234, 235, 236, 237, 238, 247, 248, 249, 254, 257, 258, 261, 267, 268, 271, 273, 274, 275, 276, 277, 279, 281, 282, 283, 284, 285, 286, 287, 289

**Investment allocation:** 278

**Investment asset:** 278

**Investment real estate:** 99, 197, 278

**Investment strategies:** 10, 16, 29, 118, 139, 189, 230, 278

**IPO (initial public offering):** 277

**IRA (individual retirement account):** 57, 59, 65, 79, 109, 127, 135, 178, 193, 194, 195, 196, 198, 199, 200, 201, 202, 231, 244, 247, 259, 270, 277, 284, 286, 287, 288

# J

**Joint finances:** 238, 279

# K

**KISS (Keep it simple, Stupid):** 225, 238, 279

# L

**Large cap:** 279

**Large-cap growth:** 230, 279

**Large-cap value:** 230, 279, 288

**Legacy:** 243, 244, 245, 246, 251, 260, 279

**Leverage:** 18, 115, 116, 119, 120, 121, 122, 159, 222, 228, 231, 279

**Life expectancy:** 64, 279

**Life insurance:** 7, 79, 163, 164, 166, 174, 175, 190, 193, 194, 195, 198, 202, 229, 244, 249, 251, 274, 278, 279, 286

**Line 39:** 104, 279

**Line of credit:** 102, 279

**Liquidate:** 31, 168, 172, 173, 279

**Liquidation:** 169, 270, 280

**Liquidity:** 6, 8, 30, 127, 165, 173, 176, 178, 179, 194, 195, 280, 284

**LLC (Limited Liability Corporation):** 182, 229, 279

**Load:** 14, 16, 136, 176, 280, 281, 285

**Long-term care insurance:** 280

**Long-term goals:** 43, 44, 119, 280

# M

**Margin account:** 280

**Market decline:** 280

**Maturity:** 8, 269, 279, 280

**Mentor:** 116, 117, 119, 262, 280

**Mid-cap:** 230, 231, 268, 280

**Milestone:** 97, 98, 147, 151, 158, 213, 217, 280

**Monetary value:** 28, 32, 36, 47, 280

**Monthly obligations:** 37, 280

**Mortgage:** 36, 66, 71, 74, 79, 88, 89, 103, 126, 134, 156, 175, 190, 193, 194, 195, 196, 197, 198, 199, 200, 201, 202, 233, 234, 272, 273, 275, 277, 278, 281, 282, 283

**Mortgage payment:** 234, 277, 281

Municipal fund: 281
Mutual fund: 269, 281, 288

# N

Nasdaq or NASDAQ (National Association of Securities Dealers Automated Quotation system): 281

Net worth: 74, 94, 165, 189, 208, 209, 210, 217, 224, 225, 234, 237, 239, 240, 289

No load: 281

# O

Operating expenses: 174, 179, 281

Options: 6, 7, 15, 20, 30, 31, 43, 49, 61, 66, 67, 103, 130, 132, 134, 145, 147, 164, 165, 176, 183, 200, 211, 212, 245, 246, 250, 251, 267, 280, 281, 286, 287

Overhead: 65, 72, 73, 74, 78, 79, 80, 81, 82, 101, 102, 105, 161, 182, 239, 269, 274, 275, 281, 288

Overtime: 189, 281

# P

Passive investing: 166, 167, 168, 181, 282

Patient advocate: 226, 282

Pension: 13, 14, 15, 17, 20, 36, 49, 54, 55, 60, 61, 62, 65, 68, 84, 96, 117, 118, 167, 183, 187, 191, 192, 193, 194, 195, 196, 198, 199, 200, 201, 202, 259, 282, 284, 285

Personal loan: 164, 282

Planned giving: 245, 246, 282

Portfolio: 8, 9, 37, 38, 85, 104, 119, 135, 148, 155, 157, 172, 173, 179, 183, 193, 195, 197, 208, 231, 234, 238, 247, 249, 267, 268, 269, 271, 277, 278, 282, 286, 287

Precious metals: 164, 268, 270, 282

Pre-tax savings retirement plans: 282

Principal: 5, 7, 30, 89, 103, 155, 156, 227, 269, 271, 272, 276, 278, 279, 280, 281, 282

Principal balance: 279, 282

Private equity funds: 164, 282

Private investment: 181, 171, 282

Probate: 228, 283, 288

Profit: 94, 126, 128, 134, 155, 170, 267, 271, 273, 278

Prospectus: 174, 283

Purchasing power: 206, 283

# R

Rate of return: 31, 62, 64, 134, 166, 168, 169, 170, 171, 177, 198, 208, 278, 283, 284

Real estate: 6, 9, 29, 46, 65, 74, 89, 99, 109, 118, 125, 127, 134, 135, 164, 166, 167, 170, 177, 193, 194, 195, 196, 197, 228, 229, 238, 268, 270, 278, 283, 284, 288

Real estate investment trust: 6, 118, 135, 164, 268, 283

Reallocate: 232, 283

Recession: 199, 234, 269, 283

Refinance: 71, 103, 112, 134, 169, 283

Regulation T: 283

Rental property: 135, 283

Residential real estate: 170

Retirement: 6, 13, 15, 16, 17, 21, 30, 32, 36, 37, 38, 45, 48, 54, 55, 57, 60, 61, 62, 63, 65, 66, 67, 68, 73, 75, 84, 85, 87, 89, 103, 104, 107, 118, 139, 144, 146, 156, 157, 164, 167, 175, 176, 177, 181, 187, 188, 189, 190, 193, 195, 196, 197, 198, 199, 201, 202, 203, 204, 209, 212, 213, 214, 217, 222, 233, 235, 236, 244, 249, 254, 259, 264, 267, 268, 272, 277, 282, 284, 285, 287, 288

Retirement pension: 54, 284

Revenue: 6, 267, 269, 270, 274, 275, 281, 283, 284

Revenue source: 95, 284

Rider: 176, 284

Roth IRA: 57, 65, 79, 109, 135, 193, 194, 195, 196, 198, 200, 247, 270, 277, 284, 286, 288

Rule of 72: 98, 284

## S

**Salary:** 102, 128, 236, 270, 273, 284

**Sales tax:** 284

**Savings:** 13, 36, 48, 49, 55, 64, 66, 69, 74, 75, 104, 105, 107, 118, 134, 164, 175, 191, 196, 199, 200, 209, 212, 214, 215, 216, 233, 234, 246, 249, 250, 254, 255, 267, 270, 275, 277, 282, 284, 285, 286, 287

**Security:** 5, 8, 9, 14, 15, 17, 19, 20, 23, 33, 36, 55, 60, 62, 67, 72, 85, 89, 90, 91, 96, 118, 128, 144, 146, 155, 192, 217, 244, 251, 275, 276, 280, 281, 284, 285, 286

**SEP (simplified employee pension):** 99, 193, 277, 285

**Severance pay:** 75, 284

**Share:** 10, 19, 37, 131, 135, 153, 172, 173, 235, 253, 259, 260, 261, 262, 273, 279, 280, 281, 282, 284, 285, 286

**Share class:** 285

**Short sale:** 285

**Short-term bonds:** 231, 285

**Short-term goals:** 43, 161, 162, 280, 285, 288

**SIMPLE (savings incentive match plan for employees) plan:** 164, 277, 285

**Small cap:** 285

**Social Security:** 17, 19, 20, 23, 36, 55, 60, 62, 67, 72, 96, 144, 192, 244, 251, 285

**S&P (Standard & Poor's) 500:** 31, 209, 210, 217, 284

**Speculative investment:** 285

**Stock investment:** 29, 285

**Stock market:** 37, 65, 163, 194, 273, 277, 282, 285, 286

**Stock market volatility:** 286

**Stock option:** 15, 286

**Stocks:** 6, 8, 9, 31, 89, 154, 155, 164, 171, 193, 195, 201, 208, 230, 231, 234, 247, 268, 270, 274, 278, 281, 283, 284, 285, 286, 288

**Strategy:** 9, 30, 36, 57, 60, 61, 65, 87, 89, 103, 104, 109, 119, 125, 128, 130, 134, 137, 143, 172, 173, 191, 226, 230, 232, 234, 235, 237, 245, 247, 248, 249, 250, 256, 257, 258, 259, 267, 268, 271, 274, 276, 280, 282, 286

**Sub-account:** 174, 286

**Surrender charge:** 30, 174, 176, 177, 179, 182, 286

**Systematic saving:** 13, 175, 268, 286

## T

**Target:** 7, 25, 26, 27, 28, 29, 31, 32, 34, 35, 47, 200, 209, 264

**Taxable:** 7, 10, 31, 232, 233, 235, 236, 247, 268, 277, 282, 283, 286, 287

**Tax bracket:** 104, 175, 247, 286

**Tax credit:** 164, 286

**Tax-deductible:** 95, 108, 248, 284, 286

**Tax-deferred:** 6, 30, 232, 247, 270, 287

**Taxes:** 9, 32, 64, 66, 72, 79, 81, 89, 102, 104, 110, 175, 181, 222, 223, 228, 229, 235, 236, 237, 244, 245, 246, 247, 248, 249, 250, 267, 272, 274, 277, 278, 279, 281, 282, 283, 286, 287

**Tax harvesting:** 286

**Tax liability:** 104, 246, 247, 287

**Tax withholding:** 287

**Ticker symbol:** 287

**Ticket charge:** 287, 288

**Tipping:** 287

**Tolerance zone:** 208, 287

**Total return:** 172, 287

**Trade fee:** 287

**Traditional IRA:** 277, 288

**Trusted advisor:** 288

# V

**Value fund:** 279, 288

**Values:** 9, 17, 25, 26, 28, 29, 30, 31, 32, 33, 34, 35, 36, 38, 39, 40, 41, 47, 48, 123, 131, 158, 159, 226, 227, 234, 244, 251, 261, 268, 275, 288

**Variable annuity:** 196, 200, 288

**Variable expense:** 288

**Venture capitalist:** 288

**Visionary goals:** 43, 45, 47, 48, 288

**VRBO (vacation rental by owner):** 46, 288

# W

**Wealth accumulation:** 17, 22, 30, 72, 95, 210, 217, 234, 235, 258, 274, 275, 289

**Wealth management:** 22, 289

**Wealthy:** 13, 18, 22, 23, 68, 69, 74, 77, 84, 86, 87, 94, 96, 98, 104, 105, 107, 133, 136, 144, 158, 192, 221, 224, 225, 263, 280, 289

**Windfall:** 64, 87, 188, 289

# Y

**Yield:** 31, 167, 169, 231, 276, 277, 279, 289

*James P. Studinger*

# About the Author

James P. Studinger believes that every important journey must begin by plotting one's course—and that an informed client is the best client. He is author of *Wealth Is a Choice,* his first book, and owner of the JPStudinger Group, a wealth-management company.

Growing up in Manistique, Michigan, young Studinger knew at an early age that he would be a businessman of some sort. But when he got to college, he quickly incurred some hefty credit card debt. Although very challenging at the time, these early financial missteps shaped Studinger's future and convinced him that financial education was a vital life tool.

Once on steadier financial footing, Studinger continued his pursuit of financial acumen, working early in his career as a financial advisor with one of the largest financial planning firms in the country. In 2002 Studinger opened his own company, JPStudinger Group, a firm that specializes in education and meeting clients' needs rather than the sales side of the business. Studinger's initial motivation for writing down his principles was to create a road map for his children to follow, should anything happen to him. This passion blossomed into *Wealth Is a Choice,* a book intended to educate readers and help them embrace, not fear, financial decisions.

Studinger's expertise was recently called upon by the State of Michigan where he was instrumental in the passing of a new 529 College Savings Plan. For his participation, Studinger received accolades from Governor Jennifer Granholm, as well as from the bill's sponsor, State Representative Tim Melton of Pontiac/Auburn Hills and chairman of the Committee on Education. Studinger was happy to participate in a plan that helps Michigan families educate their children.

When not writing and advising, Studinger enjoys the outdoors: hiking, camping, hunting and fishing. He is also a fitness buff and likes to run, bike and play hockey.

The author and his wife reside in Bloomfield Hills, Michigan, with their two sons.

To inquire about booking James P. Studinger
to speak at your next event, please contact:

## JPStudinger Group
On the Web at: www.jpstudinger.com

Toll-free: (800) 975-6550